Mike Jay is the author of *The Air Loom Gang*, *Emperors of Dreams: Drugs in the Nineteenth Century*, *Blue Tide: The Search for Soma* and *Artificial Paradises: A Drugs Reader*, and editor of *1900: A Fin-de-Siècle Reader*.

www.booksattransworld.co.uk

The Unfortunate
COLONEL DESPARD

MIKE JAY

BANTAM BOOKS

LONDON • TORONTO • SYDNEY • AUCKLAND • JOHANNESBURG

THE UNFORTUNATE COLONEL DESPARD
A BANTAM BOOK: 0 553 81608 X

Originally published in Great Britain by Bantam Press,
a division of Transworld Publishers

PRINTING HISTORY
Bantam Press edition published 2004
Bantam edition published 2005

1 3 5 7 9 10 8 6 4 2

Copyright © Mike Jay 2004

The right of Mike Jay to be identified as the author of
this work has been asserted in accordance with sections 77
and 78 of the Copyright Designs and Patents Act 1988.

Set in 11/13pt Bauer Bodoni by
Falcon Oast Graphic Art Ltd.

Bantam Books are published by Transworld Publishers,
61–63 Uxbridge Road, London W5 5SA,
a division of The Random House Group Ltd,
in Australia by Random House Australia (Pty) Ltd,
20 Alfred Street, Milsons Point, Sydney, NSW 2061, Australia,
in New Zealand by Random House New Zealand Ltd,
18 Poland Road, Glenfield, Auckland 10, New Zealand
and in South Africa by Random House (Pty) Ltd,
Endulini, 5a Jubilee Road, Parktown 2193, South Africa.

Printed and bound in Great Britain by
Cox & Wyman Ltd, Reading, Berkshire.

Papers used by Transworld Publishers are natural, recyclable
products made from wood grown in sustainable forests. The
manufacturing processes conform to the environmental
regulations of the country of origin.

CONTENTS

ACKNOWLEDGEMENTS

I'm very grateful to Simon Thorogood, my editor, and Andrew Lownie, my agent, for all their help in realizing this project; to Herbert Despard, for access to his absorbing family archive and for the valuable time, thoughts and assistance he offered me in assembling Edward Marcus's story; to Peter Linebaugh, for the inspiration of *The Many-Headed Hydra*, and for his subsequent kindness in sharing with me his unpublished material on Despard; to Mary Vickers, for her permission to use material compiled by her late father, Tom, during his time in Belize; to Hal Cook and Tom Pocock for their careful readings of the manuscript; and, as ever, to Louise Burton and Michael Neve for their support and encouragement throughout.

LIST OF ILLUSTRATIONS

Prologue

THE HANGED MAN

The day of Colonel Edward Marcus Despard's execution is one of the most dramatic, and strangely forgotten, in British history. In this, as in much else, his death mirrored his life.

He was to be publicly hanged, drawn and quartered for high treason, a punishment that had barely been carried out in London within living memory. Its most vivid associations were still with the Jacobite rebellions over fifty years before, the days when the British state's greatest fear had been that a Catholic monarch might seize the throne. Those days were now long gone, and, many thought, the old ceremony with them; Despard, as it turned out, would be the last person on whom the sentence would ever be passed. As specified by the Lord Chief Justice, the colonel and his six confederates were 'to be drawn on a hurdle to the place of execution, there to be hanged by the neck, but not until you are quite dead, then to be cut down and your bowels taken out and cast into the fire before your faces; your heads to be taken off and your bodies quartered'.

Intimations of the drama had already begun to

transform the city the day before – Sunday, 20 February 1803. At first light, carpenters had begun to assemble scaffold and gallows, large enough to accommodate the seven men, on the roof of Surrey County Jail in Horsemonger Lane, just south of the Thames in Southwark. The jail was a plain barracks-style building, recently constructed to replace the old prison, which had been torn down during the Gordon Riots some twenty years before. The roof had been built flat for precisely this purpose, and this was the first occasion for its use. The main gates of the jail opened to admit seven plain wooden coffins.

According to contemporary witnesses, even as the preparations began 'vast multitudes of people immediately began to assemble'. It was noted that the throng consisted 'chiefly of the lowest of the vulgar', but that, unusually for a public execution, 'a considerable number of persons of genteel appearance were observable'. The forces of law and order, too, were out in unprecedented numbers. Every single member of the Bow Street police patrol, the other London patrols at Queen Street, Marlborough Street and Hatton Gardens, and a 'numerous tribe' of petty constables from the outlying London boroughs, were placed on duty. The jail and its surrounds were emphatically staked out, surrounded by a cordon two officers deep. All 'the public houses and other places of resort for the disaffected' bristled with police. A detachment of mounted Horse Guards cavalry clopped into Horsemonger Lane; all the infantry regiments in the city, at the Tower of London and at Knightsbridge Barracks, were placed on the highest alert. The head keeper of the jail was issued with six sky rockets, each containing a pound of explosives, 'to be let off as a signal to the military, in case of any disturbance'. London's entire martial forces were instructed not to leave their posts until the danger was past.

The impending execution had dominated the news all week. The *Times* had led its news pages with testy dismissals of the rumours that were spreading around the city: that Despard and his confederates were being cruelly chained together, that they were being tortured for their confessions, that a last-minute reprieve was in the air. It was beginning to dawn on the authorities that the graphic medieval ritual they had scheduled might be counter-productive, inflammatory and unpredictably dangerous. The Police Magistrate of Southwark had expressed grave concerns, pointing out that the question that had been on the common people's lips during the week was 'When are these poor men to be murdered?' It had been hard, apparently, even to find labourers prepared to erect the scaffold. When the warrant for the execution was issued on the morning of 20 February, it became clear that these anxieties had led to a change in the sentence. Exercising their statutory discretion, the magistrates announced, 'we have thought fit to remit part of the sentence, viz. the taking out and burning their bowels before their faces, and dividing the body severally into four parts'. Despard would now be drawn – to the place of execution on a carriage without wheels – hanged until dead, and then beheaded. The *Observer* commented with relief that 'the cutting out of the heart of the malefactor, quartering &c is very humanely and properly to be dispensed with'.

On the day of the execution, 21 February, the pace quickened long before dawn. 'A vast number of police officers' were soon massively outnumbered by the spectators streaming through the bitter cold and darkness. Southwark was a hard area to police at the best of times, a hinterland to the city of London proper characterized by unedifying activities that were prohibited across the Thames. A warren of timber shacks among the marshy waste ground and garbage landfills, it had long been a teeming red-light district; in recent times it had become dominated by malodorous and insanitary industries – distilleries, tanneries and vinegar mills – that had been forced south of the river by City of London edicts. It also had a long history of insurrection. In 1381, Wat Tyler had led the Peasants' Revolt through the same streets; in 1450, Jack Cade had set up camp here with his Kentish rebel army. Despard's sentence of high treason had more powerful resonances with this period than it did with the freshly minted nineteenth century. Most of the crowd had never seen a treason execution; now, jostling to witness one, they were passing shops selling roller-skates, umbrellas, toothbrushes, matches, alarm clocks, condoms, Twining's Tea and Pears' Soap. Part of the appeal of the spectacle must have been this lurid collision of the old and the new; part, also, the uncertainty on all sides as to whether the crowd had really assembled only to stand and watch. It was widely rumoured that the execution would not take place as planned – or, if it did, that the main event would turn out to be an entirely unscheduled one. The people of London had rioted countless times over much less, and, given the nature of Despard's alleged crime, there were an unknown number among the crowd who might attempt to turn a riot into a full-scale revolution.

The character of execution crowds seems, as with most crowds, to have been largely in the eye of the beholder. For many, they were simply the scum of society: crude, vulgar, leering, gawping, sadistic. For others, though, they were the salt of the earth, good men and true come to witness and legitimize the exercise of state power. Despite the rough spectacle they presented, they were often visibly

The eighteenth-century public execution, as seen by William Hogarth in 1747

civic-minded: rescuing stranded children, or crying 'shame' if one of their number insulted a woman. The beholder's view of such crowds tended to reflect their attitude to public execution itself, as the most graphic and visceral demonstration of the ultimate power of the state. There were many who were already campaigning for its abolition on the grounds, as one put it, that 'the real effect of these scenes is to torture the compassionate and harden the obdurate'. There were many more, though, who thronged to such occasions in high spirits. Their hilarity and ribaldry – the proverbial 'gallows humour' – may have been heartless mockery, but it may also have been a response to the unspoken but unmissable tension between the pomp and solemnity of the occasion and the ghastly reality of the act.

This tension reached its high watermark with Despard's

execution. There had been a long-observed trend in Britain towards public disrespect at hangings: the victim cheered, the executioner and officials booed and mocked. But the crime of high treason placed an unprecedented focus on the legitimacy of the act, a focus sharpened by the fact that the majority of the onlookers believed Despard to be innocent of it. He had been accused and convicted of a shocking, cold-blooded plot to overthrow the state, an accusation he had consistently and calmly denied. Now, at the moment of the state's cold-blooded retribution, he had a final chance to speak the case for his defence. Part of the unique appeal of executions was always that the victims, in the moments before their death, might say anything; it was often the only time the unspeakable could be spoken in public. But if Despard chose to speak the unspeakable, it would be more than a howl of rage, a fruity obscenity or a cheeky quip. The danger he posed might yet be far from over.

The bell of St George's Church began tolling at five, and continued for about an hour. By the time it had finished, every conceivable vantage point was packed solid. It was estimated that there were twenty thousand people jammed into the carriageway of Horsemonger Lane and spilling onto every nearby roof and patch of open ground 'that afforded the least prospect'. It was evident, too, that this was no ordinary gallows crowd, just as it was no ordinary hanging. The packed observers were almost completely silent: 'no tumult, no disorder appeared among the multitude . . . all was stillness and expectation of the approaching event'. For the massed guards and officers, this must have been considerably more unnerving than the unruly mob they had feared. It might be an expression of uncertainty, of a crowd unsure of the tone of the event, and too diffident to break the silence. But it could equally, and perhaps more plausibly, be read as a mute but chilling sign of prearranged intent.

Inside Surrey County Jail, as the prison bell struck seven, Despard was invited into the chapel for a service of last rites. He politely refused the invitation, and remained in his cell. At seven thirty, his arms were bound with ropes and he was led out into the walled prison yard. He was still a colonel, and still entitled to wear the uniform of his rank, but he appeared instead in his favourite dark greatcoat and boots, bare-headed, without wig or powder. His solicitor was waiting for him outside his cell and, manoeuvring around his ropes, he shook hands with him 'very cordially'.

Awaiting Despard in the prison yard was a very strange sight indeed. Two horses were harnessed to a small cart that contained two trusses of clean straw, and whose floor rested directly on the ground. Behind the cart stood the Sheriff of Surrey, behind him a fully robed priest, and behind the priest the head keeper of the jail, Mr Ives, solemnly holding a white wand. Behind Ives stood a line of high constables, and behind them a line of duty policemen. Bringing up the rear was the executioner, holding up a drawn sword.

The quartering and dismembering had been waived, but there had never been an execution for high treason without the victim first being drawn through the streets to the scaffold. It was integral to the ceremony, but today it was out of the question. The ritual was intended to allow the people to vent their feelings towards the traitor, to abuse him and spit on him; today, though, no-one was minded to test how the ominously silent crowd outside would react if Despard was paraded among them. Apart from anything else, the packed streets made it logistically impossible. It had hastily been decided to switch the ritual to the privacy of the enclosed prison yard.

Outside the yard, the traditional gallows humour might have been conspicuously absent, but Despard himself was unable to keep a straight face at the furtive display of pomp that confronted him. 'Ha! ha!', he exclaimed with a laugh, 'what nonsensical mummery is this?' The solemn procession was not programmed to respond. Despard was ushered into the cart, seated backwards on the straw bales and, as the dawn spread grey over the prison walls, bumped around the cobbled yard until it was deemed that the drawing had been completed. There was to be no thwarting of justice, but neither would the ancient ritual of drawing a traitor survive that morning's embarrassment and ridicule. Despard, though powerless against it, had nevertheless passed a sentence of death on the sentence itself.

As day broke, officials could be seen making the gallows ready on the prison roof. The seven wooden coffins were brought up; the drop was erected; bags of sawdust were arranged to catch the blood when the heads were severed. Still the crowd watched in oppressive silence. At eight thirty, the prisoners began to file up to the scaffold.

First was John Macnamara, a stout, florid Irishman, who looked down at the packed streets and exclaimed loudly and devoutly, 'Lord Jesus, have mercy upon me!' Next came Arthur Graham, at fifty-three the oldest of the traitors, who looked shaken, 'pale and ghastly'. Next, James Wratton, a thin, pinched-looking shoemaker, who 'ascended the gallows with much firmness'. The carpenter Thomas Broughton followed, then the two tall, amiable-looking soldiers, John Wood, then John Francis. Finally, the colonel took the steps up to the drop. He was impassive; 'his countenance underwent not the slightest change' as the rope was fastened around his neck and the cap placed on his head. He assisted the executioner in adjusting the noose, taking care to tie the knot under his left ear; he had presumably witnessed enough hangings to be aware that this arrangement offered the best chance of a broken neck and a speedy death. John Macnamara is reported to have muttered to Despard, 'I am afraid, Colonel, we have got ourselves into a bad situation.' Despard replied, 'There are many better, and some worse.'

Two priests arrived on the platform: a Roman Catholic who read the last rites to Macnamara, and the Anglican prison chaplain, Revd William Winckworth, who did the same to the other five associates. Despard himself declined any religious absolution. It had emerged during his imprisonment that 'although he thought the institution of religion politic, he had no faith in its efficacy'. When pressed by Winckworth, he had admitted that, as far as he was concerned, 'the opinions of churchmen, dissenters, Quakers, Methodists, Catholics, savages or even atheists were equally indifferent'.

By this time nearly a hundred officers, dignitaries and guards had joined the condemned on the roof. When all was ready, Despard turned to the Sheriff of Surrey, who was presiding over the event, and asked permission to address a few words to the people. The sheriff told him that he had no objection, 'provided nothing inflammatory or improper was intended'; but if Despard were to speak a single word of that kind, the platform would be immediately dropped. Given Despard's situation, this was a difficult tightrope to walk, but he was ready for the challenge. What followed was, even in the remarkable annals of gallows speeches, perhaps the most notorious and best remembered.

Despard stood up straight and, in clear tones, addressed the crowd, beginning with 'Fellow Citizens'. It was a carefully judged phrase, with clear republican associations, yet in itself some way short of an incitement to revolution. Despard may have used it to gauge the crowd's mood, or the sheriff's tolerance, but its reception is impossible to judge today. The accounts of Despard's speech perfectly illustrate the paradox that the more witnesses present at an event, the harder it is to establish exactly what happened. Robert Southey, the future Poet Laureate, was among the packed crowd; he recorded that 'the mob applauded him while he spoke'. Others maintained that his speech was received 'in the most perfect silence'. Still others squared the circle by reporting that the speech 'was applauded by certain persons who appeared to have placed themselves near for the purpose', presumably attempting to incite the crowd to a frenzy, but that the crowd refused to join in. Doubtless others still would have suspected – and with some justification – that the vocal front row were government *agents provocateurs*, trying to encourage Despard's fellow traitors in the crowd to reveal themselves in the presence of the massed guard.

'I come here, as you see,' Despard continued, 'after having served my country faithfully, honourably and usefully served it, for thirty years and upwards, to suffer death upon a scaffold for a crime of which I protest I am not guilty. I solemnly declare that I am no more guilty of it than any of you who may now be hearing me.' Again, a judicious combination of plain speaking and hidden meaning: Despard's not-guilty plea was a matter of public record, and he was perfectly entitled to repeat it. Yet, as everyone knew, much more depended on the statement than the colonel's own innocence or guilt. If the government was prepared to use the ultimate penalty to silence him, and unjustly, then they were themselves condemned. For Robert Southey, this was Despard's sly masterstroke. 'This calm declaration of a dying man', he wrote later, 'was so well calculated to do mischief.' It was, for Southey at least, the perfect instrument of malice and revenge, far more plausible than a rabble-rousing denunciation. But the majority of the crowd would have taken it as a simple statement of record. So much of what was known of Despard's views had been disputed, attributed, denied or fabricated that simply hearing him in his own words would have conveyed a forceful impression of truth.

But now Despard set his sights more broadly, and edged towards the unspeakable. 'Though His Majesty's ministers know as well as I do that I am not guilty, yet they avail themselves of a legal pretext to destroy a man, because he has been a friend to truth, to liberty and to justice, because he has been a friend to the poor and the oppressed.' Here was an obvious cue for applause; the next day's *Times* reported 'a considerable huzzah' from the front rows at this crescendo. But it was still the crowd's forbearance rather than its clamour that struck most observers. The sheriff, too, kept silent, and Despard went on. 'But, Citizens, I hope and trust, notwithstanding my fate, and the fate of those who no doubt will soon follow me, that the principles of freedom, of humanity, and of justice, will finally triumph over falsehood, tyranny and delusion, and every principle inimical to the interests of the human race.'

This, now, was enough for the sheriff; he moved over to Despard and told him that any more in this vein and the platform would drop. Despard nodded his understanding and fell silent. Then he raised his head and spoke once more. 'I have little more to add,' he concluded, 'except to wish you all health, happiness and freedom, which I have endeavoured, so far as was in my power, to procure for you, and for mankind in general.'

It was a gentlemanly sign-off, courteous both to the crowd and to the officials clustered around him, but it smuggled in another subtle barb. It was the references to tyranny and falsehood that had prompted the sheriff to put an end to Despard's speech, casting aspersions as they did not just on the government of the day but on the monarchy and the entire political establishment. Yet 'mankind in general', added to his previous and precise use of the term 'the human race', made a larger point. Who or what, precisely, was he referring to? Many in the crowd would have assumed he was referring to them, the disenfranchised masses, and implying that his cause was theirs: liberty and justice for all, not merely for the few. Those of Irish background or sympathies, of whom there were undoubtedly many, might have construed it more pointedly in terms of their own struggle for self-government. In fact, if Despard had anyone particular in mind, it was most likely to have been those for whom he had first taken it upon himself to seek justice: a small and scattered tribe of creoles, Irish convicts and freed black slaves in a remote part of the world most of the crowd had never heard of.

Some among the crowd, though, would certainly have caught this drift. Pamphlets and memoirs telling the rollicking tale of Despard's life had been circulating widely in recent weeks. Many would have known, for example, that his wife, Catherine, was a black woman with whom he had returned from his years of military service in the Caribbean and the Spanish Main. Despard's conviction for high treason had been secured, contentiously, on allegations of a plot against the British Crown; but his final exhortation expanded the frame to a panorama beyond Britain's shores. It might have been the struggle for British liberties that had finally claimed him, but he had been forged in a wider world of which most in the crowd were yet unaware. The British might celebrate that they never would be slaves, but what right had they to celebrate if their liberty was founded on the slavery of another portion of mankind? Few among the crowd could have conceived that within twenty years sovereignty over two hundred million people – a quarter of the world's population – would be claimed in their name. Yet this was a future Despard had already seen; his life had unfolded there, and its front line was perhaps still the closest he had to a home.

John Francis, next to Despard, looked straight ahead. 'What an amazing crowd,' he observed.

Despard looked up, and spoke his final words: ''Tis very cold; I think we shall have some rain.'

The moment around which all the activity of the last two days had centred could be put off no longer. At seven minutes to nine the signal was given to drop the platforms, beginning with Despard's. In the first unambiguous expression of their feelings since they had assembled, the crowd removed their hats. The rope was jerked, the platform gave way; Despard uttered no sound and betrayed no struggle. He clenched his hands in spasm twice, and then hung perfectly still as he was, in the words of one eyewitness chronicle, 'launched into eternity'.

Yet, as Despard hung in the massive silence, everyone was well aware there was more to come. In the days before measured ropes and weighted drops, death by hanging was an uncertain business. It was thirty-seven minutes before the executioner finally cut him down and wrestled his corpse over the block. Despard's dark coat flapped back to reveal a blue undercoat with gilt buttons, a cream waist-coat trimmed with gold lace, and a strip of scarlet flannel turned over the waist of his grey breeches. The executioner stepped back to make way for the surgeon with the dissecting knife.

This was the part of the ritual that had barely been seen

within living memory and, as soon became clear, had never previously been attempted by anyone present. The surgeon aimed at a joint in the neck vertebrae but missed it, and was soon reduced to nervous hacking. The executioner barged him out of the way and began twisting Despard's neck this way and that, a spectacle that 'filled everyone present with horror'. (Again, other sources – whether from restricted view or self-censorship – recorded that the head was 'severed in an instant'.) When Despard's head was eventually separated, the executioner picked it up by the hair, carried it to the edge of the parapet in his right hand and held it before the crowd. As he did so, he spoke the words that had for centuries marked the climax of the ceremony, but which were now ringing out for the first time over the modern world: 'This is the head of a traitor: Edward Marcus Despard.'

Robert Southey recorded that the crowd broke their silence at this point to hiss the executioner. Others claim that they remained mute to the end, when the freezing rain began to bucket down.

PART ONE

The Spanish Main

1

PATRIOT

The hanged man card in the Tarot deck is often read as the archetype of a character suspended between two worlds. There is no more graphic illustration of its appropriateness to Edward Marcus Despard than the images of him that were published around the time of his death. The National Portrait Gallery holds three engravings, all drawn or copied in 1803 and 1804. They are more or less mutually unrecognizable; surrounded by a random line-up of likenesses of his contemporaries, it would be hard to identify them as the same man. This, in turn, reflects the striking lack of consensus about who Despard actually was, and what his dramatic death signified.

The image of Despard delivering his gallows speech was the last to be published, and bears the least resemblance to the other two: a thick-set, jowly man, stiffly posed and rendered somehow anonymous by his execution cap. Without the crowd in frame to illustrate the public nature of his hanging, this image seems to project Despard into the future, suggesting a twentieth-century war traitor hanging behind closed prison doors. With the cut of his

WONDERFUL MUSEUM.

Sketch'd by a Gentleman who was permitted to take a place up on the Building, the only likeness ever take...

COL. EDWARD MARCUS DESPARD,

*At the place of Execution upon the New Surry Goal, just as he
appeared when addressing the Spectators, a few minutes before the
Platform dropped.*

Pub. by Alex Hogg 16 Paternoster row Feb. 1803.

coat slightly altered, he might almost be mistaken for his fellow Irish gentleman-traitor Sir Roger Casement, or even William Joyce, Lord Haw-Haw. But the two other images show a very different man – or, perhaps, two different men.

The other likeness from 1804 shows Despard in wig, silk frock-coat and cravat, unmistakably an officer and a gentleman. It may have been modelled on earlier likenesses, and it certainly harks back to his distinguished military career. It is reminiscent of no-one so much as the great patriotic hero of the age, Admiral Horatio Nelson, and the similarity is more than coincidental. Nelson and Despard went back a long way. They had fought together as young men, with heroic bravery and against impossible odds; they had faced death in action for the first time together, and both had survived by a whisker. Their mutual admiration had lasted a lifetime. The most publicized event of Despard's trial had been the appearance of Nelson as the star character witness for the defence; he had publicly stated that he had the 'highest respect' for Despard, and that 'no man could have shown more zealous attachment to his sovereign and his country'. Each man would die in the service of his cause, and both their ends were public sensations: the London crowd at Despard's execution would not be surpassed until the extraordinary scenes at Nelson's funeral after Trafalgar two years later. History would record them as opposites, the epitomes of hero and villain; in each other's eyes, they were closer to brothers.

This Nelsonian image of Despard is the one recalled in the epithet that attached itself so firmly to the hanged man at the time: 'the unfortunate Colonel Despard'. It was originally coined by his supporters to denote a man of principle and a loyal servant of his country, whose silencing

Etched by J Chapman

COL DESPARD.

on trumped-up charges was a national disgrace. But the epithet stuck so universally because of its multiplicity of possible meanings. As well as the literal sense of 'unlucky', the word 'unfortunate' also had a second, colder and more ironic usage, one which is preserved today in phrases such as, for example, 'an unfortunate turn of phrase' – unfortunate not just for the protagonist but for everyone concerned. This is the sense in which Despard was unfortunate for most of the British establishment: regrettable, even pathetic, someone to be glossed over quickly and dignified with as little comment as possible. In this sense, though, Despard's death was unfortunate not just for the man himself but for those who executed him. They had their day of pomp and ceremony, their unarguable show of strength, yet they were left to explain why it had become necessary to execute a loyal and heroic army officer whose dignity in the face of his punishment had not cracked and who had left a far more positive impression on the crowd than those who had sentenced him to death.

Over the years, perhaps as an alternative to explanation, 'unfortunate' came to acquire a third sense as an epithet for Despard: a pointed euphemism for mentally unbalanced. In the ever more cursory tellings of his tale, Despard became 'crack-brained', 'deluded', 'disturbed', his conspiracy a 'crazed scheme' or a 'mad plot'. Increasingly, over the next 150 years, the standard explanation for Despard's actions came to include this sense that he was, to a greater or lesser degree, insane. Even some of his apologists joined in with the insanity plea, suggesting that he had been 'touched' by the sun during his time in the tropics, or 'made mad by official persecution'. This was perhaps not so much a serious clinical diagnosis as a shorthand for the way in which Despard's motivations became ever more incomprehensible

Etched by Barlow, from a Sketch taken at his Trial.

COL. DESPARD.

to history. There is no contemporary evidence that he was mentally unbalanced, even though it remains hard to say exactly how a sane man ought to act under such circumstances. On the contrary, from his trial through his final imprisonment right up to his carefully measured gallows speech, observers on all sides were struck, even haunted, by his eerie dignity and unbreakable commitment to an exacting code of honour.

The final portrait, sketched at Despard's trial and published before his death, shows the artist playing up to his viewers' expectations of rough-hewn villainy, but is perhaps as close to life as the previous one. Here is another man entirely: no wig or finery, wild hair and a craggy face, unmistakably a man of action with a life of weatherbeaten experience behind him. This is a portrait that suggests not so much the future as the past; nothing so much as a buccaneer or privateer from the golden age of piracy, Henry Morgan perhaps, or Captain Kidd. This image dovetails with a different aspect of Despard's story. His career unfolded in the piratical wilds of the Caribbean, part of a British colonial presence that had evolved slowly, and less than completely, from the days of state-sanctioned piracy against the Spanish. The accusation of piracy in these parts was still a potent one, and one which was levelled against Despard; it was an accusation that was instrumental in setting him on his trajectory towards the gallows. He hung on the cusp between the age of piracy and the age of revolution.

All these images of Despard – traitor, pirate, freedom-fighter, noble scapegoat – are still left hanging in the air. No consensus was forged after his death. The cloud of treason obscured the man, and then evaporated as other news took its place. For many, the case was closed, an ugly episode put to rest. For others, it was deeply regrettable, gone but not forgotten. For a minority it was a festering sore that would not be healed until it was avenged with the same brutality with which Despard had been executed.

This lack of consensus manifested itself not in continued controversy, but, as the crowd had witnessed it, mostly in silence. Histories during the nineteenth century mentioned Despard less and less; chronicles dropped the day of his execution from their lists. He became a footnote, and gradually even less than a footnote. Throughout most of the twentieth century, he receded further from memory. His period of history took on a character imbued with triumphal hindsight, dominated by Nelson and Wellington, Trafalgar and Waterloo, the era that birthed a new national anthem and a new Great Britain, and dispelled the eighteenth-century bogeys of violent mobs and insurrections with a golden age of trade, prosperity and empire. By the 1920s, the historian H. W. C. Davis could assert in passing, and without fear of contradiction, in his Oxford lectures that the 'hare-brained and desperate plot' that preceded Despard's execution was 'hardly possible to explain except on the supposition that his mind was disordered'.

This was an assertion that would be repeated un-challenged for a further generation. Within this confident imperial narrative Despard, who had been the harbinger of a quite different story, sank without trace. It was only in the 1960s that his world began to be revisited by scholars seeking the roots of another grand story: the origins of democracy, political reform, the labour movement, the revolutionary working class and racial equality. In the landmark work of this movement, his *Making of the English Working Classes*, E. P. Thompson reversed the certainty of over a century by arguing that Despard's treason had been 'an incident of real importance in British political history'.

Assembling this story has awoken Despard from the sleep of history, because his causes are now the rights and liberties we take for granted in modern democracies. It is no longer possible to ignore the match between his gallows speech and, for example, the UN Charter of Human Rights, which enshrines the 'democratic principles of the dignity, equality and mutual respect for men', or UNESCO's rejection of the 'ignorance and prejudice of the doctrine of the inequality of men and races'. The *Times* denounced Despard's gallows speech as the most 'flagrant high treason' ever spoken in public; today, it is the opposition to Despard's sentiments that is a crime. There is no longer any difficulty in understanding Despard's political views; the difficulty now lies in understanding what it meant to hold such views two hundred years ago.

Yet the attempt to shoehorn Despard into this modern story is still problematic. All too often within its scheme he becomes a satellite: a postscript to the radicalism of the French Revolution, or a precursor to the next generation's struggle for democracy and political reform. Such schemes, by their nature, risk turning him into an abstraction, a figurehead for broader social currents and political forces. But Despard was a practical man, not a political theorist; he played his cards as they lay, and his contested death was the outcome of a life like no-one else's.

To locate Despard in his place in history, it may be necessary to grasp the paradox that he was indeed an important figure, but to a history that never quite took place. In the first great age of revolutions, from 1776 to 1848, Britain was a conspicuous island in the tide that swept most of Europe and America. Why did a British revolution never happen? Many reasons have been cited. Britain was indeed an island, partially sheltered from such tides by its geography. Its people were less intensively armed and militarized than many of their neighbours. Its state apparatus of law and order was highly developed. It was constantly unified by real or imagined dangers from beyond its shores. But there are two reasons that are pressed into service most frequently. The first is that, unlike most of Europe with its despotic monarchies, Britain already had a constitution and a parliamentary democracy, established by its own Glorious Revolution of 1688. The second is that, with one major exception, it won every war it fought throughout the eighteenth century. It was a winning formula, and its people had neither the need nor the desire to overthrow it.

These may well have turned out to be the salient factors, but such analysis was not possible from Despard's vantage point in 1803. Then, an entirely different view was possible, and at least as plausible. Britain had spent much of the previous century at war against the absolutist monarchies of France and Spain, fighting proudly and righteously in defence of a state that enshrined a far greater degree of liberty and justice for the common people. But it had then lost, catastrophically, a war against its American colonies for their right to set up an independent and constitutional republic based far more explicitly on the consent and freedom of its citizens. In 1803 Britain had once again been at war with the ideologically driven republic of France, and had just been forced to sue for an ignominious peace after years of near bankruptcy, mutiny among its troops and the imposition of draconian state powers to suppress its own dissenting population. The conclusion was easily drawn at the time that, when Britain had been fighting with justice on her side, she had always won; but that the beacon of liberty that had inspired her was now dimmed, perhaps even tarnished beyond repair. With hindsight, Britain might have been on her way to a manifest destiny of global empire, but at the time the writing seemed to many to be on the wall, and its message unambiguously clear.

Despard's execution prompted Robert Southey to take stock of which way the tide of history seemed to be flowing. 'Do I then', he asked, 'think that England is in danger of revolution?' His answer was grim: 'I believe that revolution inevitably must come, and in its most fearful shape.' This was no isolated or partisan view. Southey, like his fellow Romantics Wordsworth and Coleridge, had long since retreated from the zealous republicanism he had championed loudly after the fall of the Bastille; he had, though, maintained throughout his hatred for Prime Minister William Pitt, whom he still thought of as a vain, power-obsessed warmonger. 'What a blessing that it did not happen under Pitt,' he observed of Despard's execution; no-one at all would have believed the charges, and revolution would surely have come sooner rather than later. But Pitt had resigned in 1801, and had been replaced by his childhood friend Henry Addington. Although there was little to choose between their political orientation and vested interests, Southey found himself able to approve of the new man. Addington's evident weaknesses – lack of colour, will and conviction – were for Southey good points: they made him less belligerent than Pitt, more disinterested, more likely to preserve the peace with France and loosen the state's grip on British liberties at home. Yet there was a strong hint, too, of Southey's relief at finding himself back in the mainstream of politics, able finally to distance himself with dignity from his youthful ardour. His assessment of the threat of revolution might have been tinged with an alarmism that became more theatrical as he got older, but it was essentially offered from the cautious centre ground by a man who was soon to be honoured as the nation's poet. Whether or not Britain came close to revolution around 1800, the threat of revolution was a major driving force in its politics, and one which would be drastically underestimated by historians to come.

Yet to patch Despard into a history that never happened is still, perhaps, to bend him out of shape. He was, by his own account at least, no violent revolutionary. This was precisely the charge he had denied at his trial, and continued to deny to the end, even in front of a partisan crowd and with a rope around his neck. He was much judged at his death, but little observed during his lifetime, and consequently such judgements reflected the prejudices of those who held them, and the bitterly contested political debate of the time, more than the man himself. Even today, the greatest challenge to understanding his life is to avoid the rush to judgement: Despard's story cuts to the quick of our instinctive modern certainties about the politics of left and right, and challenges them by refusing to sit neatly within either frame.

The lack of consensus about Despard represented, and still represents, far more than the disputed facts of his fatal crime. There was no-one who had shared all or even most of his life with him; it had unfolded in distant colonies and in the shadows of London's underworld, among Miskito Indians and army officers, freed slaves and colonial dignitaries, peers of the realm and outlawed freedom-fighters. Its most striking feature was the breadth of experience it had taken in, its vertiginous heights and depths: from heroic soldier to political dissident, from Irish gentleman to colonial governor to pirate. In every telling, its hallmark was its contrasts: it was irresistibly read as a morality tale of pride and fall, hubris and nemesis. Yet when his story is assembled without moral or political intent, it is not Despard's contrasts but his constancy that is most striking. It was not the man who changed, so much as the world around him.

When Despard was executed in London, it was still in many ways a foreign country to him. There were two countries that had a better claim to being his home: Ireland, where he grew up, and Jamaica, where he came of age and served out his career. These two cultures were not as remote from each other as might be imagined. Both were colonies of Britain; both were ruled by a class of people who regarded themselves as British first, and Irish or Jamaican an often distant second. His own family were Anglo-Irish, by which they would have meant that they were British Protestant landowners who felt more kinship with their fellows in Yorkshire, Canada or Barbados than with the indigenous Gaelic and Catholic culture that surrounded them.

Despard was twenty-one when he arrived in Jamaica as an army officer in 1772 and he served the British Crown in the Caribbean and Central America, with only two brief visits home, until he was forty. In one sense, Jamaica was a backwater: a remote island colony, six weeks' journey across the Atlantic from Britain, its few thousand plantation farmers dwarfed by their slave labour force, presided over by a small military presence and riddled with tropical disease. But in another sense, it was a pioneering, if unwitting, experiment in the next stage of human history. Many of the revolutions that were to transform the following century – imperial, industrial and political – were incubating in the Caribbean colonies more intensely than anywhere else on the globe. The relations between trade and war, rulers and ruled, capital and labour, productivity and profit, were all being crucially reworked on the coastlines, plantations and mountain plateaux of Despard's adopted home. When his life came to its notorious conclusion, his time in this melting-pot would be the basis for his quiet conviction that he had seen the future more clearly and accurately than most.

There had never been a time when Despard had not been destined for the army. He was the youngest of seven brothers, six of whom survived infancy; the eldest inherited the substantial family estate, and the rest entered the armed forces as soon as their childhoods came to an end. Two of them, John and Andrew, would serve with distinction in the American War of Independence and reach the ranks of general and major. Edward's rise through the ranks would be faster than both of them, though its trajectory would be cut short.

The family estate centred on a tall, rather forbidding manor house near Mountrath in the centre of Ireland, whose ruined and ivy-covered gables still stand. The family were Protestants, descended from Huguenots named D'Espard who had fled France two hundred years before, and who regarded England as their cultural and religious motherland. Although subsequent generations of Despards would campaign for Irish home rule, Edward's later and passionate identification with the Irish political struggle was not inherited. His childhood was a cloistered one, where casual mixing with the local culture was not indulged. The tenor of home was set by religious observance, correct manners and the prospect of a life of military discipline.

Although reckoned to be the most talented of the family, with precocious abilities in drawing, mathematics and engineering, Edward was steered into army service exactly as his brothers had been. Before school he was placed as a page in the family of Lord Hertford, the Lord Lieutenant of Ireland, a notoriously strict and unsentimental education during which any chafing against authority was suppressed – or perhaps, in Edward's case, postponed. School itself was the military academy in Dublin Castle, from which he graduated at the age of fifteen. His father immediately bought him a commission as an ensign in the 50th Infantry Regiment, and he passed through to his coming of age as a footsoldier. When the 50th was posted to Jamaica in 1772, he was promoted to lieutenant.

Despard's arrival in Jamaica was part of an extended wave of military reinforcement against the Spanish, the first time that the island had hosted a substantial British army presence. This militarization had begun during the Seven Years' War with Spain, which had ended with British victory in 1763, and was a marker of the ways in which the island was becoming a crucial focus of British economic strategy and a coveted prize in the conflict between European powers that was soon to transform the New World.

The first transatlantic visitor to Jamaica had been Christopher Columbus, who landed on its north coast on his second voyage in 1494. Like so many subsequent visitors, he was staggered by its natural beauty: white-sand beaches and coves leading up to lush savannah and, unlike many of its low-lying neighbours in the archipelago, towering mountains covered in dense mahogany forests, their peaks vanishing into columns of mist. It was immediately apparent that the island was well settled. The Tainos, an Arawak-speaking Indian people, had been crossing over from the mainland in canoes for centuries, setting up communities around the fresh water sources and gradually evolving a loose political system of provinces controlled by tribal chiefs, or *caciques*. Despite a brief, suspicious stand-off – the explorers' reputation had

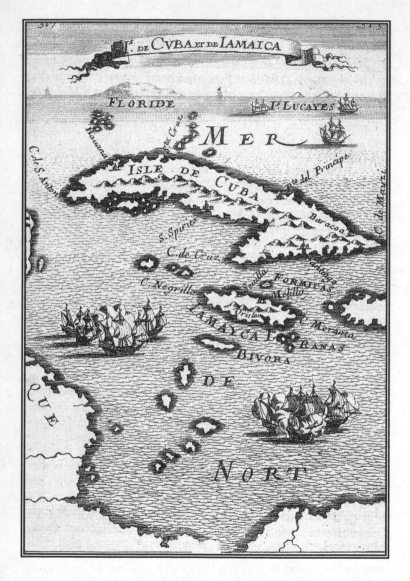

Jamaica and the Caribbean, seventeenth century

preceded them – relations settled into functional co-existence. The Tainos respected the new arrivals' property, and Columbus was delighted to report that 'we lost not the value of a pin'. In fact, it was the new arrivals who borrowed from the locals: they became converts to the Taino habit of smoking. The name of their pipes was *tabaco*, although the plant itself, which they cultivated extensively, was known as *cohiba*.

Columbus had little interest in Jamaica, his sights still fixed on navigating his way through to China; but he had, naturally, claimed the island in the name of the Spanish Crown, and a period of sporadic settlement followed. A base named Spanish Town was set up near the south coast as a staging-post, and handfuls of Spanish colonists moved in to make a living from the lush interior. But the colony was slow to prosper. Gold and silver were what the Spanish merchants were after, and hopes had been raised by the discovery that the Tainos possessed some items of gold jewellery, but these turned out to have been brought from the mainland. The island itself seemed to offer little but unprofitable subsistence crops such as maize and cassava, and some virulent and previously unknown tropical fevers.

The early Spanish settlers had a far more dramatic effect on the people than on the landscape. The Columbian exchange of diseases was, as everywhere, fatally loaded in the Europeans' favour. Smallpox in particular swept through the indigenous population; the weakened tribes were sent into a terminal decline by Spanish territorial raids. Captives were corralled into forced labour on largely unsuccessful plantations, where thousands were worked to death. The Spanish administration eventually proposed reservations for the dwindling population; the Tainos themselves were in favour, but the planters objected that such a measure would compromise their workforce.

Spiralling towards extinction, Taino tribes committed mass suicide by drinking poison extracted from cassava roots. By the seventeenth century, the original settlers were virtually extinct.

Thus Jamaica at the dawn of the mercantile era was, from the colonists' perspective, more or less virgin territory. What made it most attractive to visitors over the next hundred years was not its physical assets but its location. Its many hidden coves and bays were easy sailing distance from the transatlantic routes plied by merchant ships returning from the coast of Panama, where the prodigious treasures being plundered from Peru and Mexico were transported and stockpiled in remote and vulnerable shanty ports to await shipping to Europe. Jamaica, during the course of the seventeenth century, became synonymous with piracy.

Piracy took hold in a political and military vacuum. Although the island was technically Spanish, the colonists lacked the manpower to secure it, and it rapidly evolved into a no-man's land in the shadow war between rival European nation states. Pirates offered themselves as paramilitary forces for their native lands in exchange for legal immunity; commissioned state vessels presented themselves as pirates so that they could raid during peacetime without diplomatic consequences. In times of delicate negotiation between Britain, France and Spain, acts of piracy could be disowned, lamented or plausibly denied; in times of diplomatic sabre-rattling they could be claimed as famous national victories. Someone like Francis Drake could be – as he remains to this day – a patriotic hero to the British and an infamous villain to the Spanish. Drake's methods were, from his victims' perspective, indistinguishable from piracy: he disguised himself as a Spaniard to case out the Panama ports, anchored in hidden coves, and ambushed mule trains and treasure stores in the middle of the night with a motley crew armed to the teeth. The only difference – that he sailed his haul of gold and silver ingots back to Britain and presented it to the monarch – was negligible from the vantage point of the sacked and torched ports he left behind. Piracy, like treason, was and would remain a slippery concept, subject to the vagaries of perspective and timing.

Jamaica's transition from pirate haven to legitimate British colony was similarly opportunistic and piecemeal. In 1655 Oliver Cromwell despatched a fleet to take the island from Spain. He had asked the Spanish ambassador for the right to trade from Jamaica, but had been refused; he had several naval detachments he suspected of royalist sympathies, and which he wanted to utilize as far away from England as possible; he also wished to carve out some Protestant territory in the overwhelmingly Catholic Americas. The original target had been the far more profitable and well-settled Spanish colony of Santo Domingo – present-day Haiti – but the fleet was fought off easily and headed for Jamaica instead. The Spanish settlers here had dwindled to fewer than two thousand, mostly in Spanish Town, and they sued for peace as soon as the English arrived. Over the next few years the resistance from outlying Spanish enclaves was rooted out, a small Spanish fleet was seen off, and several thousand planters and traders arrived from New England and the British Isles. A new capital was established on the archipelago of tiny coral islands, or cays, flung like an arm across the huge natural harbour on the south coast, and in 1660, on the restoration of Charles II, it was named Port Royal.

Jamaica's change in colonial status led not to an extension of government and the rule of law, but to a massive resurgence of piracy. Port Royal looked like an English port, complete with brick and half-timber houses arrayed along Queen Street and Thames Street, but functioned as an enclave where privateers – pirates operating under letters of marque from the English Crown – could refit their ships, buy provisions and sell goods looted from the Spanish ports in Panama. Their numbers were sufficient to scare off the Spanish, and they operated free of charge to the English government, on a commission basis of 'no prey, no pay'. Port Royal swiftly gained a reputation as a sinkhole of depravity where freebooters, filibusters, buccaneers and privateers squandered vast sums on drinking, gambling and prostitution. The Spanish government protested vigorously and persistently to the English court, and the two nations signed a treaty whereby the Spanish recognized English rule in Jamaica in exchange for the appointment of a state-sanctioned governor accountable for reining in the pirates. The governor, Sir Thomas Molyford, followed the now-standard diplomatic practice of deploring the extent of piracy but pleading his powerlessness to act effectively against it.

The piratical heyday of Port Royal came to an abrupt end on 7 June 1692 when a massive earthquake ripped the cays of Port Royal from the sea bed and plunged virtually the entire town into the ocean. In a biblical apocalypse widely seen as divine retribution for the city of sin, the churchyards opened up to disgorge decades' worth of putrefied corpses into the harbour; buccaneers paddled through the wreckage in canoes, stripping the cadavers of their jewellery. The town was abandoned, and trade and government administration relocated across the harbour to the small settlement on the more sheltered mainland known as Kingston.

The 1692 earthquake at Port Royal

The destruction of Port Royal turned out to be the cue for another reinvention of Jamaica. At the same time that the increasing settlement of the Caribbean was beginning to squeeze old-time piracy out of range of the larger islands, the influx of planters was also beginning to make the interior of the island profitable for the first time. Tropical crops such as tobacco, indigo and cocoa were being successfully cultivated, and a better-policed maritime trade was gradually making their export to Europe more economically attractive. But the new enterprise that was really beginning to transform the Caribbean islands was the growing and refining of sugar. By the time Despard arrived, the sugar trade had become far more valuable than the gold and silver that had motivated the original colonists. Despard was witness to a powerful tide of change that was not only economic but social and political, the consequences of which were transforming the destiny not only of the Caribbean but of the entire developed world.

The individual most emblematic of the early stages of this transformation was Henry Morgan. A Welshman from a distinguished military family, he was born around 1635, entered the army as a youngster, arrived in Jamaica with Cromwell's fleet and participated in the island's capture. Installed in Port Royal, he took his pick of the most hardened pirates and buccaneers and launched a series of daring raids on the Spanish ports along the Panama coast, locating the best-concealed treasure stores by torturing the inhabitants and extracting huge ransoms from the Spanish government under the threat of burning their harbours to the ground. He returned to Jamaica several times with enormous cargoes of loot, and led the most prodigious orgies of drinking, whoring and gambling in Port Royal's history. When the diplomatic heat became too great for

Henry Morgan

him to continue, he was arrested with much fanfare by the English navy and hauled back to London. There, though, he was not imprisoned but consulted in detail by the government about how to manage their affairs in Jamaica, then sent back as a poacher-turned-gamekeeper with the title of lieutenant-general. He used his position and salary to buy a thousand acres of sugar plantation and grew fat – spectacularly fat, by all accounts – on his new trade. He became a folk-hero back in England, where he was knighted, and he successfully sued the author of a chronicle that referred to him as a pirate. When he died in 1688 he received a state funeral, complete with twenty-one-gun salute.

The change in the fortunes of men such as Sir Henry Morgan led to a new system of government in Jamaica, one which was operating on Despard's arrival and would continue to operate until long after his death. The Crown – which after the Act of Union of 1706 became British rather than English – appointed a governor to oversee its interests and enforce British law. This led to a brief secondary burst of notoriety for the remnants of Port Royal which, by virtue of its conspicuous position at the entrance to the new Kingston harbour, was reconstituted as a site for public execution by hanging. By the 1720s, the last recalcitrant buccaneers such as Charles Vane, Calico Jack and the female pirate Anne Bonny could be seen swinging over the half-submerged cays.

Under the new administrative system, the governor's power was balanced by that of an elected Assembly, composed overwhelmingly of wealthy planters representing the colony's economic interests. This gave a degree of balance to the crucial arrangements for trade and its protection, issues that involved the planters directly. Britain was under an obligation to protect the planters and traders by force of arms; Jamaica, in turn, was obliged to trade exclusively with Britain, even if more money could be made by piracy or trade with rival colonial powers. From the start, the details of this arrangement set up tensions between the rival administrative bodies. When the Assembly's local regulations and codes shaded into laws, the prospect of Jamaica's legislature drifting apart from the mother country began to alarm the British government, and they imposed their own laws to override them. The Assembly tested its strength by refusing to accept certain laws; its members were sporadically dragged back to London, sometimes under arrest. After several years a compromise emerged: the Assembly would make its own laws, but the governor would send them to the Crown to be ratified. New British laws, similarly, would be passed to the Jamaican Assembly for approval.

Behind these tensions lay a struggle between money and power that could never be entirely resolved, as the balance was constantly in flux. The planters, the power behind the Assembly, were becoming phenomenally rich. By the time Despard arrived, Jamaica was Britain's wealthiest colony, yielding substantially more at this point than India and China combined. But the planters in turn were dependent on the British army and navy for the protection of the island. Just as Jamaica's location had made it an ideal remote base for pillaging the Spanish empire, it conversely made it a vulnerable and increasingly attractive target for Spanish aggression as its wealth swelled.

Despard's career in the Caribbean would be defined by this power struggle. As an army officer he represented the Crown, and was under the immediate command of the governor; yet the army's overwhelming imperative was to protect the planters and their trade. As the ambiguities of the chain of command became more apparent, Despard would remain unambiguously loyal to the Crown, but in doing so he would become a thorn in the side of the British government.

Refined sugar is a food, but it is also a drug. Its effects, most noticeable in children and those unaccustomed to it, or in anyone who has had a large dose, are almost instantaneous: energy, euphoria, physical excitation. The corollary of the 'sugar buzz' is a set of negative effects, less often noticed because they occur at a further remove from the ingestion of the dose: lethargy, nervous irritability, and a surge and drain of energy that can induce depressive mood swings. But its most classic effect as a drug is to generate a metabolic addiction, which manifests itself in the cycle of craving, tolerance and withdrawal. When refined sugar is introduced into a diet for the first time, it is powerfully self-reinforcing. Doses that initially produced excitation or nausea are quickly tolerated, and withdrawing sugar from the diet produces a desire and sense of need for it that were absent until it was first introduced.

On an individual level these effects are usually mild, but when observed macroscopically, on the level of cultures, societies and epochs of history, they are momentous. Refined-sugar dependency began to transform the modern world in the eighteenth century; the society that became addicted was Europe, and the one that supplied the drug was the colonial Caribbean – and, more than anywhere else, Jamaica. In 1650, refined sugar was absent from all but the most luxurious European diets; throughout the eighteenth century, both production and consumption increased by an average of 7 per cent every year. During the nineteenth century, the annual increase rose to 10 per cent. In 1700, the average per capita intake of refined sugar was 4lb a year; by 1800, it had risen to 18lb, and by 1900 it was rushing towards 100lb – often 20 per cent of the entire calorie intake – with new technological drivers such as refrigeration, carbonated sugar drinks and processed foods poised to raise it even higher. Today, the wave of refined-sugar consumption that overwhelmed Europe in the eighteenth century is still breaking on the furthest and most remote reaches of the globe. No society in history has yet kicked the habit.

Jamaica was the epicentre of this revolution, and it was the first to feel its unprecedented social and economic consequences. The logistics of the sugar business rewrote the rulebook for the creation of wealth, announcing a new relationship between capital, productivity and profit. The mechanics of mass sugar production drove a new set of economies of scale and prompted the creation of a new type of labour force, and the race to cash in on the endless spiral of demand pioneered many elements of what would soon be called the Industrial Revolution. The global trade in sugar entwined business and politics in new ways, testing the old system of national markets with ever-escalating demand that could only be met by more vigorous trade protection and military intervention. Every settled society in history had thus far been maintained by a 'core carbohydrate' – wheat, rice, cassava, maize, sago – which functioned as the staple of its domestic food economy. The escalation from core carbohydrate to the high-powered, labour-intensive production of a refined carbohydrate – sugar – was intimately involved in the parallel acceleration from disparate regional trade networks to an increasingly unified global capitalism.

Sugar cane was not native to the Caribbean. It originated in the South Pacific, New Guinea and Indonesia, and had travelled around the globe the long way. It had been cultivated in China and India, adopted as a sweetener in the Arab world, and had 'followed the Koran' to Spain. The Spanish had cultivated it in the Canaries and Madeira, and Columbus had brought it to the Caribbean on his second voyage. But it had taken a conjunction of factors to get the motors of the mass sugar industry fully up and running. One was the increasing wealth of the population back home, and the trickling down of courtly and luxury items to a new class of spender. Another, interlinked, was the increasing popularity of other soft drugs such as tea, coffee, cocoa and tobacco. All naturally had a bitter edge, and stimulant beverages sweetened with sugar, or tobacco ropes cured with molasses, proved more palatable than the traditional Indian preparations. These nudges were enough to start the trade snowballing by revealing the hitherto unsuspected extent of the European sweet tooth. Sugar became medicine, condiment, preservative, sweetener; it was added to meat dishes to make them richer, to beer to make it stronger, and to tea until the spoon stood up in the cup. Medical opinion was largely behind it, recommending it as an energy source for the young, elderly and infirm, and in forms ranging from toothpaste to snuff. By the end of the eighteenth century, a medical authority could proudly write that it had enriched the daily diet to the point where 'a royal English dinner of the twelfth century would be despised by a modern tradesman'. Previous sugar sources had always been self-limiting – honey was hard to mass-produce, eating too much fruit led to stomach complaints – but refined sugar was quick to demonstrate the untapped potential of sweetness.

This escalating demand, it was soon discovered, could be matched by escalating supply. Systematic large-scale cultivation of sugar cane began in Barbados and Jamaica around 1650, and it soon became clear that its economic rewards were prodigious. A planter could invest a sum and increase it twenty-fold in ten years; he could then invest the new sum and do the same again. There were only three theoretical limits to the amount of money that could be made. One was the amount of land, but the amount of land available for sugar plantation in Jamaica was effectively unlimited. The second was the supply of capital, and this simply multiplied itself even from modest beginnings. The third was the labour required, which was massive. Sugar cultivation was hard, intensive work. Jungle had to be cleared, swamps drained, trenches dug, cane shoots planted and weeded and harvested. The cane had to be cut as soon as it was ripe, and ground down to pulp as soon as it was cut. It had to be boiled in giant vats, over fires that had to be constantly stoked; it had to be skimmed, reduced, dried and granulated. The final obstacle to turning sugar into an unlimited global money machine was overcome by intensifying the practice of slavery. It was the ramifications of this last, crucial link in the chain that would define Despard's tour of duty.

It has been argued that global capitalism could not have got started without slavery, that without the defining boost from a massive army of forced labour, themselves unpaid, neither consumers nor a drain on profits, the system could never have bootstrapped itself from its piecemeal origins into a fully global market. Whether it could have started in other ways is perhaps a moot point; the fact is that it was the trinity of sugar, slavery and private capital that gave birth to today's global economic system. It was not precisely an industrial revolution, since it did not depend on machines to substitute for human labour; rather, it depended on human labour being used for the type of work that would soon be done by machines. The eighteenth-century Jamaican sugar mill – with its boiling-houses and their vast vats dwarfing the dozens of slaves who attended to their every need; with the deafening noise of clanking metal, hissing and roaring, the already intense heat amplified by the log furnaces and the crowded trestles; with its massed ranks of drones separated into their treadmill tasks of grinding, milling, boiling, stoking and pouring – looked like nothing else in the world at that time, but very like the industrial infrastructure that would blanket Europe in the next century.

The British were not the first to bring slaves to Jamaica. The Spanish had imported them from West Africa since the fifteenth century; the Dutch and the French had previously used slave labour in their Caribbean colonies. Nor were African slaves the only source of forced labour. The British planters had long used indentured servants: Irish deportees or convicts who were worked without pay

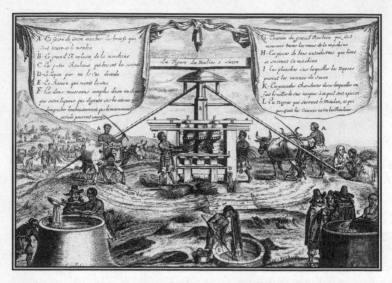

Jamaican sugar mill in the eighteenth century

for ten or fifteen years as an alternative to prison sentences. Nor was there a clear line between slavery and other forms of coercion such as naval press-ganging; sailors in the British navy were rarely allowed shore leave because so many of them would desert as soon as they were given the chance. All in all, the vast majority of those performing the Herculean labours required to turn tropical islands into economically viable colonies were doing so against their will, or at least without any choice in the matter. Nevertheless, the scale of slavery in Jamaica at the point when Despard arrived in the 1770s was unprecedented. There were two hundred thousand black slaves on the island, and twelve thousand whites. It had long been recognized that this was a ratio that was close to unmanageable. The Assembly had passed a law requiring planters to hire one white servant for every ten black slaves, but it was frequently flouted and the imbalance was constantly increasing. The brute fact was that, as far as the planters were concerned, Africans outperformed Europeans, who were unused to the tropical heat and were rarely able to survive the malaria to which many Africans had a tolerance. The economic imperatives of the sugar trade allowed for no other solution than black slavery.

But this was still an unprecedented arrangement, and one which many realized was changing the nature of the British colonial world. Previously, most of Britain's colonies – America and Canada – had been composed of white, Anglo-Saxon emigrants; it was business as usual, simply on new territory. The British army had been required to defend the colonies' borders, but not to keep order from within. Now, in Jamaica, the army needed to be permanently stationed in large numbers alongside the colony's own militia to protect the enterprise from insurrection and collapse. Where the previous system had been consensual and cheap, the new one was coercive and expensive. At the moment when Edward Gibbon was beginning to write his *Decline and Fall of the Roman Empire*, there were many who felt that, in the cane plantations of Jamaica, Britain was crossing an invisible line between a consenting network of trading colonies that was beneficial to all and a tyrannical, multiracial empire sustained by brute force and destined to grind slowly towards economic, military and moral collapse.

There was already a great deal of opposition to slavery, though most of it was theoretical rather than practical. A generation before William Wilberforce and the Clapham Sect, the abolition of slavery was close to intellectual orthodoxy. *The Spirit of the Laws*, Baron de Montesquieu's eloquent defence of natural rights – and, specifically, of the British constitutional system – had been published in

1748, and its demolition of any moral basis for slavery had been highly influential in both France and Britain. Enlightenment thinkers such as Adam Smith had stated their opposition to it on economic as well as moral grounds. Samuel Johnson, by no stretch of the imagination a political radical, raised toasts 'to the next slave revolt in Jamaica'. John Wesley had insisted that slavery was incompatible with Christian values. Lawyers had demonstrated in the benchmark ruling of 1772 known as the Somersett case that the right of habeas corpus, whereby detention without trial was presumed illegal, made it incompatible with British law. In 1758, the Quaker Society of Friends had made the first step from theory to action, prohibiting its members from any involvement in the 'iniquitous practice'. Despard was working within the slavery system and duty bound to enforce it, but his final gallows plea for justice for 'the human race' and 'mankind in general', if it was treason in 1803, nevertheless echoed a conviction that had long been deeply rooted in British public life.

The case in favour of slavery was, in the 1770s, rarely presented. There was little need to do so: the practice was in full swing, and there were no serious attempts to interrupt it. When it came, it was, naturally enough, the planters who made it most forcefully. Their appeal was also to liberty, in the form of their right to their own property, and they made it indignantly: as Dr Johnson pointedly wondered, 'How is it that we hear the loudest yelps of liberty among the drivers of negroes?' The planters, in their petitions to the British government, took the line that the abolitionists 'must show what right they have to disturb and injure the planter in the enjoyment of a property legally acquired'. They argued that Britain's primacy in the slave trade was a form of regulation, since the French, Dutch and others 'at present buy their negroes of the British traders, at very high prices, which operates as a check on their cultivation'. They appealed, too, to the creation of wealth, and the folly of Britain hamstringing itself with a unilateral ban. Mostly, however, they stood aloof from the argument. In 1800, the Surgeon-General of Jamaica, Benjamin Moseley, could still paint a sunny and lyrical picture of the sugar trade, a benign circle where the goodness of the sun's tropical energy was equably distributed around the globe. 'At home, the merchant, from this transatlantic operation, supports legions of manufacturers,' he maintained. 'He collects his rays from equatorial climes, diffuses their genial warmth over the frigid regions of the earth, and makes the industrious world one great family.'

The slaves themselves, though increasingly aware of these debates, were not counting on them for their freedom. The only practical strategies at their disposal were insurrection and escape, and they had been using them since they first arrived. The mountainous interior of Jamaica had been inhabited for centuries by maroons – runaway slaves from the Spanish days, so named from the term *cimarron*, meaning wild or untamed. There were thousands of them, at times outnumbering the slaves in the plantations; they cultivated corn, yams and plantains in the highlands, kept pigs, came down from the mountains at night to raid the settlements and retreated up to the high mountain gorges when they were pursued. As guerrilla fighters, among the limestone caves and sinkholes of the deep interior, they were untouchable; they camouflaged themselves in leaf hides and co-ordinated ambushes with bugles made from cows' horns. The British army had been reduced to scorched-earth tactics, torching their habitations with forest fires, and to the torture and execution of captives, their bodies staked on posts or hung from trees

Caribbean slave revolt

on the borders of maroon territory. Finally, in 1738, a treaty had been made with them: they were to be given their liberty in the non-cultivated parts of the island in exchange for returning to the British authorities any escaped slaves who tried to join them. The treaty held, and from this point the maroons became a priceless asset in the continuing struggle to keep the slaves in the plantations.

But the slave revolts continued. When Despard arrived, the colony was on high alert after a wave of insurrections that had come closer than any before to a full-scale slave takeover of the island, of the kind that would eventually wrest neighbouring Haiti from colonial control entirely. They had begun in 1760 with a mass rebellion known as Tacky's Revolt.

Tacky – a corruption of his Ghanaian name, Tekyi – was a recent arrival, a chief of the Coromantee people of the Gold Coast of Africa, who had a reputation among the planters for 'pride', by which was meant an unwillingness to buckle under their new regime and a powerful ability to persuade even those who had been born into slavery in Jamaica to risk their lives for their freedom. Just before

dawn on Easter Sunday, Tacky and his immediate gang
murdered their owner, freed themselves and descended on
the north-coast harbour town of Port Maria, where they
broke into the stores, killed the shopkeeper and made off
with all the muskets and shot they could carry. By the time
the sun was up, they had been joined by hundreds more
slaves who had co-ordinated their escapes with Tacky's,
and together they blazed a trail through the inland plantations, killing planters and seizing more muskets before
heading for the hills.

Pursuit came quickly. One of the slaves slipped away
from the rebels and spread the alarm, and by noon there
were a hundred armed militia on their trail, with platoons
of infantry following them and the local Scott's Hall
maroons mobilizing to intercept them in the hills. But
Tacky and his fellow rebels made it to the high mountains
and held out. Among them were several Coromantee
obeah-men, the traditional West African priestcraft, who
had reverted to their priestly regalia of teeth and bone
jewellery, feathers and masks. All such native religious
practices were strictly prohibited in Jamaica, but this
prohibition had paradoxically strengthened them:
traditionally a secret society, obeah had flourished undercover, and had become an occult focus for organized
resistance. Some of the rebels, terrified by the brutal retribution promised by the troops, had deserted and returned
to the plantations, but many hung on fearlessly among the
bushfires and army and maroon patrols: the obeahs had
mixed up a powder which they claimed would protect the
wearer from gunshot wounds. Hearing that the obeah-men
were rumoured to be immortal, the troops determined to
catch one, and when they did they hanged him
prominently on a mountaintop.

Throughout the humid, sweltering summer Tacky and

A Negro hung alive by the Ribs to a Gallows.

Punishment for escaped slaves

his men remained at large, with the risk of wider insurrection spreading every day. Finally, in August, Tacky was run to ground in a forest gully and shot dead by a maroon named Davy as they were both running at full speed through the trees. The rest of his gang were found several days later in a cave where they had all committed suicide.

The army's most conspicuous strategy for deterring revolt was an array of execution methods that made hanging, drawing and quartering look mild. Tacky's head was posted on a spike in the middle of Spanish Town, from where it was secretly and ominously spirited away under cover of darkness. Subsequent rebel leaders were burned alive, or left to die in public, chained in irons or starved to death in steel cages in the centre of Kingston. It is probable that Despard's first view of Jamaica when he arrived in 1772 included not only the breathtaking spectacle of Kingston harbour and cays rising up to the emerald slopes of the Blue Mountains, but also dozens of black slaves, in various stages of decomposition, gibbeted from the yardarms, swinging from the street signs and impaled on posts along the waterfront.

Whatever expectations Despard had absorbed from his upbringing about a career in the British army, whether of defending the Crown against foreign tyranny or participating in conquests for its greater glory, the reality was that the first years of the 50th Regiment's tour of duty in Jamaica were dominated by a state of high alert against slave uprisings. The largest conspiracy yet was uncovered just before it was due to burn Kingston to the ground, by witnesses who told of a group of Coromantees swearing a death pact by drinking a brew of rum, blood, gunpowder and graveyard dirt. Sugar mills were periodically torched;

another revolt was put down in 1775. But this was also the year that a new threat to Jamaica materialized, with the first military engagement at Lexington between the British army and the rebel American colonists.

The declaration of independence by the thirteen colonies threatened Jamaica both from without and from within. The British army, whose forces in the New World were already stretched perilously thin, found themselves sucked into a conflict spanning a huge territory; at the same time, France and Spain were already beginning to mobilize their armies and navies to take advantage of any chinks Britain might leave in her armour. But the war also crystallized Jamaica's internal divisions between the governor and the Assembly. The governor, and thus the army, were there to defend the interests of the Crown, and to provide military support for Britain if it was required. But the Assembly had long been chafing at the bit. The established and wealthy planters considered themselves to have the same rights as free-born Englishmen at home, and believed that the Assembly should be treated as an institution equal to the House of Commons, rather than the subsidiary local role to which Whitehall tended to relegate it. There were many who were quite as opposed to British rule as the most militant of the American rebels; the difference was more in the island's geography than the inhabitants' ideology. In Jamaica, the balance of military power was overwhelmingly in the mother country's favour. Without Britain's navy, the planters would be defenceless against the French and Spanish; without her army, they would be defenceless against slave revolts from within. Any act of rebellion against the Crown could be put down in days with a naval blockade. Ultimately, too, unlike most of the American colonists, the Jamaican planters were wealthy enough to sell up and buy their way into the landed gentry back home if they wished.

Nevertheless, much of the dissent in America had also played out in the Jamaican Assembly. Its members, too, had bitterly resented the Stamp Act of 1763, which had obliged them to commit all legal documents, deeds and contracts to government-issued stamped paper on which a tax was levied. In 1775, as the American crisis broke, a militant faction in the Assembly issued a strongly worded statement affirming their loyalty to the King but warning that 'no law could bind Englishmen unless it had received the assent of their representatives'. Parliament, they asserted, should leave the colonists' business alone; centrally imposed taxes weakened the colonists' obligations to the mother country. They appealed for reconciliation between Britain and the American colonies; the Americans extended a vote of thanks to Jamaica for its support. This was a strong statement of dissent in a time of national crisis. The Earl of Dartmouth, British Secretary of State for America, called it 'indecent, not to say criminal'.

Although the Jamaican Assembly could never push from dissent to full-scale rebellion as the Americans were doing, the schism was both serious and unresolved. Over and above the Stamp Act, the Assembly remained extremely resentful of the Sugar Act, which obliged them to sell all the sugar they produced to Britain. The truth was that this was an overwhelmingly advantageous arrangement for the planters. In exchange for it, large duties were levied on any sugar that came to Britain from outside its own colonies; without it, French sugar would have flooded into Britain well below the Jamaican price. The planters had the British market sewn up, and it was a huge market, with the British at this point consuming eight times as much sugar per head as the French, and at twice the price. The Jamaican planters were hardly in dire financial straits: 'as rich as a West Indian planter' had become a common turn of phrase all over Europe. Demand continued to outstrip supply, and they were nowhere near producing at capacity; in fact, they had deliberately restricted the amount of plantation land in Jamaica to keep prices high. At least half the suitable land on the island was still unplanted.

But the planters were nevertheless concerned that the French colonies were outstripping them. Santo Domingo and Martinique were by now producing more sugar than Jamaica and Barbados and selling it cheaper, and, crucially, they were permitted to sell it direct to the American colonies, thus cornering the short-haul market. In 1775 the Jamaican Assembly lobbied the British government to change the terms of the Sugar Act, threatening them with dire consequences if they refused. 'The French planter', they urged, 'can undercut the British planter by above twenty per cent.' It was no longer a question of capacity – 'the French as well as the English have each of them lands enough in their hands to produce as much sugar as will supply the whole consumption of Europe' – it was a question of winner-takes-all. 'In a small course of years one or other of them must become masters of that trade, and beat the other out of it,' they argued, stressing that the French were not unaware that the economies of scale offered by mass production cut both ways. The only way for the British colonies to survive was to take the fight to the enemy, and that would require a new arrangement: 'we should have a liberty of carrying our sugars directly to a foreign market, free from the charges, encumberances and restraints which presently lie upon us'. It was not yet the principled American call for no taxation without representation, but it was a clear sign that the Jamaican Assembly was also looking for a new dispensation, and would not be accountable for their actions if they were refused.

*   *   *

The records of Despard's life at this point are limited to army despatches; if he expressed his political views in private correspondence, it has not survived. But despite his later revolutionary career, there are no grounds for assuming that he felt sympathy for the American colonists' cause; some of his later correspondence certainly suggests that he found it dishonourable in important ways. Many of the British officer class took a dim view of the Jamaican Assembly's complaints against the Crown: the protection of the planters' trade was an expensive and dangerous business, and they were at the sharp end of it. This was the lens through which the struggle in America presented itself to them. The mainland colonies were not yet a nation, and there was a world of difference between the Boston lawyers who presented the most visible face to Britain and the wealthy slave-owning planters in the American South, who were the closest in distance and ideology to the Jamaican Assembly. From Despard's vantage point, there were principled objections to an independence that might allow those colonists who had wealth, land and property to abandon the precepts of universal justice guaranteed by Britain's constitutional monarchy. The American Revolution was many things, but it was not a social revolution: almost all its disparate voices enshrined the sanctity of property, to the benefit of those who already had it.

The non-white populations of America were a case in point. The British government, for example, had proposed a Proclamation Line to set western boundaries on white expansion and thus to maintain Native American territory; Thomas Jefferson, by contrast, had called for the 'termination of the history' of native land rights, and for the entire continent to become a blank slate for the colonists. When Native Americans joined battle, it was mostly on the British side. Black slaves, too, were joining the British in great numbers, aware of the contested legal status of slavery on British soil and hoping for better treatment under British rule. According to various estimates, including Jefferson's, some thirty thousand black slaves in Virginia defected to the British side, amounting in some areas to half the labour force. By contrast, many slaves were excluded from fighting for the rebel militias, whose codes often specified 'no blacks, no lunatics, no idiots'. British opposition to American independence was caricatured, then as now, as imperial arrogance; while there was plenty of that, there were also appeals to justice and liberty that were not the monopoly of the rebels.

Much of this debate turned on the question of slavery, where neither side had convincing claim to the moral high ground. Jefferson's first draft of the Declaration of Independence would attempt to outlaw it as a 'cruel war against human nature itself', but the clause would be struck out by a committee driven by the same economic imperatives that had transformed Jamaica into a forced-labour colony. American rebels such as John Adams and John Dickinson might insist that 'those who are taxed without their consent are slaves', but British abolitionists were quick to point out that the taxed were themselves slavers. Their American counterparts, in turn, were equally quick to ask who had brought the slaves to America in the first place. Meanwhile, both sides continued to practise slavery unabated. From the perspective of Jamaica the planters, and by extension the American rebels, appeared to many British soldiers not as freedom-fighters against despotic rule so much as a selfish, wealthy and unprincipled elite, an 'arbitrary aristocracy' whom Despard would later encounter in another form. He might end his life as a traitor, but there is no reason to suppose that when American independence was declared in 1776 he was anything other than a sound patriot.

More immediately, the War of Independence brought Despard the prospect, after three years of policing slave plantations, of true military action. The armed forces were being pulled in two new directions at once, by quite different forces. Once it became clear that the American insurgence was no small-scale rebellion to be quickly put down, and that the French were engaging alongside the colonists, regiments such as the 50th, already ferried across the Atlantic, were at the front of the queue for active service. But, at the same time, the war threatened Jamaica directly. The French, Spanish and Dutch navies were all roaming freely around the Caribbean, and had all been scouting Britain's possessions with reconnaissance patrols. Despard's regiment would certainly be valuable in America, but it might be absolutely crucial where it already was.

The decision, as it happened, turned not on military or naval strategy but tropical disease. After three years in Jamaica, the 50th had been comprehensively ravaged by the savage cocktail of Old and New World diseases that had bred and multiplied in the 'torrid zone' of the Caribbean to the point where the islands had become almost uninhabitable for recently arrived Europeans. Every morning and evening the mosquitoes descended in clouds; there were even said to be cases where men had died from their stings alone. The only defence was to cover the skin with vinegar and sit in the smoke of fires. The connection of mosquito bites to the 'intermittent fevers' of malaria was unsuspected, but the 'intermittents' were as ubiquitous as the mosquitoes; even old Jamaica hands could expect chills, sweats, fevers and stabbing pains in the bones for days or weeks at irregular intervals.

Tropical diseases in Jamaica: 'langorous noons and the hells of yellow fever'

'Peruvian bark' – quinine – was claimed by some to be a specific against 'intermittents', but the success stories were still largely anecdotal, and many of the Peruvian bark samples that were traded were from the wrong trees.

Intermittents often came in tandem with the 'bloody flux': dysentery, violent diarrhoea accompanied by physical collapse and delirium that could produce lasting mental impairment or fatal dehydration. There was a 'putrid bilious fever', which produced a deep-yellow, bile-laced diarrhoea, not to be confused with yellow fever, an exotic import that had come to the Caribbean in a merchant ship from South-East Asia and which produced black vomiting, a black tongue and yellow skin; the quicker the onset of the vomiting, the more likely it was to be fatal. For all of these, the remedies available were variations on the themes of bleeding and purging. Then there were 'putrid diseases', sores and infections: gangrene, yaws, tetanus, cancerous ulcers, weeping and necrotic cancers that could only be burned out with corrosive mercury preparations. The fauna included chiggers – bugs that deposited eggs in the feet which erupted in blue gangrenous boils – scorpions, tarantulas, centipedes, coral snakes, rabid dogs and sharks, which were frequently caught in the bays with human heads in their stomachs. It was a fearsome assault course: the percentage of European arrivals that died as a result of it varied, but it was always high. Many of these were whites' diseases, hitting the governing class more heavily than the slave population. African folk medicine, too, was probably at least as effective as its European equivalent.

Faced with all these competing demands and limitations, the Governor of Jamaica, Major-General John Dalling, a distinguished veteran who had fought the French at Quebec with General Wolfe, decided to split the 50th Regiment up. Many of the troops were invalided out of service; some of the able-bodied were despatched to New York; a few were hand-picked for special duties in Jamaica. Edward Despard fell into the last category. His childhood aptitude for engineering had developed into a level of practical competence that had caught his superiors' attention, and he was reassigned to the 36th Regiment and detailed to the crucial, if unglamorous, task of repairing and strengthening the island's fortifications.

There were about twenty forts around Jamaica's coast, of varying sizes and states of repair. Some were imposing, with hornworks, retired flanks, cannon emplacements and covert passages for running artillery in and out; others were simple stockades surrounded by ditches. Reinforcing them required a combination of technical and improvisational engineering skills, and a vast amount of

John Dalling, Governor of Jamaica

back-breaking labour. Despard was assigned a 'motley crew', which meant a workforce of mixed races: some were sappers and infantrymen from his and other regiments, some were local 'poor whites', some were 'trusty' black slaves who had been promised their freedom in exchange for joining the war effort. It was Despard's job to assess the structural integrity of the buildings and decide what to shore up, what to blast and rebuild, what to extend. Having made his decision, he was responsible for dividing his workforce into crews – for dynamiting, digging, shoring, underpinning, trenchwork, damming and flooding – and for co-ordinating the effort to time and budget. It was the grunt-work of empire, but his reward of command and glory would come.

After two years of this, Despard was despatched back to England as part of a reshuffle of the depleted and overstretched military structure. A new battalion within the 79th Regiment was being created, pulling together new recruits and the older hands who, like Despard, had become scattered around the colonies. Financed by patriotic public subscription, assembled in Liverpool and assigned a royal blue stripe, they were dubbed the 'Liverpool Blues'. Despard, trailing glowing recommendations from Jamaica, was promoted to quartermaster in command of a small company; his older brother Andrew, just returned from action in America, was also commissioned as one of the officers. It may have been during this short visit that the only surviving oil portrait of Edward Marcus was painted. It is attributed to George Romney, who was rapidly becoming the most famous and certainly the most prolific society painter of the age, holding five or six separate sittings daily and, during the manic phases that punctuated his working life, turning out several portraits a week. Here, in his Liverpool Blues

Edward Marcus Despard, attributed to George Romney

uniform, is a Despard of austere face and piercing, intelligent gaze, only distantly recognizable from the confusion of images that would emerge after his death.

Once assembled, the Liverpool Blues shipped out via Philadelphia to Jamaica, where Despard was promptly reassigned to his old engineering duties. But this would be a shorter stint. In the summer of 1779, the military picture in the Caribbean altered drastically, and Despard's life switched abruptly from gruelling spadework to high drama.

For three years, military tensions in the New World had been wound ever more tightly, and on 16 June 1779 they erupted into war. Spain, officially at peace with Britain since her defeat in the Seven Years' War in 1763, decided that the balance of forces was once again in her favour; now was the time for Britain to be forced to choose between the conflict in America and her precious jewels in the Caribbean. The Spanish declared war, and the French, scenting blood, profit and victory, despatched a huge fleet to their strongest base among the islands, Santo Domingo. Jamaica was now officially encircled by enemy powers. A British naval fleet was rushed across the Atlantic; while it was awaited, Despard's engineering crews were multiplied and worked double time. Rumours abounded that the French fleet, under the Comte D'Estaing, was assembling an invasion force. But the French decided to wait; time, they calculated, was on their side. The immediate crisis passed, and Despard returned to quartermastering the Liverpool Blues.

Britain, now at war, had to devise an immediate strategy to protect her distant wealth. The Secretary of the Colonial Office in London, Lord George Germain, sent a set of directives to Governor Dalling outlining where Jamaica now fitted into the broader theatre of operations. Germain, a brisk and capable Secretary of State, took the view that it was under serious threat, but perhaps also presented with opportunities. The Spanish, drawn out by war from their mainland and island strongholds, were likely to stretch themselves thin; the best form of defence might be a pre-emptive attack. If Dalling could pull together an expeditionary force to strike at one of their possessions, they might not only have some quick and morale-boosting success but also draw the predatory Spanish fleet back into its own waters. He proposed that they should investigate the possibility of sending a war party down the wild, sparsely populated and still piratical eastern coast of Spanish Central America, the Mosquito Shore of Honduras and Nicaragua.

It was a promising idea, but it had also occurred to the Spanish, whose fleet was already placed to turn it into action. By the time Germain's brief arrived, they had performed exactly the operation he was proposing. The Mosquito Shore was also home to a few informal colonies of British loggers and planters, including St George's Cay, just north of present-day Belize. The Spanish descended on it at dawn on 15 September, burning its houses, bundling the British colonists into their warships and sailing them back to captivity in Cuba.

Dalling was crushed by this pre-emption of his own preemption, which exposed alarming weaknesses in his position. The Colonial Office brief made it clear that Germain had a worryingly inflated notion of Jamaica's military capacity. Even before war was declared, it had been undermanned, under-resourced and ravaged by disease. Now he had serious fears that the colony might be lost on his watch, and he disgraced; the sack of St George's Cay painted an all too plausible picture of exactly how this might happen. Mounting a military campaign seemed out of the question; apart from anything else, the Assembly would refuse to countenance it. In their view, the sole purpose of the army in Jamaica was to defend their own commercial interests, vast and indispensable to Britain. If he risked them for a quixotic military adventure and failed, he could expect no mercy. 'Both men and things', he confided in a letter, 'appear now in so many points of view, and all so complicated, that they puzzle and perplex me exceedingly.' If he were still the fighting man of Quebec, he could simply follow orders and do his best and bravest, but now 'I am obliged to profess myself in every respect, saving the military line, unequal to the task'.

Yet a ray of hope emerged to strike through his gloom. A small British force had been sent to try to retake St George's Cay but, finding it too well defended, had sailed south down the coast and attempted a daring raid on the Spanish port of Omoa. Despite being outnumbered two to one, they had stormed the fort in the middle of the night, surprised it into surrender, and even found a large stash of gold bullion there. They sailed back into Kingston to wild acclaim, unloading their booty with a flourish; it was a moment freighted with the romance of the glory days of privateering, of Francis Drake or Henry Morgan. Suddenly the idea of another pre-emptive raid struck Dalling as a solution of genius, and he began once more to study his map of the Mosquito Shore.

The map in question was the same one Germain had been studying in London: the *West Indian Atlas*, which had been produced by Thomas Jefferys, the royal cartographer, a couple of years before. It was beautifully produced and quite up to date, and peculiarly intoxicating in the magisterial bird's-eye view it offered of the jumbled terrain of islands, cays, shifting channels, swamps, reefs

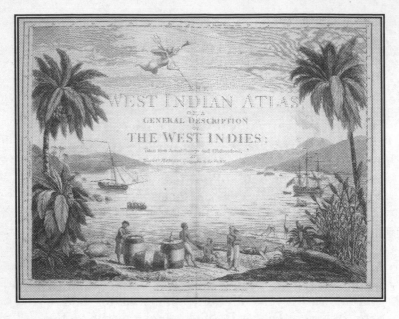

The West Indian Atlas, *frontispiece*

and indented coasts experienced by actual voyagers. What struck both Dalling and Germain was the way that Spanish America, which neither of them had visited, narrowed down to quite a thin isthmus as it approached Panama; moreover, that there was a point where this thin isthmus was largely composed of an inland lake, Lake Nicaragua. On the east coast was the sparsely inhabited Mosquito Shore, with a river, the San Juan, running down into it from the lake. From the western reaches of the lake, it was barely a fingertip's length on the map to the Pacific Ocean.

This was a geographical arrangement that had been noticed before. In fact, the fleet that had originally captured Jamaica for the British in 1655 had been sent by

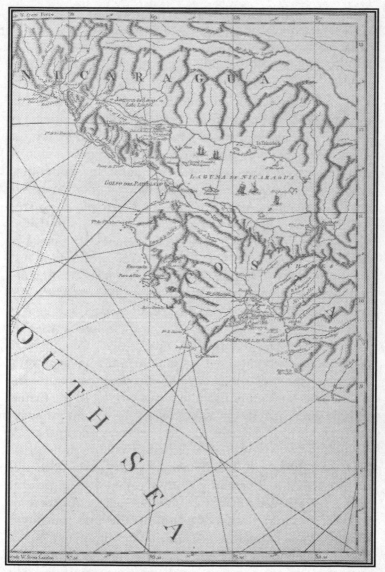

The Mosquito Shore and Lake Nicaragua: a route to the Pacific (West
Indian Atlas)

Cromwell with what he called the 'Western Design' in mind. If this narrow strip of land could be taken and held by the British, it would not only slice Spain's New World dominions down the middle, it might also provide access for the British navy to the Pacific Ocean. The risks were great, but the prize would be greater than any hoard of bullion. Dalling immediately sent a letter outlining the idea to the senior British army representative on the Mosquito Shore, Superintendent-General James Lawrie.

Lawrie was the most important man on the spot only in the absence of any competition. He had arrived there a few years before as an army captain, and had stayed to represent the interests of the straggling communities of British loggers and planters who had long occupied the coast in small and inconsequential settlements to which they had clung tenaciously enough to see off the few Spanish ships that patrolled the waters. By assiduously petitioning the Colonial Office, Lawrie had eventually persuaded them to give him a grander title, even though the colony was an ad hoc and unofficial one that, given Spanish dominance in the area, seemed destined to remain so. Thus, for him, Dalling's letter was the chance he had long been awaiting to patch his backwater battalion into the rest of the British military presence. By the same token, he was not the best man to ask for advice. His report was glowing. The Mosquito Shore, he replied, was lush, fertile, a grand prize. The possibilities for cultivation were boundless, the pasture was extensive and already stocked with cattle: 'the beef I have killed there would not disgrace Leadenhall market'. Dalling's notion of a raid up the San Juan River, moreover, was eminently feasible. The river opened out on to a 'commodious harbour' at the small settlement of Greytown 'where ships of the largest size may lie'. The river up above the harbour was 'pretty broad', and in favourable conditions flat-bottomed schooners could ply the thirty or so miles up to the first Spanish fortress, known as Fort Immaculada. This was a frontier outpost, guarded only by a small and poorly equipped militia; beyond it, it was plain sailing into Lake Nicaragua, which would 'present an easy channel for distressing [the Spanish] in some of their richest provinces'.

Dalling, freed from politics and once more on his home turf of military strategy, had the bit between his teeth. The scale of the forces he would need to take the San Juan fort was probably within his grasp. If they were successful, they could continue to pump reinforcements up the river and carve a huge hole in the heart of the Spanish empire. In time they might even dig a canal from Lake Nicaragua to the western ocean and accrue territory that would make the loss of the American colonies little more than a temporary setback. In a matter of days he had swung from nightmares about losing Jamaica to visions of opening up the entire Pacific. He wrote back to Germain not the plea of helplessness he had been dreading but a firm and states-manlike acceptance of the Colonial Office's suggestion, concluding, 'I see hardly a possibility of not succeeding in whole or in part'.

Given the six-week time lag in communications, he received the swiftest possible response from London encouraging him to put some flesh on the bones of his proposal. Dalling had about fifteen hundred regular British troops to call on in Jamaica, with some three thousand more expected within weeks; in addition, there were perhaps a thousand 'irregulars', local militiamen, un-employed whites and slave volunteers. He calculated that the expedition would need a total of around two thousand men. He wrote back to Lawrie, asking how many he could supply from his end. Lawrie made a commitment to have a thousand men standing by: some British settlers, some of their slaves whom they would 'volunteer', and several hundred of the indigenous inhabitants, the Miskito Indians, who hated the Spanish and would be sure to join in for a share of the rewards.

The numbers were stacking up, and Dalling began to approach the higher levels of command. He would need the co-operation of the navy to ferry the troops there and back, and to stay at anchor in the San Juan harbour to repel any French or Spanish prowlers who might try to cut the troops off from the rear. He approached the commander of the navy in the Caribbean, Rear Admiral Sir Peter Parker, a distinguished old hand who had been sailing the Spanish Main on and off for forty years. Parker, though, was sceptical about the idea. The navy was already overstretched and the ambitious plan would not, in his opinion, 'promise much to the adventurers'. Dalling, with his mandate from the Colonial Office, overruled him: 'I cannot be so vague and indeterminate as to lay aside the expedition'. Parker, perhaps more realistic than Dalling about the risk and also perhaps keen to escape censure if it failed, upgraded the naval support from the sloop that had been requested to a frigate, and offered Dalling the *Hinchinbrooke*, which was currently patrolling the waters around Jamaica under the command of the twenty-one-year-old Captain Horatio Nelson. Nelson and Despard were both poised for their first spectacular taste of military adventure – and, as it turned out, for a friendship which would entwine the fate of Britain's most famous hero with that of her most infamous traitor.

Nelson's tour of duty with the *Hinchinbrooke*, his first command as captain, had been relatively uneventful. It had involved hailing and boarding small private vessels to check that they were flying the correct colours – the naval equivalent of a bobby on the beat. He had missed out on the excitement of the piratical raid on Omoa, which had been carried out by the boat from which he had been transferred to assume his captaincy. Now that the *Hinchinbrooke* was to see some serious action, his excitement was tempered with some apprehension. He shared Parker's doubts about the plan; it was a small force to send so far into such unknown territory, and at the same time to risk the navy's main responsibility, Jamaica. 'I do not approve', he wrote home, 'of sending so many people off this island till we are convinced of the disability of the enemy to attack it.'

With the rest of the expedition in place, Dalling now began to set up his command structure within the army regulars. His choices were limited by the number of senior officers in action in America; he settled for appointing Captain John Polson of the 60th Regiment as overall commander, temporarily boosting his rank to lieutenant-colonel. Polson brought about a hundred of his regiment with him, and was offered 140 of the Liverpool Blues. He picked Despard, now a lieutenant, as chief engineer officer – a crucial role. Despard would act as scout and cartographer, proceeding upriver with an advance party, assessing the navigability of the river, picking campsites and mapping as he went. When they reached the fort, he would be responsible for choosing the site for defences, batteries and gun emplacements, and for getting them built. He would have a couple of dozen men at his disposal: labourers, blacksmiths and carpenters who would have to rig up everything from boats to ladders, floating platforms to levers and cranes. As they made their way through uncharted and hostile territory, there would be any number of possible situations where he would stand between the expedition and total disaster.

The force was scheduled to leave Jamaica at the beginning of January 1780, but was delayed several times. Even before it left, the cracks were beginning to show. The irregulars, the non-military Jamaican contingent, began last-minute renegotiations for shares of rewards in the light of disputes about the shares of the Omoa bullion, which were still unresolved and over which Dalling and the Assembly had fallen out badly. Enough salted meat, rum, flour and basic provisions for six months had to be located, commandeered and stowed. January turned into February. Not only was the expedition losing its element of surprise, but every day was bringing its arrival closer to the beginning of the humid 'sickly season', which would begin in late spring and bring downpours that might make traversing the river impossible.

Finally, on 3 February, they were ready to depart. Dalling was still preoccupied with his disputes with the Assembly, which had escalated into sackings and complaints to London, and he excused himself from the public ceremony of seeing off the expedition. His place was taken by his new second-in-command, Major-General Archibald Campbell. Campbell turned up in his formal dress of red jacket and tricorn hat, and had a rude awakening to the type of display he was to see in Jamaica more often than he had imagined. The Jamaican irregulars were 'half-clothed, half-drunk, they seemed to possess the true complexion of buccaneers and it would be illiberal to suppose their principles were not in harmony with their faces', he recorded. 'I thought it good policy to order ten guineas for them to be drunk in grog on board.' He 'embarked them with three cheers to the great satisfaction of the town of Kingston'. Desperate as the Jamaicans might have been for protection, this was a motley crew they were quite happy to despatch to parts unknown.

2

HERO

The Mosquito Shore is still a remote and dangerous place. While most of Despard's theatres of action are now diving resorts, tax havens or marinas, the eastern coast of Honduras and Nicaragua remains characterized by the same features that marked it two hundred years ago: mangrove swamps, unbearable humidity, under-population, piracy, suspicion and violence between its scattered communities, and perhaps the most savage insect population on the planet. For a thousand miles, from Belize to Panama, the coastal jungle, savannah and swamps east of the dividing mountain range are mostly trackless wilderness, until recently easier to reach from New Orleans than from their own national capitals. The land is riddled with brackish lagoons and deluged with over 250 inches of rainfall a year, making agriculture almost impossible. The rains constantly erode the soil, flood the rivers and change the shape of the land; where the ground is stable the mangroves and jungle growth choke out crops. The coast is scattered with abandoned compounds, sawmills and factories, the remnants of boom-and-bust mining, logging and rubber enterprises. Settlements destroyed by the constant succession of hurricanes rot into the mud. The few inhabitants mostly live in villages that are often temporary and therefore unmarked on maps. There are more guns than people, more suspicion than welcome. Today's pirates, cocaine traffickers, ply the coast; links with the governments and cities to the west are made still more tenuous by pockets of rearmed Contra rebels. Most visitors still find the dense clouds of malarial mosquitoes that descend at dawn and dusk intolerable, but even more virulent, along with the ticks and screw-worms, are the sandflies – 'no-see-ums' – which bite painfully and persistently even through thick clothing, immune to all insect repellents.

Lieutenant-Colonel John Polson, leading the expedition, was under firm instructions from Governor Dalling to traverse this coast as fast as possible to maximize the element of surprise, and, newly and generously promoted to command, he was eager to impress. But the expedition's progress was far slower than he had hoped. First the fleet had to detour to an offlying island to pick up local guides; then it had to stop at the northern end of the shore to join forces with Superintendent-General James Lawrie and his local volunteers. On 14 February it arrived at the rendezvous, the small estuary settlement of Cape Gracia a Dios, but there was no sign of Lawrie; apparently he was further up the coast, rounding up his contribution to the expedition. Polson, informed by the chief medical officer that the crew's health was already deteriorating in the cramped ships, reluctantly decided to disembark and camp ashore until the reinforcements arrived.

Crew, provisions and ammunition were hauled into small boats and laboriously installed about a mile inland, where the mud and lagoons gave way to savannah. At dusk the mosquitoes descended with a ferocity unknown even in Jamaica, and the troops were obliged to drape themselves and their beds in linen and keep fires burning throughout the camp. The next morning they realized that the lie of the land was less than ideal. It was swampy, the sea water at high tide only a foot or two below ground level, and it was cut off from the sea breeze by salt grasses and mangroves 'so as to generate an unwholesome air'. The first meal cooked with the local water produced an out-break of stomach cramps and diarrhoea, and even boiling it thoroughly failed to make it entirely safe.

The expedition was on the fringes of a vast wilderness territory unknown to almost all of them, but one which had in fact been occupied by British settlers since 1633, before even Jamaica. It was known as Mosquitia, or the Mosquito Shore (or simply the Shore), not on account of the prevalent insects but after its distinctive inhabitants, the Miskito Indians. The first people to arrive here, prob-ably around AD 1000, they were originally not Mayans or Mexicans from the central highlands but South Americans, perhaps related to the Caribs, who had made their way up the coast in canoes from the low-lying jungles of Venezuela. They had lived in small, isolated communities, subsisting on wild crops such as bananas and cacao and using their skills with poison spears to hunt fish and turtles on the coast and pigs and tapir in the forest. The Spanish, when they arrived, had found it both impossible and unnecessary to subdue them; instead, they had fortified a few settlements at the mouths of rivers and cut trails into the gold and silver lands of the interior, leaving the majority of the Shore to the Indians.

As in Jamaica and elsewhere, the Spanish power vacuum had created a haven for buccaneers. British, Dutch, Portuguese and others had learned their way

A Rebel Negro armed & on his guard.

London, Published Dec.r 2.d 1794 by J. Johnson, S.t Paul's Church Yard.

Miskito Indian

around the treacherous no-man's land of reefs, cays and sandbanks that offered limitless possibilities for ambushes and stashes of loot. They had also formed a loose alliance with the Indians, based partly on their shared hatred of the Spanish and partly on trade, the backbone of which was guns to the Indians and women to the almost exclusively male buccaneers. The blurring ethnicity of the locals was further compounded by a steady trickle of freed or escaped black slaves, with occasional mass arrivals such as the cargo of a wrecked Portuguese slave ship in 1571. Thus the inhabitants gradually drifted from full-blood Indians to a confederation of mixed-race peoples living off a mixture of traditional hunting and gathering with trade, smuggling and piracy. In the north of the Shore, where black skin and African tribal politics were more dominant, they were sometimes known as Zambos; more generally, and particularly in the more Indian south where the Jamaican expedition was headed, they were called Mosquitos or Miskitos, perhaps from the Spanish *mixtos*, referring to their ancestry, or perhaps from the fact that they were conspicuous among Indians by being armed with muskets. They were a people who belonged neither entirely to the old world or to the new, defined not by their origins but by their shared ability to inhabit a frontier regarded by everyone else as too harsh to settle. At the time of the expedition there were perhaps ten thousand of them on the coast, their hostility to Spain well known, but their devotion to the British cause a matter thus far of historical expediency rather than patriotic conviction.

Just as the indigenous Indians had blended slowly into an autonomous native-creole society, so the buccaneers had evolved gradually into semi-legitimate loggers and planters. Although the Shore sat squarely in the middle of the vast Spanish-American kingdom, its remoteness and lawlessness encouraged increasing numbers of British to base themselves there. Some were buccaneers who, like Henry Morgan, settled down; others were new settlers who used the buccaneers as cover and protection for their own operations. As Jamaica shifted gear into the mass production of sugar through black slavery, many of the white indentured labourers were released from the small tobacco plantations and drifted south. There was logwood to be cut there, and pitch pine ideal for refitting ships with masts and spars, and in some of the upland savannahs sugar could be grown. But the greatest money-spinner throughout the seventeenth and eighteenth centuries turned out to be smuggling. Both Britain and Spain had hedged their colonies around with trade barriers and injunctions that all goods must be sold directly back to the mother country. This meant that neighbouring colonies, even those within sight of one another, could not legally trade without their goods travelling to Europe and back again, and this in turn made small-scale contraband deals routine. Most of the British 'Shoremen', as they became known, had cheap, untaxed goods to offer to the Spanish ports along the coast, and most of the Miskitos spoke good enough English to supply the Shoremen. Enforcing the laws against smuggling was virtually impossible in a lawless territory where almost all the inhabitants were accomplices.

Within this *laissez-faire* arrangement, the British had long tested the degree to which they could safely antagonize the Spanish. In the late seventeenth century they had begun referring to the Shore as the 'Kingdom of Mosquitia', claiming it not for the English crown but as a sovereign state of Miskitos loyal to England. In 1680 the first Miskito king was crowned Jeremy I, a lace hat placed over his long black hair. He was presented with a treaty the English representatives explained to him as a 'treaty of friendship', but to which they referred in private as a 'ridiculous piece of writing'. Its terms as understood by both sides were that Jeremy and his successors would offer the Jamaican governor a shortlist of candidates for the role of monarch, who in return would receive fancy uniforms, English clothes and rum. This arrangement bore no relation to any Miskito tribal or political structure – there had never been a 'king' over the autonomous communities – but it offered a largely symbolic conduit for the Miskitos' dealings with the outside world, and it had persisted. The British had, in the same tradition of antagonism, upgraded the ranks of their few soldiers on the Shore so that they nominally represented a colonial presence. Thus Polson, himself overpromoted, was sailing down to rendezvous with a supporting force that officially comprised a royal sovereign army and high-ranking British command but which was, as the expedition would soon realize, perhaps unique in the terms of the gulf between its badges of rank and its reality.

After two weeks on the rank and humid savannah, the expedition experienced the first of the season's tropical storms. It ripped through the camp, drenching everything and flattening many of the tents. But, as it blew over, it brought the first of the reinforcements behind it. A few canoes showed up, with an array of Miskito dignitaries bearing honorifics such as the Duke of York and General Tempest. They wore a mufti of cast-off army uniforms decorated with gold braid, and raised the expedition's spirits with fresh turtle meat, rum, music and dancing; they were gratefully honoured and presented with the traditional gifts of cutlasses and muskets.

The next day they were followed by a dozen small craft carrying remnants of the 79th Regiment, which had fought in the Omoa raid. But these troops brought less welcome gifts: intermittent fevers, dropsy and bloody flux, which they had incubated en route from Jamaica. Sickness began to spread through the expedition, and within days they were burying the first casualties in the swamps around the camp. Polson decided to abandon the wait for Lawrie, and to head on to Greytown, the settlement at the mouth of the San Juan River.

The journey down the Shore was once again slower than anticipated. The local pilots had no experience of leading a large flotilla and guided the *Hinchinbrooke* and its convoy onto a submerged reef, damaging several boats. Halfway down the coast they finally encountered Lawrie, on his way back up to collect some scattered groups of volunteers. It quickly became clear that his original estimate of a thousand fighting men had been optimistic; now he was promising a handful of white Shoremen, a few dozen of their slaves and perhaps three hundred more Miskitos. When they arrived at Greytown on 24 March, after a fortnight at sea, they anchored in the harbour off the tiny settlement of hurricane-beaten shacks and saw for the first time the green wall of palms and lianas throbbing with the distant shrieks of parrots and monkeys which was to be their next, and more serious, challenge.

If there were those who were beginning to feel that the raid, let alone the grand scheme that lay behind it, was looking less plausible by the day, Despard was not visibly among them. He was first ashore; as chief engineer, he had the job of selecting a site for the onshore battery that would serve as base camp both for the upriver expedition and for the fleet guarding the harbour. He surveyed and sketched, and made his recommendation; within two days the battery was constructed and stocked with artillery, ammunition and provisions ferried precariously from the flotilla in Miskito canoes – as it turned out, the only craft that could negotiate the muddy shoals that stretched out into the harbour. Polson, agitated that his plans were already weeks behind schedule and facing the intractable hazard of the advancing rainy season, found himself once again paralysed, waiting in a muddy estuary for Lawrie's reinforcements. Dalling, corresponding from Jamaica with a time lag of two weeks, was assuming that they had already reached Lake Nicaragua. This time, Polson resolved to dispense with the ever less promising local assistance and on 27 March ordered the army into action.

The evening before their departure, Captain Nelson approached Polson with the request that he might be allowed to leave the *Hinchinbrooke* and join the assault on Fort Immaculada. He had been dubious about the expedition from its conception, and less than impressed by the logistics of his first engagement thus far; nor had Polson inspired much confidence in him. But he had recognized fellow spirits among some of Polson's officers and had struck up a bright friendship with Despard in particular.

It is in the company of Nelson that Despard begins to emerge from the broad colonial and military story as a character and a force in his own right. On the trip upriver, Nelson and Despard would share a tent, eat together, and gradually become the combined driving force behind the entire expedition. In Jamaica, records show only that Despard performed the tasks he was set with distinction; on the San Juan raid, he would quickly distinguish himself as an individual with a distinctive style and character, to the point where his initiatives would begin to chafe against the directives of his higher command. But the character who emerges is still one-dimensional, an artefact of military despatches and other official paperwork, and while the picture they paint is unusually vivid, it is still barely detailed enough to separate Despard and Nelson from each other. Both were energetic, practical, capable and ambitious; both had served lengthy apprenticeships of routine work that they felt had already taught them all they ever would. Both, too, were aware that, whatever its risks, the San Juan raid had the potential to be a legendary and glorious engagement that might turn the colonial map of Central America on its head and propel its heroes down the fastest possible track to career advancement. Whatever their opinion of the expedition's planning and leadership, they had no sense of being exploited or betrayed. All its shortcomings and dangers would be grist to their mill if they were to succeed.

Polson selected six hundred troops for the raid, leaving a small command behind to follow with whatever re-inforcements might belatedly show up, and gave Despard the command of a small reconnoitring force of Miskitos to explore ahead and plot the route upstream. From the first morning, it was clear that Lawrie's upbeat assessment of the journey had been highly misleading. The passage upriver was nearer sixty miles than the thirty he had claimed, and at the end of the dry season the San Juan was a tangle of shallow tributaries and sandy shoals barely navigable in anything more than a Miskito canoe. Almost from the outset, most of the upriver progress involved disembarking from the boats and dragging them up the best route through the ribbons of shallows Despard had been able to identify the previous day. Clouds of mosquitoes and sandflies blurred the gloom of the forest canopy, and when the shade broke over the river channel the men were working in full sun, glaring off the shoals, for seven or eight hours a day.

These conditions were a surprise to the expedition's

planners, but not to the hired help. It rapidly became obvious that this was not to be a British army operation with some Miskito assistance so much as a classic Miskito raid alternately helped and hindered by its British contingent. Few of the army and volunteered irregulars had the stomach for the exhausting and debilitating labour; the Miskitos, despite their smaller size, did most of the hauling, as well as catching plenty of birds and fish to eke out the army rations of grain and salt meat. Some of the British officers persisted in exasperated attempts to force the Miskitos to observe military discipline, but Despard took the opposite route, slimming down his advance party to its Miskito component and following their lead.

Ten days into the uninterrupted wilderness of the river trail, Despard's advance party had their first sight of the enemy. Searching for a path around a stretch of white-water rapids over shiny mica rock, they stumbled on a cut path that looped through the jungle and emerged below a small island in the river known to the Spanish as St Bartholemew which was roughly fortified in a horseshoe shape by ramparts with nine or ten gun emplacements mounted on them. Despard scribbled a note to Polson and sent one of his Miskito crew to deliver it. He recommended that his party should remain in hiding to observe the post, and that Polson should bring a contingent up to join him for an attack. The main force should follow up the cut track he had discovered, and some of the boats should also be dragged up over the rapids, but with great care and only by night so as not to alert the Spanish garrison.

Polson concurred with Despard's plan, and set off with Nelson among his detachment. For most, it was their first experience of the jungle interior – as the medical officer called them, 'these horrid woods'. They soon found themselves among tangles of thorns and razor-grasses, leech-infested and humming with vicious insects; one infantryman of the 79th Regiment walked into a snake hanging from a tree that bit him under the left eye. To the horror of the medical officer, when a following party was sent to attend him, 'he was found dead, with all the symptoms of putrefaction: a yellowness, and swelling over his whole body; and the eye, near to which he was bitten, all dissolved'. The transit of the rapids was hardly any better: the heavier boats had to be emptied entirely and dragged over the slippery rock shelves by all hands. But by nightfall the various parties were in place. Despard recommended an attack at dawn, with a small boat leading the assault covered by British and Miskito musket detachments hidden in the woods.

Nelson and Despard volunteered to command the boat. It slid silently enough into the water, but hit a deep and choppy channel; the splashing of the oars was met by an alarm cry in Spanish from the garrison. Nelson ordered the boat to move on to the island at top speed through the popping of musket-fire; two of the crew were hit. As soon as it grounded, Despard and Nelson led the charge, the first moment of real military action for them both. Despard's was notably unfortunate. He leaped from the boat onto the red mud of the island, only to sink in it up to his knees. He struggled to free himself, muskets swivelling towards him from all directions, but his boots remained stuck so he continued his charge in bare feet. Crackles and billows of smoke burst from the green canopy on the bank, and the Spanish musket-fire stopped. Despard followed Nelson over the ramparts. The enemy had fled, and the post was theirs.

Miskito sharpshooters cut off the fleeing Spanish as they scrambled upstream, and fourteen of the garrison were taken prisoner. Two, by Despard's reckoning, had succeeded in escaping. Polson was rowed over to the island, where he congratulated Despard and Nelson, and interrogated the prisoners. Fort Immaculada, it transpired, was only five miles upstream. Nelson and Despard recommended that as the expedition's element of surprise, whatever it had been, was now almost certainly lost, they should press on to the fort immediately. Despard set off with his Miskito advance party.

Fort Immaculada was over a hundred years old, and had for most of its life been the largest fort in Central America. Neither Dalling nor indeed Cromwell had been the first to spot the Achilles heel of the Spanish empire that Lake Nicaragua and its narrow surrounding isthmus represented. Originally the San Juan's source had been guarded by a wooden stockade on the lake to deter buccaneer raids from the Shore, but this had been a remote rearguard, too far from any viable reinforcement in a crisis, and had rotted in the jungle heat. In 1670 it had been replaced with Fort Immaculada, situated commandingly a few miles downriver from the point where Lake Nicaragua emptied into the vast forest. It was a structure of massive stone bastions a hundred feet wide and twice as long, with four-foot-thick walls surmounted by fourteen cannon emplacements studded along its river side, all surrounded with a ten-foot moat and drawbridge.

Immaculada had never been taken, and only one attempt had been made. In 1762, during the skirmishes preceding the Treaty of Paris, it had been attacked by a motley crew of British buccaneers and Miskitos who had succeeded in shooting its commander but were defeated by the bravery of Rafaela Herrera, the commander's daughter, who took charge of the cannon herself, killed the buccaneer leader and earned herself an eternal place in Spanish colonial legend. As both British and Spanish empires had come to their uneasy truce over the no-man's land, the threat of invasion via Fort Immaculada had become remote to the point where Dalling, seventeen years later, had had to consult a map published in London to locate it. For the Spanish it had become something of a white elephant, a commitment to garrison and arm with few benefits and many disadvantages. In the century during which it had been constantly manned and guarded with barely a whiff of action, it had become one of the army's most hated tours of duty and revealed some serious potential weaknesses. Cannon and musket rusted in the humidity and soaking dews; thousands of infantry had died from the fevers that were almost impossible to escape within its damp walls. It had no internal water supply, and was vulnerable to being cut off by the surrounding river. There was also a hill that overlooked it from the north bank. But it was from the rapids below the fort that, at dawn on 10 April 1780, Edward Despard, accompanied by Horatio Nelson, a dozen Miskito Indians and a Spanish prisoner of war, had his first leisurely look at it.

Despard and Nelson quickly arrived at the same conclusion. Immaculada was essentially St Bartholemew's island writ large, and the best strategy was the same: storm it as quickly as possible. There was little evidence that the Spanish were busying themselves to resist an attack. The only question for the invaders was whether they should approach it by land or river. They made the short and straightforward passage downstream to the main expedition, and offered their views to Polson. But the lieutenant-colonel was paralysed once again. In Despard and Nelson's absence, Lawrie had finally arrived, and had struggled up from Greytown with the news that his four or

Fort Immaculada, in a sketch attributed to Despard

five hundred reinforcements were finally ready for action, and were making their way upstream to join the main party. At the third time of asking, Lawrie's long-promised troops were now on the way, and Polson decided that the expedition would wait. Despard and Nelson, frustrated, pressed him: if the Immaculada garrison knew anything, they knew how to dig in, and delay would play into their hands. Polson wavered, then compromised: the advance to the open ground below the fort would be staggered, and would begin the next day.

Inside Immaculada, the element of surprise had indeed been lost. Hours before the stragglers from St Bartholemew had made it back, the fort's commandant, Juan de Ayssa, had seen the smoke from the musket-fire in the forest, realized that he might be facing the greatest crisis in Nicaraguan colonial history, and moved to battle stations. The two hundred or so troops inside Immaculada had armed themselves and taken up position around the walls; the handful of Spanish settler families who tended vegetable plots in the surrounding area had been hurried inside; all the water tanks and barrels had been filled from the river; and messengers had been sent up to Lake Nicaragua and the distant capital, Granada, requesting at least five hundred reinforcements at the double.

Despard and Nelson ferried the troops as swiftly as possible up to the last easily navigable point, just below the fort and out of sight behind a bend. As the troops massed, Polson had to decide again. His pair of young officers were still recommending a frontal assault up the river, under the enemy's fire but with enough force to burst through; delay might bring him reinforcements, but it would also make this strategy a great deal trickier. Polson opted for caution once more, ordering the troops to cut a path through the jungle by which they could reach the top of the overlooking hill without being seen. But these 'horrid woods' were even worse than the last. There was no trail; the steep slopes of the bank were covered in dripping moss and stinking, rotting vegetation. The more the troops tried to force their way up them, the more they collapsed, quickly becoming no more than vertical mud. One of the soldiers inadvertently flushed out a very indignant jaguar, and the company behind him panicked and started a landslide. Polson was forced to rescind his own orders and bring the land party back.

Already acutely conscious of the question marks hanging over his experience and judgement, he quickly conceived another alternative to Despard and Nelson's strategy. He ordered the troops to move up the other, flatter bank of the river and try to find a spot for an artillery emplacement. This was more successful: a fortified outpost had been abandoned by the Spanish as they had retreated, and the work of lugging a cast-iron cannon up to it began. Despard simultaneously organized a construction crew to protect the post with a rough rampart and conceal the gun from enemy fire. Once the emplacement was set up, Polson delegated command of the cannon to Nelson. On 13 April, Nelson fired the first shot of the battle for Immaculada, sending the Spanish on the ramparts scrambling for safety. Polson was encouraged, and sited three more cannon under his own command down below, but they were ineffectual from the position he had chosen. He gave command of them to Nelson and Despard, who had already worked out how to redeploy them. One more would be dragged up to join Nelson's; the other two would be sited on a new emplacement to the south that Despard had already scouted.

There were few cannon, and even fewer cannonballs; after the first day, they could only be replenished by the Miskitos clambering down into the river after dark and rescuing the spent ammunition. For this reason, it was critical that the few shots they had were well aimed, and thus entrusted to experts. But there were no specialist artillerymen on the expedition, and several soldiers had tried and failed to master the three cannon downriver. Nelson had proved his ability with the first volley; by the time the rest of the cannon had been set up, it was obvious that Despard had the combination of engineering and tactics, mathematics and bravery that was needed to make the shots count from the other emplacement. For the next three days, as Polson wrote in his despatches, 'there was scarcely a gun fired but was pointed by Nelson or Despard'. These despatches, which also commended Despard as a chief engineer 'who has exerted himself on

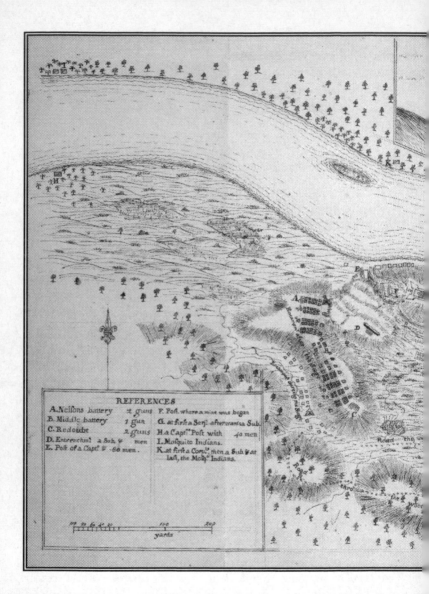

Plan for the siege of Fort Immaculada, probably by Despard

every occasion', were eventually published in the *London Gazette*, giving both men their first taste of patriotic acclaim back home.

The cannon exchange produced an initial surge in morale, especially when Nelson smashed down the fort's Spanish flag with a direct hit on its flagpole, but the garrison was well dug in and the massive stone structure impervious to long-range attack. Scaling ladders and ropes were assembled, but Lawrie's straggling contingent were still mostly downriver and Polson, despite Despard and Nelson's argument that Spanish reinforcements would inevitably be on their way, was still unwilling to launch a direct assault. On 13 April, both sides settled in for a siege.

Over the next few days, what had been immediately clear to Despard and Nelson dawned on the rest of the British expedition: this was a strategy that favoured the Spanish in almost every respect. The cannon-fire ground to a halt; the Spanish kept hold of all the ammunition that landed inside their ramparts, and the Miskitos ran out of spent cannonball to scavenge and reuse. The fort was effectively impregnable, and the besieged at least as well stocked with provisions as the besiegers. There were virtually no casualties on either side; among the few was a Jamaican irregular who had been chasing a wild pig while drunk, had strayed into the line of enemy fire and been shot through one testicle. In an attempt to break the dead-lock, Polson gave Despard a team of sappers to dig a tunnel towards the fort and plant explosive charges under-neath its walls, but the soft mud rapidly gave way to solid bedrock and the initiative was abandoned. The British had some reinforcements on the way but the Spanish had, in theory, their entire mainland Nicaraguan forces to call on. Despard and Nelson were frustrated, with nothing to do but kick their heels and eke out their dwindling provisions;

the Miskitos, who had been summoned for a swift raid with a hard-negotiated share of the plunder as their reward, were tiring of the waiting game and the onerous camp discipline, and talking about drifting back to the coast.

After a week of this, on 20 April the stalemate was broken by the arrival of Lawrie's Shore contingent, under the command of Major James Macdonald. But with them came a less welcome arrival – the seasonal rains. The anvilhead clouds that had been sailing overhead with increasing frequency erupted into sheeting downpour, thunder growling continuously around the forest from every direction, lightning discharging across the fort and the smell of ozone sharpening the gunpowder-saturated air and setting teeth on edge. There had been a few sudden rains on the upriver trip, but this was different; it might last for weeks, even months. With it, too, came an even worse problem. Intermittents and fluxes sprung up among the troops; Nelson found himself gripped by hot and cold chills, blinding headaches and convulsive vomiting. It was thought by some that the 'miasma' had come with the rains; others noted that it was three weeks since they had arrived at San Juan, and suspected the sickness might have been incubating all along. In neither case was the prognosis good. Most troublesome of all was that the Miskitos were falling victim to it faster than anyone else. The medical officer was frustrated in his attempts to treat them with purgatives and sweating medicines, all of which they refused. 'It is a kind of custom among them', he discovered, 'never to regard or pay any attention to their sick, further than to place them under some tree or hut, and giving them water.' As events unfolded, it would become clear that there was little to choose between European and native medical care.

Lawrie and Macdonald's arrival, it transpired, made less difference to the balance of power than Polson had hoped. They had brought provisions only for themselves, with the result that all the invading forces would be on reduced rations within three more days. Of the two hundred four-pound cannonballs that had left Greytown, most had been lost in transit as a result of capsizing relay craft; only fifty remained, and the prime marksman, Nelson, was too sick to aim them. Macdonald, once he had taken stock of the situation, concurred with Despard and Nelson that a siege in the rains was little better than slow death. Polson, pressured from all sides, finally consented to drawing up attack plans. He issued orders to assemble the few scaling-ladders and round up the remaining hand ammunition and explosives, and committed the expedition to throwing everything it had at Immaculada in a frontal assault.

On 28 April Polson was as ready as he ever would be, and he assembled the entire party on the river bank below. In accordance with the rules of engagement, he sent a Spanish-speaking officer up to the gates with a white flag, offering Commandant Ayssa the chance to surrender. It was met with a drum roll from inside the castle, and an answering white flag.

The Spanish surrender astonished the British, who had not the least expectation of it. It transpired that while Polson had been considering the logistics of forced entry into Immaculada, a skirmish on the fringes had fortuitously located the most significant chink in its armour. Two days earlier an impatient British detachment had been given permission to capture an abandoned build-ing down by the river that had formerly been Commandant Ayssa's residence. Unexpectedly, the Spanish had sent a unit down immediately to recapture it; the Miskitos, hungry for some action, had swarmed over it under fire from the ramparts and retaken it, sending the Spanish scurrying back inside the walls. This, as it turned out, was the cover the garrison had been using to sneak down at night and refill their water-skins; without it, they had only a couple of days' supply within the fort. At the moment when Polson made his move, they were just beginning to contemplate the certainty of dying of thirst within days.

Despard, who spoke Spanish, was deputed to handle the surrender talks. Ayssa accepted the standard terms for prisoners of war, but asked that they should be freed after six months if they had not already been exchanged for British prisoners. Despard relayed this condition to Polson, who promised to make representation to Dalling in Jamaica. He then returned with a guard to take formal possession of Fort Immaculada. Despard's was the first British foot over the threshold.

If Polson was surprised by the turn of events, he was also delighted. He installed himself in Ayssa's office, and wrote triumphantly to Governor Dalling in Jamaica: 'I have the honour to inform your excellency that this castle surrendered to His Majesty's arms yesterday at 5 o'clock pm.' Dalling, who had privately shared Polson's darker fears, was equally delighted, and equally prompt in informing his superiors. As soon as the news reached him, he wrote excitedly to Lord Germain at the Colonial Office to trumpet the capture of 'the inland Gibraltar of Spanish America', and to spell out its implications for the grand and long-forgotten Western Design. 'It must', he concluded, 'necessarily lead to other objects with a facility that must surprise even ourselves.'

But once again the diplomatic exchanges were wandering from the reality on the ground. Long before these letters reached their destinations, the moment of victory had curdled. All through the weeks of negotiating the strange desolation of the Shore and battling the hazards and horrors of the upriver trek, the expedition had been sustained by the faith that, increasingly improbable though it came to seem, there was a massive and well-equipped European fortress somewhere in the horrid woods ahead of them. They had found it, and they had somehow taken it; their mission was seemingly accomplished. But what they had grasped was a poison chalice, and their success had landed them in their worst predicament yet. It was the British turn to discover what the Spanish had kept quiet for a century: that Fort Immaculada was a death-trap.

The garrison inside had no treasure, a poor selection of rusty cannon and muskets, and fewer provisions than the expedition outside. All it had to offer were slimy walls and damp quarters that were, in the medical officer's view, 'only calculated for the purpose of breeding infection'. Underfoot were rotting animal skins, 'semi-putrid' and 'yielding a most intolerable stench'. There was nowhere within its walls where the sick could escape the miasma and recover; it was 'not merely an improper hospital but a certain grave'. The expedition was now 'falling down in great numbers', infection spiralling out of control towards the tipping point where the sick would outnumber the healthy. There were barely enough able bodies for basic guard duty, and soon not enough spare to act as orderlies for the sick. The rain fell relentlessly, day and night; when it paused, the heat and humidity built up until the fort became a pestilent steam bath. The Miskitos, ravaged by disease, were outraged at the state of their destination. They had been promised a share of treasure that was non-existent, and the few black and Indian prisoners they might have sold or ransomed were claimed by Polson in the name of the British Crown. Once the truth dawned, most of them simply melted away into the forest, leaving their sick and dying comrades behind.

The regular British forces, though, were finally building up a head of steam behind the advance party. Colonel Stephen Kemble, Dalling's original first choice for expedition leader, had returned from fighting in America and was now anchored at Greytown, asking for instructions before heading upriver to join the push for Lake Nicaragua. Polson asked for all the supplies, ammunition and troops he could muster; but the same messenger also announced a blow for the expedition's command. Nelson, now bedridden, shaking with fever and with little chance of survival in the middle of a jungle epidemic, was summoned back to Greytown. On 1 May he appeared at the mouth of the rain-swollen San Juan, his uniform with its gold naval braid flapping around a skeletal, almost unrecognizable figure clinging to the bow. He signed over command of the *Hinchinbrooke* in an illegible scrawl, was carried onto another frigate and collapsed into a bunk, where he shivered and shook uncontrollably as she cast off from the fatal Shore back towards Jamaica. There he was nursed back to health by a freed black slave woman named Cuba Cornwallis, who isolated him from his contagious fellow invalids and plied him with herbal remedies and heated blankets rather than the British medical regime of communal bleeding, purging and emetics. He arrived back in Portsmouth in December, and recuperated at Bath for the rest of the winter. It would be twenty years before he saw Despard again.

Despard, meanwhile, remained in the healthy minority within the fort, and had found another like-minded officer in Major James Macdonald. Despite the weakness of the party, he and Macdonald were still of the opinion – as

Nelson would have been – that the expedition should be moving forward. A small raiding party had ventured further upriver, and had established that Lake Nicaragua was not far, poorly defended and well supplied: they had returned with a couple of canoes filled with turtle, grain and chocolate. The Western Design could not possibly be furthered by sitting out the rainy season in a filthy barracks where disease was doing far more damage than the enemy had. There were more troops coming up the San Juan behind them, and there would be still more if there were a prospect of a greater success. Once again, Polson found himself resisting the pressure from his officers to strike boldly and fast. An unofficial consensus was emerging that, if they could move their healthy forces up to the mouth of the lake, they could leave Immaculada manned by no more than doctors, the sick and the dying. They could raid for supplies and hold off any Spanish retaliation until Colonel Kemble's detachment made the fort once more a formidable bulwark.

But again paralysis took hold. Kemble's journey up the swollen river was even more hazardous than Polson's had been, undertaken in the teeth of muddy torrents that splintered supply vessels on the rocks and sent supplies tumbling downstream in the frothing floods. Despard finally succumbed to intermittent fevers, along with Lawrie and most of the officers, leaving a rump of thirty or so volunteers as the only available strike force. It was the end of May before Despard, recovered temporarily, led the first reconnoitring party up to Lake Nicaragua. He followed the source of the San Juan round to its northern shore until he came within sight of a Spanish garrison; they gave the alarm and fired, and he retreated downriver. For the next three weeks he scouted the lake and its surrounding jungle, until one day he returned with his fever so high that 'it rendered him unable to see, or make any remarks'.

When Colonel Kemble arrived, he stepped into the breach opened up by Polson's insistence on holding the fort and Despard's impatience to advance. He was unimpressed by many of Polson's decisions, particularly the rigid insistence on protocol that had denied any spoils to the Miskitos and forfeited their services. But neither did he concur entirely with Despard, Macdonald and Nelson. He was no dashing young blade but a seasoned commander, and he knew a lost cause when he saw one. Even pulling together every man still standing would yield, according to Despard's estimates of the forces massing on the lake, a British force that would be outnumbered by as much as five to one. On the other hand, Governor Dalling's excited claims about the prospects opened up by taking Immaculada meant that it was necessary at least to make a show of advancing. On 26 June Kemble sent a gunboat with about seventy men up the river, and began to pull as many more as he could into fighting shape. Despard was no longer among them, once again laid low by fever and dysentery. By 8 July Kemble had another two hundred or so of his men at arms, though half of them were sick and some barely able to stand. After slogging upriver for a few hours, they found the gunboat lodged on a shoal where it had been stuck for the previous ten days. Despard struggled up from his bed to join them a few days later, but by the time he arrived they were already in retreat. Sickness was ravaging the last of the healthy contingent, and Kemble had given the orders to withdraw and hold the fort.

Conditions on their return were worse than anybody present had ever witnessed. Men were dying at the rate of nearly ten a day, and there were scarcely enough left standing to bury them. The stench of dysentery, septic wounds and boils inside the castle was unbearable, and its walls were surrounded by piles of filthy linen and uniforms and rows of shallow graves, all rotting in the torrential rains. Kemble bit the bullet, and wrote to Governor Dalling disabusing him of his intoxicating fancies of conquering Spanish America and announcing that the only option was to retreat downriver and regroup at Greytown. He left a small garrison in command of Immaculada under Despard, with instructions to hold it as long as he could – if possible, either until reinforcements arrived from below or Spanish forces from above.

Dalling, in receipt of Kemble's bleak letter of capitulation so soon after Polson's intimations of triumph, was shattered. He accused his colonel of 'retiring from uncertain danger to certain destruction', and immediately began plans for a second expeditionary force to follow up the gains. More troops were due to arrive in Jamaica under General Garth, and when they did, on 1 August, he attempted to reassign them to the Shore. But they were in little better shape than the ones languishing in Fort Immaculada. Almost half were dead or dying from the 'sickly season', and he was forced to set up makeshift camp hospitals around Kingston to contain them.

Worse was happening at Greytown. Kemble's flotilla arrived from the mouth of the river overjoyed to reach the sea air, feel the breeze and eat as much fresh fish and turtle as they wanted. But, to the despair of the medical officers, the new conditions 'served rather to hasten their exit'. Whether it was the diet, the sun or simply the inexorable progress of the epidemic, the survivors developed painful and disfiguring dropsies, the death rate doubled, and the scene on the frigates and gunboats became as putrid and appalling as that in the fort. Kemble, laid up in the harbour and living on wild bananas and roast monkey, recorded that many of his crew's 'limbs are swollen to an enormous size, and fountains of water issue from their legs, feet and thighs, attended by fluxes'. At the mouth of the river the Spanish had long called 'Rio Morte', he was surrounded by death. His mission had telescoped down to the grim imperative of getting out alive as many men as possible.

Despard, meanwhile, was still on the battlefield, and almost single-handed. He had fewer than a hundred men in his garrison, and most of them were helpless invalids. He also had, if he could live long enough to use it, plenty of time. There was little possibility that reinforcements would arrive for a second push for at least a couple of months; the Spanish were unlikely to make an attack on Immaculada before the end of the rainy season, which would probably last at least that long. His thoughts were probably drifting in rather different directions from Kemble's. Had he and Nelson been in command from the first, events would have played out quite differently. They would not have waited for Lawrie; they would have been upriver much sooner and would have taken the fort before the rains set in. They would have pushed forward and would now be sitting on Lake Nicaragua, feeling the breeze of the inland sea rather than suffocating in the rolling clouds of the jungle. They would have escaped the disease, and would be sitting exactly where the Spanish were now, massing at leisure, waiting for the rains to stop before embarking downriver to pick off any of the invaders who had managed to survive. The historic grand scheme of the Western Design would still be in play, and the new theatre of operations would be transforming the balance of power between Britain and Spain.

Throughout August and September the rains continued

to fall incessantly. There was little for Despard to do but make small scouting missions upriver when the weather permitted, and to bury the dead. Sporadic messages came up from Greytown, and on 8 November he received his final orders, the culmination of the extended exchange between Kemble and Dalling. Despard was to salvage everything possible from Fort Immaculada and use the rest of the explosives and ammunition for 'a total and effectual demolition of the castle'.

For the expedition leaders in Greytown and Jamaica, this was the quickest and most emphatic ending to the raid that they could conceive. For Despard, it was a long and arduous job. It involved sinking mine shafts into the bedrock into which the fort itself had been dug, and blasting each bastion down separately; this, in turn, required as much labour as he could get his hands on, and most of the able-bodied crew were still engaged up towards the lake in freeing the gunboat from the shoal on which it had been beached. He sent a message back estimating the job at eight to ten weeks. This was far more than Kemble had envisaged, and risked running past the end of the wet season and into the time when he expected the Spanish to make their counter-attack. 'I cannot pretend to give you directions in your line of department,' he replied to Despard, 'but I think it advisable to hasten affairs.'

Despard began digging and sapping as fast as he could with the few men at his disposal. It was 18 December before he had the gunboat crew to help him, but by 1 January 1781 he had sunk, loaded and primed twenty shafts, and the next day he sprung the first set of mines. He brought the north curtain wall down completely, blowing the ramparts, he recorded, thirty-six feet away from their foundations. The demolition brought down the western corner of the bastion and tore away a chunk of the tower's foundations, splitting it from top to bottom.

The following morning, a scout returning from upriver confirmed what Despard must have suspected: the Spanish were coming. The blast had been spectacularly visible from the lake; they had decided that the waiting game was over, and it was time for them to counter-attack while there was still a fort left for them to occupy. Despard had until midnight; the Spanish could be expected at dawn the following day, by which time his garrison had to be on their way. He loaded half the explosives he had left into the shaft he had sunk beneath the tower, and crammed the other half into a pit under the southern curtain wall. The Spanish, two hundred troops under the command of Captain Tomás de Juliá, were already visible upstream by nightfall. At midnight Despard embarked all the remnants of the British troops and sent them off downriver towards safety. He himself ran back into the fort and touched off the fuses before leaping into the last boat and rowing down the swollen river. As they rounded the first bend, the explosion shook the river banks and filled the air with rolling clouds of dust and smoke. At dawn, Despard moored the boat and scrambled up the overlook hill, where he 'perceived that the tower was rent in several places and dispersed about the fort'.

As the flotilla struggled back up the Shore towards Jamaica, the death toll continued to rise. By the final count, more men died on the sea voyage back home than had perished in the jungle. The *Venus*, the new frigate Nelson was to have captained until he was invalided out of action, hit heavy storms on its way to Cuba with the Spanish prisoners of war, was blown off course and ran out of food; nearly a hundred crew and prisoners died of scurvy. In the main convoy, the sick found 'the air of the ship's hold very mortal to them', and three quarters of them died before making landfall. In Jamaica, the survivors found themselves stretchered on the ground in the camp hospital, which was still struggling to contain the epidemic of fevers and fluxes among General Garth's recent arrivals. The 'raw European troops' were crowded together in the suffocating heat, with yellow complexions, emaciated bodies and swollen livers, raddled by fever and dysentery. Some shook off the fevers, but the delirium that had accompanied them persisted, and they 'wandered about in a frenzy, and died raving mad'. The final body count was shattering. Of the nearly two thousand men, British, black and Miskito, who had been despatched on the expedition in its various stages, the total number of survivors was around 380.

The San Juan raid came to be remembered as unfortunate in many of the senses in which the epithet would later attach itself to Despard. In the literal sense, it was dogged by bad luck and unfavourable conditions, dealt a set of cards that turned out to be impossible to play. But it was also unfortunate in the more pointed and ironic sense: a regrettable decision, poorly judged, and a discredit to the British military command. It is still remembered as a prime example, in the words of one historian, of 'those nightmare expeditions to which British statesmen, who used small-scale maps of America, frequently condemned a handful of British soldiers'. It remains an exemplary and cautionary tale of the folly of ignoring tropical seasons and the defencelessness of a European army against endemic tropical disease. It is still emblematic, too, of a classic military miscalculation: distraction from the main theatre of war by the prospect of a dazzling and unexpected triumph on its margins.

None of these accusations, then or subsequently,

attached themselves to Despard; on the contrary, they served to make his personal heroism stand in sharper relief. At the time, the expedition was predominantly presented as unfortunate in the sense of bad luck rather than poor strategy, for which its command was to blame. Lord Germain and the Colonial Office were devastated by the 'dreadful havoc death has made among the troops', but their reprimands to Governor Dalling were limited to wishing that the Miskitos had been given greater concessions, which might have kept them fighting alongside the army. Dalling was hauled up before the Jamaican Assembly, who were furious that the safety of their trade had been endangered by such a quixotic mission, but escaped with the verdict that the plan itself was not to blame, simply its failure to beat the rainy season. This consensus was close to the view of Nelson and Despard, and Nelson's account back in Britain was probably influential. Its effect was to heap the blame onto the shoulders of Lawrie and Polson, whose delays in assembling volunteers and taking the fight to the Spanish were seen as the root causes of its calamitous outcome. Gradually, though, the plan itself came to be regarded as unfortunate in the second sense – something to be passed over quickly – and, in the words of Jamaica's surgeon-general, Benjamin Moseley, 'buried, with many of its kindred, in the silent tomb of government'.

It was Despard, though, who emerged from the disaster in better shape than any of his two thousand comrades: not only alive, but with a luminous halo of glory. He had been the first man into Immaculada and the last out; he had shown bravery so far beyond the call of duty that it was almost alarming. He had dug his own superiors out of holes of their own making on several occasions; he had emerged as the most liked and trusted British officer among the Miskitos and the rest of the Shore's motley crew. The only blame attached to him came from Kemble, who implied that Despard's carelessness in allowing his search party to be spotted on Lake Nicaragua had contributed to the weakness of the eventual attack. But it was clear to most that Kemble was casting around for excuses to justify his retreat, and the insinuation damaged the accuser more than the accused.

Despard's bravery on his first engagement cannot be doubted, but it can perhaps be examined and separated into a number of overlapping motives. As with Nelson, it surely had a strong tinge of personal ambition. Both had waited long enough for their first chance to prove themselves, and both knew it was not a question of performing adequately: they had to excel, and to be seen to excel. From the moment Despard was born, the army had been his destiny, and he had channelled his youth into fulfilling this destiny rather than breaking the mould. An army career was, even for the best and brightest, a triumph against the odds, contingent on the luck of the draw, on the display of excellence in whatever form was demanded and in any situation that came his way. In this sense, it might perhaps have been harder for him to beat a judicious retreat than to die fighting with infinite courage against the odds. Life and death were a lottery; the true soldier was one who grasped that neither bravery nor cowardice made either one more likely.

For both Nelson and Despard, this unconditional commitment to battle was and would remain the cornerstone of a sense of personal honour that would shape their lives, and their deaths. It remained an imperative for both of them that they should be prepared to sacrifice themselves for a just cause – an imperative not necessarily compatible with those of their superiors. Colonel Kemble,

The young Horatio Nelson, depicted with Fort Immaculada in the background

by contrast, had seen just causes come and go; his job was to temper bravery with judgement, and to make a cold assessment of the art of the possible. But both Nelson and Despard, after nearly a year on the San Juan raid, returned with an understanding of heroism founded on unswerving loyalty to a cause that was greater than themselves. This sense of honour would remain a defining character trait for both of them, though it would ultimately propel them in very different directions. Both Nelson's heroism and Despard's treason were forged in the same crucible; it would be for posterity to judge whether the qualities that emerged from their shared baptism on the San Juan were the mark of a hero or a martyr, a patriot or a fanatic.

3

COLONEL

Despard's heroism was swiftly rewarded with promotion. Not only was he one of the few to make it back alive from the San Juan raid, he was also in the minority who survived the carnage of the makeshift hospital camps in Jamaica. His recurrent bouts of fever had left him weak but, unlike most, he was now a veteran of the 'torrid zone', and he pulled through. On recovery, he was given a leave of absence to gather his health and strength. But such had been the devastation of the army that he had effectively no regiment to return to. His 'Liverpool Blues' now existed in name only; they would never fight again, and would be formally disbanded within two years. Nor were the Blues the only casualty. Governor Dalling, urgently needing to reconfigure the British defence of the region, found himself with a regimental structure broken beyond repair.

Despard was one of the few bright hopes Dalling had to draw on. He had emerged from the San Juan raid with singular credit and, along with Nelson, had provided loyal and valuable support for Dalling's case that the expedition had not been fundamentally misconceived, merely poorly

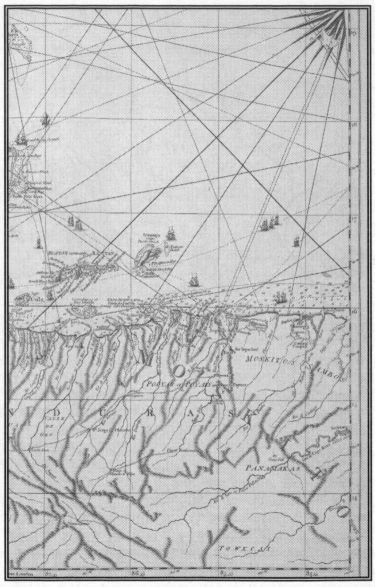

Roatan and Black River (West Indian Atlas)

executed. The two men enjoyed a warm personal relationship; discussing military tactics and past heroics with enthusiastic young officers was perhaps Dalling's favourite pastime on the island. He assigned Despard to commander-in-chief of Roatan, the largest island off the northern coast of the Mosquito Shore. Now it was Despard's turn to benefit from the inflationary promotion system that had long made the British possessions on the Shore seem grander than they really were: with his new post came the impressive rank of lieutenant-colonel.

Roatan was a remote island outpost, significant only because it was directly across the Bay of Honduras from Black River, the largest British settlement on the Shore and the headquarters of Superintendent-General Lawrie, the senior commander of the British forces in the region. This was a trading post originally carved out by pioneer planters who had arrived in 1699 and set up moorings and stores where the Black River – Rio Tinto to the Spanish – churned down from the tropical forests of the Honduras mountains and disgorged into a humid, sodden landscape of muddy estuaries, lagoons and flatlands.

Since that time, the British settlers had carved out of this unpromising terrain a prosperous little colony. The Miskitos in this northern area of the Shore were mostly of African descent – the Zambos (or 'Samboes') – and they had a reputation for ferocity that had made the Spanish keep their distance. Within this informal no-go zone the settlers had some freedom to expand, and the site had been well selected for its natural resources. There were stands of pitch pine growing nearby, the timber of choice for masts and spars, and Black River became a haven for refitting trading ships on the unhospitable Shore. There was also logwood, in high demand back in Britain, which made timber a profitable business. Bananas and cacao grew plentifully, and the land rose quickly up to a savannah that proved amenable to sugar cultivation: some of the original settler families had managed to raise plantations fifty miles long. This small but wealthy planter trade had drawn in a steady trickle of Shoremen – traders, smugglers, distillers, freed slaves, hired hands – who set up clusters of shacks nearby that inspired descriptive names such as Brewer's Lagoon and Nasty Creek. By the 1760s the Spanish, who kept as close an eye on Black River as they dared, estimated that the total number of settlers was pushing four thousand.

In April 1780, just as Despard and the expedition were hacking their way up the San Juan, the Spanish had made a strike on this far-flung British outpost. From their largest garrison on the northern Shore, Trujillo, a hundred miles to the south, they had sent a small fleet into Black River and sacked it. Shacks and sugar mills were burned to the ground; the inhabitants were scattered but not pursued, and the Spanish abandoned the smoking remains. Governor Dalling had been outraged, and had written to the Governor of Honduras protesting the wanton destruction of the 'poor and defenceless settlement', calling the burning of mills 'Don Quixote like' and the ungentlemanly raid 'derogatory to the arms of Old Spain'. He had threatened revenge, but was in no position to exact it, and nor were his protestations taken seriously once it became apparent that he was simultaneously attempting to sack and destroy Fort Immaculada. But the Spanish showed no interest in actually occupying Black River, and gradually the inhabitants returned, along with refugees from the previous sack of St George's Cay, some to the old settlement and others to the island of Roatan across the bay. It was these displaced and undefended settlers whom Despard was deputed to protect.

Roatan is a large, sickle-shaped island, closer in feel if not in distance to the Caribbean than the Shore, surrounded by arcing white-sand bays and reefs alive with fish. Its history, like its landscape, was a smaller-scale version of Jamaica's. It was originally inhabited by Pech Indians who had been wiped out by the Spanish, who in turn had lost control of the island to British pirates and buccaneers. Its buccaneer harbour was even named Port Royal. But the British had never fully settled it, and even with the recent influx of refugees Despard found it sparsely populated. Whether as a cause or effect of its depopulation, it was also nowhere near adequately defended: Despard's first glance told him that a small fleet from Trujillo could take it at will. There were no stockades, virtually no stores or ammunition, and a frightened population of a couple of hundred Shoremen delighted to have been sent a lieutenant-colonel but dismayed that he had arrived virtually alone. Despard responded to their protests by setting off almost immediately back to Jamaica to petition for reinforcements.

This was no easy venture. The rainy season was once again upon him; hurricanes were blowing up across the Caribbean, and the only boat at his disposal was too small to make the passage safely. But again, danger played little part in Despard's calculations: there was no possibility of fortifying or defending Roatan without getting back to base as quickly as possible. Arriving in Jamaica in his small sloop, he was received once more as a hero; Dalling cited his personal bravery in a despatch to Lord Germain at the Colonial Office. But the settlers of Roatan were to have a long and, as it turned out, fruitless wait. Once again, Despard had risked his life for a mission his superiors were in the process of abandoning. Dalling's plans had been hijacked by reports that the allied French and Spanish navies were massing for a full-scale assault on Jamaica. Despard was reassigned post-haste to his old fortification duties, working double time as superintendent of construction on the island's defence works.

He would be back to his old drudgery, though with a more exalted rank, for nearly another year. Meanwhile, the Spanish took advantage of the final defeat of Britain by the American colonies in Yorktown, and the massive death toll among the Jamaican regiments, to intensify their raids on the outlying territories of the Shore. On 14 March 1782, a fleet of twenty ships sailed out of Trujillo and took Roatan in a bloodless and uncontested exercise. Two weeks later, a larger force once more headed for Black River. This time Lawrie was awake to the threat and, despite having no more than a couple of dozen full-time soldiers, dug in. With the support of the local contingent of Zambos, Miskitos and Shoremen, he held for four days a fort the settlers had constructed over the previous year, but was eventually forced to withdraw and escape through the salt lagoons under cover of darkness. This time the Spanish were prepared for the possibility of a British return; they took the fort and firmly occupied the settlement. The captain in command of the new garrison was Tomás de Juliá, the man who had trooped down from Lake Nicaragua to retake what remained of Fort Immaculada after Despard had finished with it. The scene was set, as it would turn out, for a neat reversal of roles.

Despard's hard labour strengthening Jamaica's defences was to prove as pointless as his mercy dash from Roatan, but the outcome was a great deal more satisfactory to the British. The threats that had prompted Dalling to reassign him to engineering were not illusory, and the raids on Roatan and Black River were indeed a prelude to a much bigger Spanish action, one that would put an end to the decades of skirmishes, manoeuvres and reprisals between the colonial powers in the Caribbean. While the Spanish were working their way up the Shore and crushing its small pockets of British resistance, a huge French fleet was mooring off Martinique and waiting for the Spanish to join them. By 9 April it was clear that the two Catholic powers had decided that Jamaica could finally be taken. The British had lost their American colonies to the north, and their most powerful remaining bastion in the Caribbean was more vulnerable than it had ever been. If Jamaica fell now, they realized, there was little to prevent them dividing the rest of the Americas up between the two of them. Major-General Archibald Campbell, Dalling's former second-in-command who had taken over the governorship after Dalling's relations with the Assembly had finally broken down irreparably, was forced to make a fateful decision. He summoned all the naval forces at his disposal – thirty-six ships – and entrusted them to Admiral George Rodney, instructing him to intercept the combined fleet and fight it to the death.

Rodney set sail, and headed desperately towards a fleet much larger and more powerful than his own; but the wind died in his sails as he was about to engage it, and the massed vessels found themselves staring at one another across the flat, calm sea. He backed away, and the French and Spanish followed. For three days he led them through the islands, reefs and shoals between Martinique and Guadeloupe, until they finally forced him to turn and engage off a cluster of islands called Les Saintes. Outnumbered and cornered, this time Rodney found a wind springing up behind him. As his enemy struggled to retain their line of battle, he broke his fleet into small detachments that were able to force their way through the French and Spanish lines, cut the enemy into small and

The Battle of the Saints

isolated groups, and fire at them from all sides. The numerical advantage of the Franco-Spanish navy was neutralized; their big guns remained pointing out at the open sea as the British pounded away at their undefended flanks. By the end of 12 April they had lost five ships and two thousand men, and the French flagship surrendered.

The Battle of the Saints, as it became known, was seized on with great patriotic fervour in Britain, a defining triumph coming hard on the heels of a procession of humiliating disasters. But it was more than a propaganda coup. It turned out to be the spur for the British and Spanish governments, both exhausted by colonial wars that had cost more men and money than they could afford, to come to a lasting and overdue settlement of the disputed territories in the Caribbean and the Shore. As in the old days of piracy, though, there would be time for one last sacking and reprisal while the diplomats conferred in

Europe. It was to be Despard's first full military command.

With Jamaica free from the threat of invasion for the first time in living memory, Governor Campbell had the luxury of turning his attention to the few thousand British settlers on the Mosquito Shore, who had been petitioning him desperately for military support to secure their enclaves and settlements. Their calls were echoed, too, by the Zambos and Miskitos, who had also been attacked and dispossessed by the Spanish and were more than ready to lend their support to British action to reclaim Black River and Roatan. Campbell, with military capacity that could now be safely spared, calculated that a small expeditionary force from Jamaica would be enough to mop up the unfinished business left over from the Spanish raids and reprisals. He decided to send 130 of his regular infantry to the Shore.

The question of command, though, was rather more vexed. The superior British officer in the area around Black River was still James Lawrie, but his reputation for both strategy and commitment had been tarnished by the San Juan debacle. Lawrie had, in fact, fought bravely once he had arrived, but had never lived down the gulf between his glowing promises and the reality in which the expedition found themselves. He had come out of the postmortem badly, scapegoated perhaps more than he deserved as the culprit whose foot-dragging had ruined an otherwise brilliantly conceived plan. For the new raid, Campbell was counting on a swift, surgical strike, not on several weeks of paddling up and down the coast during the rains and missing rendezvous with straggling volunteers; if Lawrie failed a second time, Campbell would be doubly culpable. But he had another option: the sparse settlements of the Shore were currently home to not one but two British army majors. The second was Major Robert Hodgson, who had been in command of the St George's Cay settlement until it had been sacked by the Spanish, and had then joined Lawrie at Black River.

The two majors had a long mutual history, and none of it good. Hodgson's father had been the first superintendent of the British settlements on the Shore, a post he had held for twenty years and in which his son had succeeded him. But the son had been less popular than the father, and had gained a reputation as an old-style colonial despot, treating the planters with high-handed severity and inspiring mutterings against the whole notion of British rule on the Shore. It was these mutterings that Lawrie had orchestrated, while establishing a more effective line of communication with the Colonial Office in London, to be appointed superintendent himself. The struggle had been in abeyance for a decade, the two men dug into their petty fiefdoms hundreds of miles apart, until Governor Campbell reawoke it by nominating Hodgson to lead the expeditionary force to retake Black River.

Lawrie was further down the Shore at Cape Gracia a Dios, where many of the Black River settlers had regrouped over the last months; he had already assembled a force of eight hundred volunteers by the time instructions arrived for him to turn command over to Hodgson. He was furious, and had most of the army on his side: there were few who had a good opinion of Hodgson, and many who had scores to settle with him. The Miskitos and Zambos were among them, a population less impressed than the British by the niceties of command structure; as far as they were concerned, Lawrie had a firmer command of their loyalty than Hodgson did, whatever the contents of the governor's letter. Lawrie wrote back to Campbell, stretching the truth but not entirely breaking it with the warning that his men would refuse to serve under Hodgson.

It was at this point early in August 1782 that, quite by chance, Lieutenant-Colonel Despard turned up in Cape Gracia a Dios. He was on overdue leave and had decided to make the trip to reclaim some of his personal possessions, which he had been forced to leave on Roatan and which he had heard that the Spanish had abandoned unmolested. Lawrie greeted him warmly; once the superintendent had made his belated appearance up the San Juan, he and Despard had got on well. But Despard's glowing reputation in Jamaica also presented Lawrie with the opportunity for another of his subtle strategies, long honed in the remote backwaters, for influencing the high command. Hodgson's troops had begun to arrive from Kingston, but the major was still in transit, bringing up the rear. By the time he arrived, he found Despard appointed to command of the Black River expedition by Lawrie, technically his superior on the Shore, and a despatch announcing the fait accompli on its way back to Governor Campbell. As Lawrie anticipated, Campbell turned out to be delighted with such a popular and unexpected resolution to his knotty problem.

It was not only Lawrie who was satisfied by this turn of events. Army, Zambos, Miskitos and Shoremen all welcomed Despard's appointment warmly, and presented a 'unanimous address offering to put themselves under his command'. Some of this warmth can be ascribed to Hodgson's unpopularity, some also to the news that they were to be under the command of a rising star of the British army rather than either of the two local placemen who had tussled over the ignored territory for so long; but much of it must also be ascribed to Despard personally. As the hero of the San Juan raid, he had become something of a legend among the army in Jamaica; among the Miskitos and Zambos he had acquired a reputation as a soldier prepared to follow their advice and tactics rather than impose his own, and he had been exonerated from the general bad feeling they had developed towards the army after Polson had refused to allow them their share of the spoils. He might have been the beneficiary of petty squabbles and dirty tricks, but he was also the popular choice.

Despite this, Despard's assumption of command over his technical superior would be raked over in years to come and held up as the first incident in his career that proved that the seeds of his future treason had been present even during his years of apparently loyal service. In the history that clung to him posthumously, it was often repeated that he had roused bands of savages to anger against the British command and, like a real-life precursor of Colonel Kurtz in *Heart of Darkness*, bent them to his personal, self-aggrandizing and ultimately delusional ends. The Black River raid would not be the last time Despard commanded a mixed-race crew who were more loyal to him than they were to his superiors, but this situation was not of his making. Yet the story of his first command also hints that, from early on in his career, Despard was prepared to take risks with his authority provided that he felt such risks were firmly grounded in rank and file support. Such willingness to test the mettle of authority against popular will would indeed become a trait of his revolutionary career, and one without which he would not have got as far as the gallows. But among the small crowd of young British infantrymen and suspicious Miskitos at Cape Gracia a Dios in 1782 he was still far from this fork in the road. At this point, Nelson would have done precisely the same, and for precisely the same reasons; and had Nelson done so, his very different posthumous mythology would have found in his actions an abundance of confidence, bravery and genius for improvisation.

Once handed command, Despard laid his plans with little hesitation, and within a fortnight, on 17 August, the first phase of the expedition was launched. He sent an advance force of four hundred troops under the command of a young captain, John Campbell, straight to Black River, while he waited with another thousand men in Cape Gracia a Dios, keeping his remaining ships moored out of sight in the tangled waterways of the nearby lagoon. Captain Campbell's detachment included the main body of the local Zambo-Miskitos under the command of their leader, General John Smith. These were the force the Spanish feared most: they had been roused to fury by being dispossessed of their homelands, and had a reputation for fierce and bloodthirsty combat. Not to send them would have been a giveaway that there was another phase of the expedition to come. Both sides were well aware that they saw themselves as first in the queue for revenge.

There were two forts at Black River, and the British knew them as well: Lawrie had supervised the construction of both. The larger, in which he himself had holed up during the Spanish raid, was in the centre of the settlement; there was also a smaller one among the outlying shacks of Brewer's Lagoon, which the British had christened Fort Dalling and the Spanish had renamed Quepriva. It was this the advance party made for first. On 21 August, as soon as they had beached in the lagoon, General John Smith's Zambos made a charge for it. They encountered little resistance. There were only thirty-three Spanish inside; within minutes, there were none. One escaped across the lagoon to the main settlement, and the other thirty-two were instantly and brutally massacred.

Even by the piratical standards of Shore raids, this was an atrocity. The Spanish would long remember it as 'the Quepriva massacre', a late entry in the long catalogue of British infamy stretching back to the days of Drake and Morgan. Captain Campbell should certainly have prevented it; Despard most likely would have done. But Campbell probably had little idea that it was coming, and little chance of imposing his authority once it had begun. The Miskitos had lost their faith in the British army's promises, and had decided to snatch their revenge before they could be ordered not to. Campbell, unlike Despard, had not forged a reputation with them as an individual they could trust to share their plans.

The sole survivor escaped across the swamps to Black River, where Captain Tomás de Juliá had 140 men at arms, and within minutes they were all inside the main fort. This was a more substantial structure, and it had been renamed Immaculada Concepción de Honduras – a second Immaculada, but this time a British fort occupied by the Spanish, with Juliá inside and Despard advancing on him. Their honour satisfied and their point made, the Zambos now fell in with the British strategy, and staked the fort out for a siege. The Spanish could not hold out for long in their cramped confines but, unlike the British in San Juan, they were well placed to send for reinforcements. A messenger party cut inland across the savannah, making the hundred miles to Trujillo and alerting the main Spanish garrison on the Shore. A large Spanish troop carrier set sail for Black River immediately.

This was the trigger for the second phase of Despard's plan. He pulled his main force of ships and soldiers out of their hiding place and set sail for Black River. When the Spanish ship arrived, he was waiting for them. This time there were no escapees to send for more reinforcements, and no bloodshed either. Outmanoeuvred and outgunned, the ship surrendered, and all the Spanish troops were taken prisoner. Despard, together with Lawrie and their thousand men, moved into the Black River harbour on 26 August.

Now it was Juliá's turn to see Despard coming over the horizon with a substantial battalion behind him. Despard sent him a message, informing him that his reinforcements had been intercepted and he was outnumbered, and suggesting that he surrender. Juliá asked for time to consider terms – or, more likely, to consider how to get another message to Trujillo. Despard replied, warning him not to take too long: General Smith's Zambos had been waiting for a week already, and they were not patient men. Juliá finally acknowledged the checkmate. He surrendered, and opened the fort to the British. A total of seven hundred Spanish were taken captive and shipped up the Shore to Omoa, to be exchanged for British prisoners of war.

It was a significant victory. Following on the heels of the Battle of the Saints, it pushed the Spanish diplomats on to the defensive in their territorial negotiations. British possessions, it affirmed, were no longer to be toyed with. Where the San Juan raid had seen the British aiming high and missing, the retaking of Black River aimed low and hit hard, and in so doing it effectively cemented their claim to a permanent place on the Shore. Nor was Governor Campbell in Jamaica slow to point this out. His letter to Lord Sydney, the Secretary of State to the Home Office (which had recently taken over the administration of British territories from the Colonial Office), announced that the mission 'has succeeded equal to my most sanguine expectations'.

Campbell also gave his official, if retrospective, stamp of approval to Despard's command. The 'little army' of

'Shoremen, free people of colour, and negroes, and Mosquito Indians under their respective chiefs' had, he told Sydney, 'elected for their leader Lieutenant-Colonel Despard'. Campbell himself added 'I think it also a justice due to Lt. Col. Despard to express my acknowledgements to him, for having cheerfully, at the request of the Shoremen and Indians, taken command'. The letter was published in the *London Gazette*, to whose readers Despard was becoming a familiar name. Lord Sydney replied to Campbell expressing 'the highest satisfaction' at the news, and passing on the King's personal 'approbation of the judicious conduct and gallant services of Lt. Col. Despard'. If Robert Hodgson had been planning a complaint against the hijacking of his command, he now faced an uphill struggle.

In taking command of the Black River expedition, Despard had added a significant new dimension to his public persona. During the San Juan raid, he had shown all the qualities his role as an officer could make visible: loyalty, discipline, bravery beyond the call of duty. Emerging as a leader, he showed a good deal more. His appointment had been a recognition of his diplomacy and his capacity to engineer the consent of everyone from the motley crew to his military superiors, and to maintain that consent through a complex and difficult action. His diplomacy had even extended to the enemy: in sharp contrast to the massacre that had taken place on Captain Campbell's watch, Despard himself had taken both Black River and the Spanish reinforcements without spilling a single drop of blood, and had freed hundreds of British prisoners of war as a result. His first command had been strikingly intelligent, tidy and effective both in conception and execution, qualities which had all been conspicuous by their absence from the San Juan raid, and the swell of praise that greeted it recognized that here was someone who was more than just a first-class soldier. Despard had placed himself in the market not just for further military command, but for the higher ranks of colonial government.

Despard's fast-rising star coincided with a shift in the military balance of the New World colonies, which in turn led to a final peace settlement between Britain and Spain. Both powers had come to recognize that, across the whole of the Americas, the colonial picture was resolving itself into the same configuration presented to them by the Mosquito Shore. The British had lost their American colonies and were in political chaos; they had no appetite for another San Juan raid, and no longer any lingering ambitions to oust the Spanish from Central America. The Spanish, in turn, had been forced by Despard's Black River raid to abandon their recent hopes of banishing all British interests from the Shore, which, in truth, they had never been able fully to control. Neither had the stomach for supporting two massive garrisons, at Trujillo and Black River, in a state of permanent hostility with one another, and in all likelihood with the Miskitos as well. In November 1782 they signed a preliminary treaty ending hostilities and opening dialogue on a full and final territorial settlement.

The Shoremen up and down the coast were intensely interested in the details of this settlement, and intensely suspicious. They were used to being the poor relations in any colonial transactions, and alert to the possibility of being sold down the river in the course of the diplomatic horse-trading. Spain had many new possessions it was eager to consolidate, from Florida to Uruguay, but the British claim to the Shore had always been tenuous and they suspected that the Spanish would begin negotiating from the position that it was essentially Spanish territory, and that to concede any British sovereignty along its reaches would count as a favour that would require a corresponding favour in return. The one weapon the Shoremen had at their disposal was their bloody-mindedness. Both sides knew from extensive past experience that any deal that did not have their consent could not expect their compliance; they would continue to smuggle to both sides, raid unprotected settlements, ally with the Miskitos, extend their logging and plantation beyond agreed boundaries, dismantle their fortifications under gunboat supervision and then reconstruct them the following week.

All through 1783 they lobbied the Home Secretary, Lord Sydney, with every polite and plausible argument they could muster. They were undefended on the Shore, and until they received official territory they would be forced to 'reside in Jamaica with much inconveniency and great expense'. Their logwood plantations would remain untended, and their inability to send timber to Britain would be 'very detrimental' to her economy. They also had broader grievances about their trading status. Logwood was now used not only to make hardwood furniture; it had become an important source of red and black dyes for the booming textile trade. Since the Shoremen had been shipping logwood to the mother country, other sources of supply had been opened up around the globe, and its price had dropped from £60 a ton to £10. If they were to be bargained for by the Crown, their monopoly should also be reinstated: any settlement in British interests must 'ask for their privileges in cutting and shipping logwood to be restored'. Despard was much engaged in listening to the Shoremen's petitions and forwarding them to Governor

Campbell and the Home Office. On a short visit to Britain on leave, he lobbied for them in Whitehall.

Eventually, on 3 September 1783, the British and Spanish Crowns concluded their extensive negotiations and signed the Treaty of Versailles, formally bringing hostilities to an end and laying out the new territorial dispensation. The Mosquito Shore settlement constituted Article 6 of the treaty. 'His Britannic Majesty's subjects', it stated, 'shall have the right of cutting, loading and carrying away logwood in the district lying between the River Belize and Rio Hondo'. Within this enclave, British and Spanish officials would agree where the British settlers could build houses, and in return 'his Catholic Majesty assures to them the enjoyment of all that is expressed in the present article'. They were not to fortify the enclave, but they would be permitted to fish in its waters. It would be officially known as the Bay of Honduras Settlement.

The area outlined was essentially the mouth of the Belize River which was, along with Black River, the largest and longest-established British settlement on the Shore. It was about 150 miles to the north, on the top side of the Bay of Honduras. It was much further from Trujillo than Black River, which was to revert to Spain, and would thus place the centres of British and Spanish power at a safer distance from each other. Like all diplomatic settlements, this was a complex set of compromises, nested in such a way that every negative point could be countered with a positive, and it was sold to the Shoremen on the positives. This was the first time that the Spanish had ever conceded legitimate British territory on the Shore; their safety was now guaranteed in perpetuity; the enclave had been settled by British planters since the seventeenth century, and its true national identity was finally being recognized.

But the handful of long-established British planters and

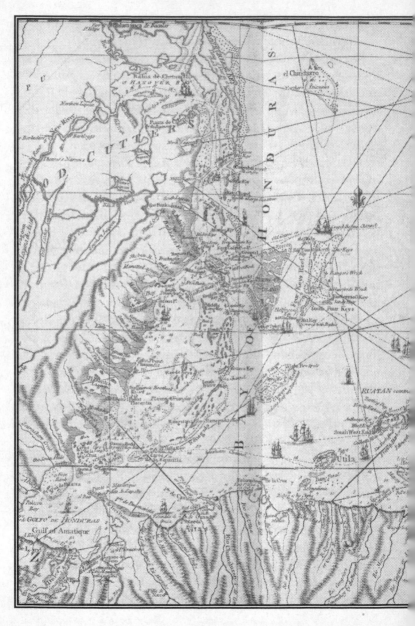

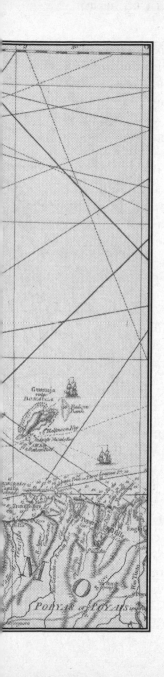

The Belize River and Bay of Honduras (West Indian Atlas)

traders at the mouth of the Belize River, known locally as the Baymen, were quick to counter with the negatives. The space and privileges on offer were 'most unexpectedly and extremely diminished from what they have always heretofore possessed and enjoyed'; they were not to own the land, merely to have logging rights at Spanish discretion. The boundaries seemed to have been fixed on a Spanish map that differed significantly from their own. They were surrounded by Spanish property, and 'as liable as ever to have their negroes and property seduced from them and pilfered'. They would have no freedom of navigation, and no rights of residency on the offshore islands, cays and atolls. They would be abandoning the Miskitos to the doubtful mercy of the Spanish. They banded together rapidly to establish a committee to represent their views and lobby for a revision of Article 6. Their nominees for the committee were three British resident planters – James McCaulay, James Bartlett and Richard Hoare – and Lieutenant-Colonel Despard, who was agreed to be ideal for 'executing the above trust and office'. All were accepted.

A few weeks later, in November 1783, Despard was nominated for promotion by the Jamaican Assembly, who had strong trade and family links with the Baymen of Belize. Their testimonial summarized his loyal and extensive service on behalf of the island: how he had 'distinguished himself in the engineering line, by constructing various works for our defence' as well as echoing the royal sentiments of his 'gallant and judicious conduct' at Black River. The Assembly rarely acted except in their own interests, and they had good reason for wishing to keep Despard in their service. He was clearly of a higher calibre than the old lags of the Shore, Lawrie and Hodgson, with whom the Baymen were used to having to make do to protect their interests; he also had the trust of the Shoremen and of the Miskitos – a scarce commodity among British army officers. Many of the Shoremen who were now to be evacuated to the new Bay of Honduras settlement were poor white settlers and freed slaves, but among their number were also British planters from the same long-established class as the Assembly members; in some cases they were the same families, even the same people. They needed a capable man to fight their corner, and such men were thin on the ground. Despard, they knew – or assumed – was ambitious, and the one inducement they could offer to him to stay in the colonial backwaters was fast-track promotion.

Their proposition was accepted by Governor Campbell, and on 19 November 1783, at the age of thirty-two, Edward Marcus Despard arrived at the rank of colonel.

It must have been clear to Despard that his duties as a colonel would, for the foreseeable future, involve little or no military action and a great deal of colonial administration. He must also have been content with this state of affairs, and probably very excited by it. The Shoremen and Miskitos had placed their trust in him, and the business of resettling them fairly and amicably was one in which the British government could not be entirely relied on. If the new colony was to endure, it needed the consent of the colonists and a reciprocal commitment from the mother country, something that had previously existed only on an ad hoc basis, subject to the tides of war that had ebbed and flowed around it. To set it on a firm footing would be an exacting and absorbing project; just how exacting Despard was soon to discover.

The Baymen, whose families had in some cases been settled at the river mouth since the seventeenth century, took the lead in renegotiating the details of the new settlement, with Despard as their representative to the British government. They focused their demands into two main categories, one aimed at the Spanish and one at the British. First, territory: they needed an extension of limits from those proposed at Versailles, and greater rights to fish, catch turtles and set up temporary shacks for such purposes around the bays. Second, they required a new internal administrative structure and chain of command to link them to Jamaica and thence to Britain. They laid out a 'Plan of Police' whereby they would create their own civil government, headed by a governor who would be answerable to an assembly, which would consist of fifteen citizens elected for every hundred inhabitants. The governor and six elected assembly members would act as a court of appeal in disputes. This government would take responsibility for regulating the logwood and mahogany trade, ensuring that all of it made its way back to Britain through legitimate sources, and that duties collected were remitted to the Crown. In return, Britain would guarantee to enforce the rights of the new colony when necessary; it would be independent of Jamaica but entitled to the same protection.

The exchanges between the Baymen and the Home Office are prosaic and focused, but it must have been clear to both sides that within this modest arrangement lay a kind of blueprint for the future of Britain and her colonies. It was the first arrangement of its kind since Britain had lost America, a catastrophe that had thrown the entire question of British overseas expansion into doubt. Not merely courts and diplomats but ordinary people around the globe were now intently engaged with the dilemmas American independence presented. Previously, it had been the colonists who had tended to demand greater involvement from Britain, to protect themselves from piracy and predatory foreign powers. Now, it was the British who had increasingly to make the case for why they should continue to monopolize and tax the wealth of their far-flung dependencies. Despard and the Baymen were working on a small canvas, but an enticingly blank one that offered the possibility of a novel and effective balance of rights and responsibilities.

This was a dialogue that was at a crossroads, as was the language in which it was conducted. The term 'British empire' had been coined two hundred years earlier by Queen Elizabeth's astrologer John Dee, but it had only recently come into common usage to denote the totality of British colonies around the world. Its sense was still far from that in which it is used today; the idea that, for example, a British queen might one day be Empress of India would have been baffling. In as much as empire had a clear meaning, it was drawn from analogy with the Roman Empire, its precise sense contested but generally taken to include the power to make laws and collect taxes in foreign lands, enforced by military supremacy. This, though, was an analogy that brought with it a set of negative connotations. An empire required an emperor. It was also something that declined and fell.

There was, however, another term that was also being used to describe Britain's relations with her colonies: commonwealth. This, too, had a very different meaning from its modern sense of an association of former colonies, and was freighted with a different cargo of political baggage. In its original meaning, dating back centuries, it had simply described public welfare and the common good: a 'commonwealthman' was a good, patriotic and public-spirited citizen. But the term had been hijacked by Cromwell, who had given it a specific meaning when he had, by act of Parliament in 1647, declared Britain a republic, 'commonwealth and free state'. Thus, after the restoration of the monarchy, a commonwealthman was no longer a patriot but a regicide traitor. Yet over the last century the word had been reclaimed, and redefined in a more abstract sense. The philosopher John Locke, for example, writing in 1690, had spelled out that 'by commonwealth I mean not a democracy or any [particular] form of government, but any independent community' with the power and the structure to manage its own affairs. Thus 'commonwealthman', by Despard's day, was an emotive but ambivalent term that on different lips could mean either patriot or traitor, or indeed neither.

What Despard and the Baymen were proposing was a retreat from the form of imperial dominance that had come so disastrously unstuck in America, and a return to the consensual and mutual arrangement for the public good which commonwealth had once represented. They might or might not have been aware of the broader political debate, but their actions fitted distinctively within it. Conditions were proposed by the colonists, not imposed by the mother country; explicit consent was sought by both sides. There was little of the traditional language of divine authority and affirmations of binding loyalty to the King. This was the bride stripped bare, an exchange of military protection for monopoly trade, with both sides equal and consenting partners. The Plan of Police was effectively an independent constitution. In its understated and modest way, the dialogue was a revolution in itself, a redrafting in miniature of the Glorious Revolution that had set Britain herself on a negotiated constitutional footing a hundred years before.

Despard presented the proposals to Governor Campbell, who forwarded them to London. Campbell advised the

Colonial Office that, in his view, the request for an extension of territorial rights was reasonable. He also commended the Plan of Police, although he struck out the post of governor at the head of the command chain. A governor would imply that the Bay of Honduras was a full British colony, rather than an enclave granted by the Spanish within their territory; technically, the treaty forbade either nation to claim sovereignty over it. The commissioners were administrators rather than ministers of the Crown, and their role should be to keep both British and Spanish governments at one remove from the territory. Campbell proposed that Despard should be given the title of First Commissioner. 'The merits of Col. Despard', he explained, 'are so well known to me that I have much satisfaction in supporting the recommendation of these settlers.' The Baymen's response was no less enthusiastic. They replied with a statement that Despard's 'thirst of knowledge, attention to their true interests, and mildness of government, has in a very particular manner endeared him to all who were so fortunate as to be under his command; and from these considerations they humbly conceive him to be the fittest of all men to preside over them'. The negotiations over the new territory had extended Despard's range from waging war to making peace, and he was showing as much natural aptitude for his new career as he had for his previous one. Ironically, it would be his attempts at peacemaking rather than war-mongering that would lead him towards his final treason.

On 15 May 1784 Despard met Juan de Aguilar, the Spanish Governor of Yucatán, at the mouth of the Belize River. They toured the territory together, navigating the rivers, noting the extent of the Baymen's logging and plantation, comparing the Spanish maps with the British, hammering boundary posts into the muddy banks and cutting marks into the trees that stood at the negotiated limits of the surrounding forest. They concluded their four-day trip with dinner on the HMS *Iphigenia* – Despard's Spanish was apparently good enough for small-talk as well as military business – and the ship honoured General Aguilar with a seventeen-gun salute. But from the shore came an ominous signal of problems ahead. Despite Aguilar's presence, and despite the treaty's stipulation that the Bay settlers were permitted to fell only logwood, the Baymen at the river mouth were clearly visible loading their sloops with huge mahogany trunks cut from the jungle interior. They persisted, nonchalantly and in broad daylight, for several days. Aguilar had no choice but to comment on it, and Despard no choice but to declare his determination to put a stop to it.

Nevertheless, on 27 May Aguilar made a formal delivery of the territory to 'Don Edward Marcus Despard' and his fellow commissioners McCaulay, Bartlett and Hoare. On 31 May Despard wrote to Governor Campbell from on board the *Iphigenia* at the mouth of the Belize River, confirming that he had been 'put into regular possession of the district'. On 12 June the new model colony held its first public meeting, voting their consent to its articles and resolutions. All future business would be conducted in Jamaican dollars, and all current debts were to be commuted into this currency. Logwood prices were to be fixed, and magistrates to be elected. 'Nothing', it was concluded, 'can contribute so much to the peace and prosperity of this country and its inhabitants than a strict adherence to and a cheerful compliance with the present regulations.' This flourish betrays, perhaps, the particular intoxication with bureaucracy unique to those who are, for the first time in their lives, settling their own affairs in their own interests.

Despard himself was also, by the same token, launched on an original, perhaps unique, course. In its exterior details, it was modest: command of a small enclave of only a few hundred citizens in a remote and pestilential corner of the globe, far from the corridors of power and the prospect of military glory. But it was potentially a game with a great deal to play for. The Shore had become the closest place Despard had to a home, and the Shoremen to a local community; if he could settle them in a land in which they had been hostages to fortune for centuries, that would be much. Beyond this, perhaps, was the inkling of a grander idea, that the Bay of Honduras might become a beacon for a shattered and traumatized British empire, a glimpse of a bright future to lighten its present darkness. Dealing for the first time with the heart of government in Westminster and Whitehall, Despard's patriotism was becoming more than a simple matter of following orders. He was now in a position to help remake the rules of colonial government for a new world, or perhaps to restore the virtues of consent and justice that many felt they had lost.

The Bay of Honduras Settlement was destined to endure, and to remain a solitary bastion of British rule in Central America for two centuries. In 1862 it would become a full colony under the name of British Honduras; in 1981 it would achieve independence as the nation of Belize. Without Despard's military command at Black River it would probably never have existed, but within a few years it would test all his promising diplomatic qualities to destruction. It would be a new battleground, one where he would come to understand that the fine-sounding ideal of commonwealth had its sworn enemies, and that their reach extended to the highest authorities in the British government.

4

DESPOT

The mouth of the Belize River had, in Despard's words, 'the appearance of an impenetrable wood'. No more than a few timber shacks were visible among the thick forest and mangrove swamps, 'which only presented the root stumps of trees almost covered with water'. But, like Black River, it had an invisible hinterland of clearings and logging camps, haulover stations and jetties further upriver, and plantations concealed in the forest. It was home to around a hundred Baymen, logwood and mahogany traders of British origin who had been there for a century or more, and around 350 of their slaves.

The first known inhabitants of the river had been the Mayans, who had left spectacular ruined cities further inland, most of which had been abandoned to the jungle by the time the Spanish arrived. Like the rest of the Shore, it had been claimed for Spain but barely settled, and the first Europeans to base themselves there were buccaneers, who had used its massive offshore reefs – the largest in the Western hemisphere – to hide in between raiding and smuggling along the Spanish trading routes. Over the years they had settled, planting and logging, filling the tidal mangrove swamp with woodchip to reclaim it as working land, and by around 1670 the river mouth was a recognizable, if not recognized, British settlement. By 1730 it had become the most important source for mahogany in the British colonies, used for the furnishing of royal residences, stately homes and government buildings such as the Admiralty Board Room. Gradually, as demand and wealth grew, Belize mahogany began to sell in large volume to popular furniture-makers such as Thomas Chippendale.

As trade blossomed and skirmishes between Spanish and British navies grew more frequent, friction between the Baymen and their Spanish neighbours became endemic. The Baymen sold British goods and provisions, particularly rum, to the nearby settlements, undercutting the official Spanish duties; the Spanish put out the word to the Baymen's slaves that they would be freed if they defected to them. The Baymen developed an informal self-organization for their own protection, which was codified in 1765 under the supervision of a visiting British admiral, Sir William Burnaby. Burnaby's Code, as it became known, was signed by the white, slave-owning, male settlers, and was intended to regularize relations between a group of former buccaneers whose wandering days were over and who needed to settle in harmony and, when necessary, speak with one voice to the outside world. It was essentially a behavioural contract to enforce new standards of law and order, but its piratical roots endowed it with a level of rough-hewn democracy that was more developed among buccaneers than the European sovereign nations. It set up rules for public meetings, a system for electing magistrates, a swear-box for public profanity, penalties for theft, and a system of regulation for ships docked in the

Mahogany logging in Honduras

river. Burnaby himself had attached little importance to the code, and had observed that the Baymen themselves had few qualms about breaking it if it proved inconvenient, but over the years it had evolved into an emotive touchstone of their rights and liberties. The code was to be superseded by the new formal arrangements with the British Crown, though as it turned out the contest was far from over.

Having led the Baymen commissioners in setting up the new Bay of Honduras Settlement, Despard was reposted to Jamaica. For most of 1785 he was employed directly by Governor Campbell, and made several trips up and down the Shore to spread the news of the treaty, discuss it with the Spanish in Trujillo and plan for the resettlement of the scattered Shoremen. In March 1786 he was ready to take up permanent residency as First Commissioner. He took a boat to the Bay, making the crossing in nine days, but when he arrived at the cluster of shacks in the river's mouth there was little fanfare to greet him. He was informed by the Baymen that there was no-one who could be spared to assist him in building a house: all the slaves were upriver cutting logwood. But there were some old houses still standing at a site called the Haulover, several miles up the river, where felled trunks were loaded into boats. He rowed the nine miles up to the spot in a flat-bottomed sloop.

The Haulover, he discovered, had been mostly abandoned, a cluster of huts and sheds with rotting timbers and leaking thatch roofs. He soon discovered why. 'The flies', he recorded, 'were so troublesome that there was no peace with them day or night.' But there was no choice but to move in, and to wait for a chance to build somewhere on the coast where there was a breeze to catch. He moved some furniture he had brought from Jamaica into the best-preserved house, but it was still 'pervious to both sun and rain', and his possessions were soon ruined. There was no escape from the mosquitoes, and the bites that covered him soon ran into the thousands; often the only way to get through the night was to walk around very fast, fully clothed, from dusk till dawn. He had nothing to eat but dry goods from Jamaica – salt pork and beef – and fresh water had to be brought from miles away. Whenever he made it downriver to the settlement, he was told that a public meeting would soon be convened where the resources would be found to build him a proper home.

In July, just as the muggy heat was building to its peak and the rains loomed, Despard received the fresh set of instructions from London he had been waiting for. Britain and Spain had been haggling for the previous two years over the stipulations of Article 6 and the petitions of the Baymen, and had finally signed the Convention of London, a tweaked and expanded version of the original

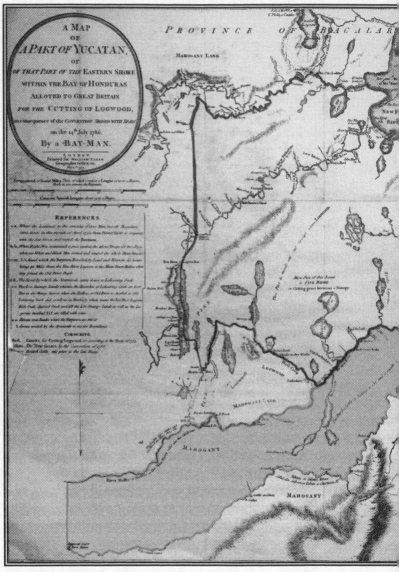

The Bay of Honduras Settlement, with the expanded territory negotiated by Despard and the Baymen (shaded)

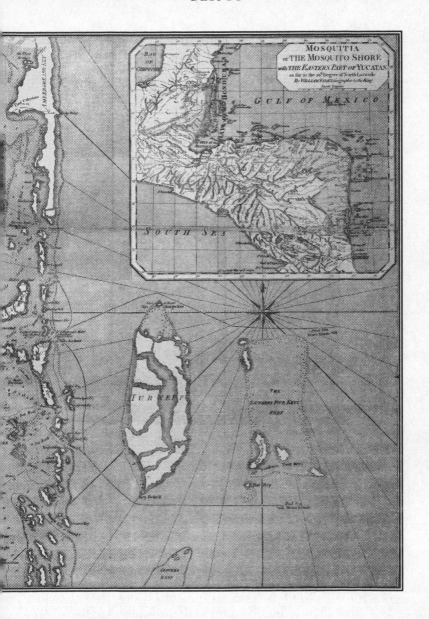

treaty. Most of the new material was in the Baymen's favour, and was testimony to the effectiveness of their, and Despard's, lobbying efforts. The Spanish had agreed to extend the limits of the Bay of Honduras, adding a swathe of territory to the south of the river mouth to accommodate the influx of British evacuees from the rest of the Shore; they had also agreed to allow the Baymen to cut all woods in the area, including mahogany, and to farm for their own subsistence provided that the right 'is not used for a pretext for establishing any plantation of sugar, coffee, cocoa or other like articles'. In addition, they could fish off the coast of the new territory. Spanish sovereignty over the settlement would be retained, and British occupation would remain dependent on the above conditions.

Notice of the convention arrived with a letter from Lord Sydney to Despard, promoting him to a new official role: Superintendent of the Bay Settlement. This was technically a military post, as the Bay was not permitted a British governor. It made Despard chief administrator not of the colony, for there was no colony, but of the British settlers, authorized to deal with Spanish governors and charged with ensuring that the settlers honoured the treaty. The post came with a salary of £500, which was modest, though equally there was little to spend it on. It also came with his first set of orders: to supervise the relocation of the Shoremen along the coast into the new Bay settlement. Despard was to be 'particularly attentive to their situation and to afford them every assistance', and to accommodate them 'in preference to all other persons whatsoever'. He was also to let it be known to the Baymen and incoming Shoremen alike, that 'infractions of the treaty will not be countenanced'.

Slowly, the Shoremen began to drift into the Bay. Unlike the predominantly landowning and ethnically Anglo-Saxon

Baymen, they were a disparate group, of various ethnic origins and arriving for different reasons. Some were planters of British origin from Black River and other points along the Shore, but many others were mulattoes, former slaves, shipbuilders, former convicts or Irish indentured labourers, brewers and traders. They were a loose community, used to living beyond the reach of the law; in the same way that the Baymen had adopted Burnaby's Code, the Shoremen had evolved 'certain rules of their own making', a frontier mutualism whereby provisions were held in common in times of crisis, and lending and borrowing were subject to informal but well-understood agreements. For many, the Bay of Honduras Settlement would be their first experience of formal administrative justice.

In addition to the Shoremen, there were also some arrivals from Jamaica, where nearly four thousand refugees from America – Quakers, war widows, loyalist planters, army surgeons – had beached since the colonies' independence. But despite Sydney's orders, Despard found as little local help in housing the new British subjects as he had in housing himself. The Baymen claimed ownership to all the land around the river mouth, and were unhelpful when it came to suggesting alternatives. Attempts to arrange public meetings were delayed. This was, Despard discovered, part of a continuing low-level resistance that predated his arrival and the Anglo-Spanish convention. During his absence on the Shore the previous year, the British government had drawn up plans to deport convicts to the new Bay settlement, but the Baymen had insisted there was no land to spare. Further, they had protested the very idea of turning the Bay into an 'open receptacle for outlaws, felons, foreigners and all such men who fly from justice, or are fond of a licentious life'.

At the same time, it became increasingly clear to

Despard that the new territorial limits were not being observed. A group of Spanish commissaries arrived, headed by a Colonel Savida, following up reports that mahogany was being logged outside the Bay boundaries. They found dozens of tracks leading beyond the boundaries to illegal logging areas managed by James Bartlett and others of the old Baymen. Despard prevailed on the Spanish delegation to stay with him for a few days so that they could inspect the disputed boundaries in detail, but one night moored outside his shack at the Haulover was enough for them. They departed on good terms, but they were terms contingent on an admission from Despard that the new logging was illegal, and a guarantee that he would put a stop to it.

Meanwhile, he also discovered, the magistrates the Baymen had appointed from their own number were meeting in his absence and passing new bye-laws, consolidating their own positions and nibbling away at the rights of the newcomers. They were also smuggling, and trading with America: their stores on the river mouth were selling luxury American goods such as embroidery and ironware, and staples at prices that undercut the duty-paid British imports. In Despard's absence they passed new regulations that taxed all shipping, British and American, entering the port. His protests were met with assertions that this was merely local regulation, not part of the business of the superintendent, which was strictly to oversee the treaty provisions to the satisfaction of the Governor of Jamaica and the British Home Office. It was becoming clear to Despard that his position was being systematically undermined, and that only explicit support of it from the very top would give him the authority to maintain it. He wrote to Lord Sydney asking for clarification of his role, and specifically 'how far I am justifiable in suffering this intercourse' with American traders.

But the Baymen, past masters at leaning on central government from a distance, had seen this coming, and they also began to take their case to London. In January 1787 Robert White, one of their number, visited London to recuperate from illness and began to pay repeated visits to Evan Nepean, Sydney's under-secretary at the Home Office. At the same time, the rest of the Baymen, who also comprised the magistrates – five of them had been elected in 1784, before the Shoremen's arrival, by seven voters – sent a series of petitions to Sydney about their plight. They had long been aware that, remote as they were from the shores and the political concerns of Britain, there was no point in understatement. 'Situated as we are without hope, oppressed both here and in Great Britain, we have no spirit or vigour left,' they moaned. 'The measure of our misfortunes is now complete, and all our remonstrances are in vain.' White, in person, was no less melodramatic: having stressed the economic value of the mahogany trade to the Home Office, he dropped dark hints that the new superintendent seemed determined to throw his weight around, and that the results might be disastrous, even forcing the planters to abandon the colony.

Despard was under no illusions about what underlay the Baymen's complaints. 'The real cause', he stated later, 'was the loss of a capital mahogany work on the Shore.' The Baymen were a handful of long-established businessmen who were, with the regularization of the mahogany trade, poised to become extremely wealthy. They had long been in the habit of dividing the Bay into large swathes and sharing it out equably, if illegally, between them; twelve of them now had over two thousand square miles of forest parcelled up between them. But they were about to be overrun: Despard's estimates from his travels around the

Shore and Jamaica was that the incoming Shoremen would outnumber the old Baymen and their slaves by five to one. Furthermore, their land claims had now been officially and explicitly invalidated. No individuals in the colony had the right to any land, which was all technically owned by the Spanish and merely administered by the British government. The Baymen had been on Despard's side while he was negotiating their treaty rights and constitutional independence, but now that he had been specifically ordered to redistribute their plantations and accommodate the Shoremen, the superintendent was an ally no longer.

The Baymen's actions and their motives were predictable, and had many precedents. Marooned in a distant and vulnerable corner of the globe, they were used to shouting loudly, overstating their grievances and reneging on agreements when official backs were turned. This was what had brought them prosperity in the past; there was no penalty for doing it, and no incentive for them to behave otherwise. Now, beneath their bluff and arrogance, they were extremely frightened. Some of the older families had lived in the Bay for over a century, and it was about to be flooded with a motley crew of dubious character who would change it beyond recognition. But if they knew their weaknesses, they also knew their strengths. The main value of the Bay to Britain was trade, and for the moment at least that trade was in their hands. They had nothing to lose from pushing their case as far as they could.

Despard took a different view. His job, which was becoming trickier by the day, was to square the circle of competing interests – Baymen, Shoremen, Spanish, British – in the new enclave, and to run it as a model independent settlement. He had no choice but to take the Spanish side against the Baymen's if they were logging illegally, because the entire project was contingent on the treaty being respected. And he had no choice but to accommodate the Shoremen, because those were his unambiguous orders from Britain. To take the Baymen's side would mean conniving with them against the Crown, and this he was not prepared to do. Their insistence on passing laws that suited their 'very arbitrary aristocracy', as Despard characterized it, was contrary not just to his instructions but to the very basis on which they were entitled to call on the British army and navy to protect their trade. Their attempt to undermine him was, in his view, 'a perfect unqualified declaration of independence'. Whatever he might become later in his career, Despard was at this point still a patriot, and the Baymen's attempt to capitalize on the benefits of British rule while avoiding its obligations was edging towards the rebellion witnessed in America. If the Baymen desired Britain's protection, they must respect its laws; if they did not, they would ultimately lose their right to call on her for defence. It was what the war in America had been fought for, and he was prepared to fight it again in miniature.

There were several among the long-established Baymen who saw it Despard's way, but they were not the cabal who had elected themselves magistrates. Despard might object to the injustice of the arbitrary aristocracy that was challenging him, but that arbitrary aristocracy had made a further calculation: that their economic importance to Britain was ultimately greater than her interest in local justice in the Bay. Both Despard's and the Baymen's were entrenched positions, and the outcome was bound to be escalation rather than conciliation. The Baymen were fighting a piratical guerrilla war of small, daily infractions and plausible deniability, nibbling away at Despard's power to act. Meanwhile, the Shoremen were begging

Despard for land to settle, homes to build and plots to cultivate, and for government hand-outs and rations to feed them in the meantime. They were Despard's greater responsibility: their livelihood was in his hands, and he was under orders to settle them in preference to all other claimants. On 9 July 1787 he published a proclamation announcing his solution: Convention Town.

Convention Town was to be a new development, owned by the British local authority, a planned settlement where the hundreds of new arrivals could be housed and could grow food for their sustenance. It was to be situated on the south side of the Belize River, the land newly ceded by the Convention of London. Together with his surveyor, David Lamb, Despard marked out over a hundred family plots, each a hundred feet by fifty, running along the bank of the river and down the coast to the mangrove swamps. He invited any Shoremen who were still looking for a home to apply for a lot, and made it clear to all that this was a temporary housing solution that would be extended or amended according to instructions from London.

The Baymen, led by James Bartlett and William O'Brien, raised immediate objections. This, they claimed, was their land; 'they had long ago cleared there, and declared they would distribute it to such of their friends as they thought proper'. They pulled up the stakes with which Lamb was marking out the land, and threatened him if he proceeded. Despard was summoned from upriver to referee. He informed the Baymen that it was no-one's land; it had only been ceded by the Spanish the previous year, and then only for housing and cultivation. If they had cleared it previously, they had done so illegally. The Baymen set up a magistrates meeting and fired off a petition to London. Despard, they claimed, was 'dividing the newly ceded district after the manner of a lottery, without preference to

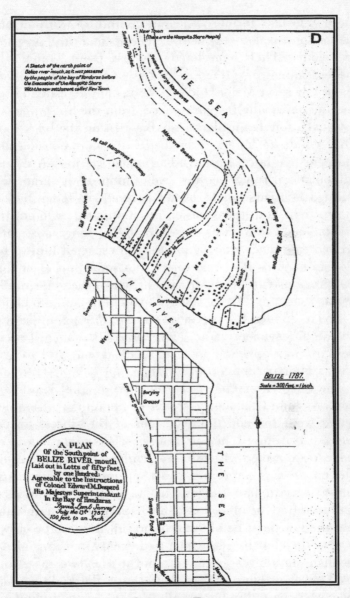

Convention Town

those who had formerly cleared ground, or without any distinction of age, sex, character, respectability, property or colour'. They hammered the last point home: 'the meanest mulatto or freed negro has an equal chance' with Major Lawrie or Major Hodgson, or any of the distinguished and unequivocally British refugees from the Shore.

Convention Town placed the Baymen on the back foot. They could no longer drag their heels or pass allegedly innocent bye-laws; Despard had taken the initiative, and without open resistance the reallocation of the land they claimed as theirs would be a *fait accompli*. They had to pick a fight, and the occasion arose promptly. One of the first ballots, Lot 69, was drawn by Joshua Jones, a recently arrived free black man, and Despard escorted him to his plot. Lot 69, as it turned out, had a small hut on it that had previously been constructed by one of the magistrates, Aaron Young, and Despard gave Jones permission to knock it down. When he began to do so, Young appeared, 'threatening violently the vengeance of the magistrates'. Despard was on hand to face Young down, and to give Jones public permission to continue.

The next morning, returning from the Haulover, Despard found an angry crowd of Shoremen assembled across from the courthouse in one of the stores. Joshua Jones, it transpired, had been arrested the night before by magistrates armed with guns and cutlasses, and locked up. The crowd was large and bad-tempered, the courthouse flimsy; several had suggested that it would be an easy matter to free the innocent man. Despard, though, insisted that the law must be allowed to prevail. He led the crowd over to the courthouse, which had twenty or thirty of the Baymen standing squarely around it and two men with fixed bayonets guarding the door. Despard asked them, by the powers vested in him as His Majesty's Superintendent, to free Joshua Jones, who was entitled to Lot 69 to do with as he pleased. The Baymen refused, claiming that it went beyond the superintendent's authority to 'accommodate a set of men of colour calling themselves the people of the Mosquito Shore'. Finally, Despard walked through the courthouse door, and found Jones sitting inside. He touched him on the shoulder and said, 'I declare this man free in the King's name.' Bartlett immediately touched Jones's other shoulder and declared him a prisoner. From outside the courthouse the crowd began shouting 'To arms!', and dispersed. Despard turned and left the court-house. A few minutes later, Jones was quietly released.

It was a crucial moment, and in an alternative history of the British empire – or commonwealth – it might have been a defining one. Joshua Jones, it declared, was as much a British subject as anyone else who lived under British law, who paid British taxes, and who was eligible – perhaps obliged – to fight for the British army, whatever his place of birth or the colour of his skin. But even as it was, an awkward little confrontation on the remote Mosquito Shore, the principle at stake was considerable. The superintendent of the new convention had finally come eyeball to eyeball with the defenders of Burnaby's Code, and Burnaby had blinked first. Any other outcome would have been the end of Despard's authority, even of his post, but he had seized the moment to establish both with greater force than before. When Lord Sydney heard of the incident, he supported Despard to the hilt. 'I am persuaded they have conducted themselves in a very unwarrantable and indecent manner,' he wrote of the Baymen. 'I am commanded to acquaint you that His Majesty is much displeased with their conduct, and expects they will demean themselves in a different manner if they value a continuation of His Royal Protection.' Sydney suggested that they might be forgiven this time for not grasping that Despard's authority overrode that of Burnaby's Code, but that this principle should, from here on, be clear to all concerned.

But there was one question that had been highlighted by the incident on which Despard and Sydney did not quite see eye to eye. Despite his support of Despard's actions, Sydney was concerned that no distinction was being made in the allocation of land 'between affluent settlers and persons of a different description, particularly people of colour'. The Baymen had offered a justification for their distinction that was framed in terms of local practices, claiming that 'in the whole of the West India Islands, negroes and mulattoes are considered in a very inferior light'; Sydney's objection was also framed in these terms. 'Free negroes,' he suggested to Despard, 'from the natural prejudice of the inhabitants of the colonies, are not, however valuable in point of character, considered upon an equal footing with people of a different complexion.' Despard seems to have been surprised by Sydney's objection, not because it was unheard of but because he thought the answer was obvious: this was a clear example of the type of policy that should be subject to British law. 'It must be governed by the laws of England,' he replied, 'which knows no such distinction.'

It is perhaps significant that this question of racial discrimination, which has loomed so large in subsequent histories of the British empire, should present itself here, when it happened to arise, as a minor misunderstanding. Technically speaking, Despard was perfectly correct: there was no colour bar or ethnic caste system in British law, and there never had been, although there were still professional bars against dissenters, Jews and Catholics. In terms of his own local experience, too, there were few grounds for such discrimination. Contrary to the Baymen's assertions, ethnicity was only one of the determinants of class in the West Indies, and not always a reliable one. Joshua Jones, for example, was a man of means: the Bay census shows that he owned seventeen slaves. Many of the black Shoremen had fought with Despard in the San Juan raid; many more who would have been under his care had died there, sacrificing their lives for the British Crown. The idea that Britain itself might limit the rights of her subjects simply on the basis of their race was still in the future – a future which, by the time of his gallows speech, Despard would have come to see rather more clearly.

Yet Lord Sydney's position was also typical of its time. Throughout the eighteenth century, all the European powers had conducted their colonial affairs in a permanent state of what is now referred to as 'imperial overstretch'. By modern standards, tiny handfuls of soldiers and officials were routinely expected to police and defend huge swathes of foreign territory; it was not only on the Mosquito Shore that British forces were supplemented, and often outnumbered, by local 'irregulars' of varied ethnicity. Britain's colonies had until recently been populated mostly by Anglo-Saxon settlers; increasingly, in the wake of war and territorial expansion, they were coming to be filled with Native Americans, freed slaves, prisoners of war and army deserters, the landless spilling into territory that had been claimed by previous – and, in many cases, very recent – arrivals. It was gradually becoming a working assumption of central government that decisions about who was to count as British were being made on a local level. When British racial policies emerged in the next century, they were not prompted by overt racist ideology so much as by the accretion of dozens of small decisions of this kind.

There was a broader debate to be had over this disputed

territory, but Despard's urgent exchange of letters with Lord Sydney was not the place for it. Nevertheless, it was a chink of light between Home Office and superintendent that the Baymen began to exploit with increasing fervour. After the heat of the Joshua Jones incident had passed, Despard ensured that affidavits were sworn by eye-witnesses – Baymen and Shoremen, black and white – to testify that no force had been used to effect Jones's release, that the crowd of Shoremen had been unarmed, and that the handling of the incident had been procedurally correct. But, as he had clearly anticipated, the account of the incident that emerged from Young and the magistrates was quite different, and was conveyed to London in vivid and urgent terms. It conjured once again the image that was later projected back to Despard's assumption of command at Black River, and which was to cling to him for the rest of his life and long after: the 'dreadful scene' of a colonel gone native, with a rabble of 'people of mixed colour and negroes' at his back, leading an armed mob through the street to terrorize the white British minority. After Despard's death and disgrace, it was the Baymen's version that was believed, not just of this incident but of the entire period of Despard's superintendency in the Bay. Colonial historians accepted it for a century or more; many of the older British generation in Belize believe it to this day. And there were more, and worse, accusations to come.

The Baymen had lost the battle of Convention Town, and lost face badly in the new community, but they had no intention of conceding the Bay to Despard's admin-istration. They held a public meeting within days and passed a new resolution that the logwood trade should be free to all, but that mahogany logging should be restricted to those with property and 'four able negro men slaves'.

Despard observed 'the partiality of this law to rich people', and also the fact that it was by this point only mahogany that was in much demand in Britain. Having secured the right to log mahogany, the Baymen had abandoned their attempts to secure a logwood monopoly, with the result, as Despard explained, that 'the cutting of logwood is at present very far from being anywise profitable'. The aim of the Baymen's regulation, as he made clear to Lord Sydney, was to ensure that none of the new arrivals would be able to get a foothold in the Bay's real business. With plantations forbidden by the Spanish, those without slaves would have no choice if they remained but to work for the old Baymen – who themselves, as Despard pointed out, had originally begun 'cutting mahogany with a single negro, some without one'. The case might be made that the convention meant that the pioneer days in the Bay were over, and that power and property should now be consolidated where they lay, but for Despard, with a duty of care to the Shoremen, it was a case without merit. He ignored the new regulations, and allowed the Shoremen to do the same.

The Baymen were prepared to keep fighting; they had little to lose, since to lose would only place them in the same position as if they conceded. But they were running out of ideas for preserving the status quo and stemming the tide. Any direct attack on Despard's authority would end in a replay of the Joshua Jones showdown; their tantrums to the British government had been thus far largely ignored; and anything more roundabout or subtle ran the risk of seeing the Shoremen settled and logging mahogany before it came to fruition. But, just as their imaginations were failing, nature intervened. Despard was woken in the Haulover on the morning of 1 September 1787 by 'a violent hurricane and inundation', the worst for many years. The wind blew over trees and tore the roofs off buildings. By the time he could fight his way down to the river mouth, the damage was tremendous. Most of the houses and huts in the main settlement had been destroyed; the shacks that had sprung up in Convention Town were flattened; every boat in the port, local and foreign alike, was 'either lost or so disabled by the storm as to prevent them going to sea without considerable repairs'. Virtually the only vessel in the Bay still seaworthy was Despard's own sloop, which had been moored at the Haulover.

Initially, this crisis seemed as if it might pull Despard and the Baymen together. He convened a meeting with his former fellow commissioners Bartlett, McCaulay and Hoare, and offered the use of his sloop to get to Jamaica with letters and requests for assistance. The Baymen leaders were grateful, and promised to spread the word among the rest of the inhabitants. Despard set off on another of his mercy dashes across the Caribbean, but it somehow slipped the Baymen's minds to pass the news on to the Shoremen. Instead, they fitted up one of their least damaged ships as quickly as they could and sent it to Bristol with a message for George Dyer, their business agent in Britain, telling him to set off immediately with provisions, which would fetch sky-high prices in the stricken Bay. Their ship slipped away quietly. When Despard returned in his sloop from Jamaica, he was horrified to discover that even those shipwrecked in the hurricane had been denied the chance of communicating their safety to their families.

A few weeks into the crisis, a merchant ship stocked with provisions arrived, and anchored off the Bay to await instructions. It was met by Bartlett and some of the other magistrates, who established that it was owned by a

Captain Josephson, and that Josephson was Jewish. They informed him that there had long been a local law in the Bay prohibiting Jews from trading with the inhabitants. Josephson appealed to the superintendent; Despard informed him that there was no such law, and even if there had been it would now be null and void. He was as free to trade here as in any British colony.

The next arrival was a schooner from New York bearing a cargo of flour, bread and spirits. It had showed up in the Bay twice before, and sold its cargo to the Baymen illegally; since Britain had declared America a hostile power and set stringent limits on its trade with the loyalist colonies, such smuggling had become commonplace, even beginning to outstrip legitimate trade. Despard impounded its merchandise and told the Americans that he would sell it and remit the money to the British government, to whom they could appeal if they wished.

This would turn out to be a decision that would dog Despard halfway around the world. He had followed the legally correct procedure, but to do so was still a risky business. Horatio Nelson, after recovering from the San Juan raid, had done exactly the same when, while captaining the *Boreas* off the island of St Kitts, he found the port full of American smugglers. He ordered them out, but they returned; when he tried to banish them again, he was accused by the British colonists of acting against their interests, and was issued with writs for loss of trade by the local merchants. He was advised against submitting himself to the kangaroo court of the island's magistrates, and was forced to remain on board the *Boreas* for two months outside the harbour. When he returned to Britain, he was acquitted of all charges, and commended by the Treasury for his 'zeal in protecting British commerce'. Despard would be rather more unfortunate.

Having impounded the American contraband, Despard sent an official request to the Spanish government of Yucatán for the right to buy emergency provisions for disaster relief. The Spanish agreed, but this placed the Bay in their debt at a time when the matter of territorial boundaries was far from settled. Subsequent visits had shown that the Baymen were still ignoring instructions from both Despard and the Spanish to stop logging outside the permitted zones; deadlines and ultimata had come and gone. A visit just before the hurricane had discovered mahogany logging some way outside the boundaries, the trees marked with the symbol of the British Crown; Despard had had no choice but to admit that this had been done without his knowledge or permission. He was now looking weak, his diplomatic credit overdrawn and the Bay's internal disputes out in the open. Although his relations with the Spanish remained cordial, there was a crisis brewing outside the Bay that was every bit as serious as the one within it.

Meanwhile, the Baymen had opened up a new diplomatic front in London. Their agent George Dyer met with the Prime Minister, William Pitt the Younger, introducing himself as the representative of the Bay's mahogany trade. Dyer stressed the value of the trade to Britain, which was by this point importing some four million feet of mahogany a year from the Baymen, and presented a petition from the Baymen complaining against the restrictions imposed on them by the British government and arguing that it would be advantageous to all parties if they were relaxed. Pitt, generally in favour of free trade, was inclined to listen, and Dyer broached the subject of the troublesome superintendent. He hinted that the disputes between the Baymen and the representative of the Crown were becoming so serious that if Despard were not replaced the main business of the Bay would sooner or later be forced to move elsewhere.

It was becoming harder, rather than easier, for Despard to weave together the contradictory demands of the Baymen, the British and the Spanish, and by May 1789 the threads were beginning to snap. A new lieutenant, Juan Bautista Gual, arrived from Yucatán with a request from the Spanish governor to accompany Despard on a tour of the boundaries. Despard attempted to engineer a delay, knowing from experience why they had asked and what they would find, but Spanish patience had run out. A new governor in Yucatán, tired of his predecessor's lack of progress with infractions by the Baymen, had decided to apply the terms of the convention to the letter. Gual announced that, this time, all settlements and logging outside the limits would have to be burned on the spot, and if any resistance was met the Spanish would send in an armed expeditionary force. Despard asked once more for a brief delay, and was countered with a further demand, this time a direct challenge to the Bay's internal affairs. The magistracy system run by the Baymen, Gual informed him, was contrary to the terms of the convention, which forbade the setting up of a system of government inside the enclave. The Spanish would no longer tolerate a code of law run by interests inimical to the Spanish Crown. Despard, as superintendent, would be permitted to set up an internal policing structure, but the existing magistracy must be dissolved.

On 10 June, Despard called a general assembly at the courthouse, announced the Spanish ultimatum and published a new Plan of Police. The authority in the Bay would now be headed by the superintendent, supported by a committee of fifteen who would be elected by all the male inhabitants. The committee might be summoned or dismissed by the superintendent, but must be called at least once every six months; a majority of the inhabitants could also call it to account. Judges were to be appointed by the superintendent, but could be removed by the committee. If the inhabitants were to vote for the plan, they must abide by it; if a new system of regulation were to be decided in Britain, it would override the stated arrangements.

Such was Despard's first and only attempt at a constitution. It was markedly more autocratic than the previous arrangement, with almost all power concentrated in himself; on this score, the Spanish had forced his hand. But it was also, at the same time, markedly more democratic, with his power triggered or annulled by a simple majority of the population, with no oligarchies or second-class citizens. Overall, it was far more limited in its scope than its more ambitious predecessor – a policing arrangement, little more or less. It awaited the judgement of the people as to whether they would hand him autocracy by consent. They did, by a landslide, in by far the largest vote ever seen in the Bay. One hundred and thirty inhabitants assented to it; twenty-four, the hard core of the Baymen, rejected it. Despard noted their disapproval, and also their vested interests. 'It cannot be expected', he commented, 'that I can now pay attention to the partial objections of a few individuals.'

For the Baymen, this was everything they had feared since the arrival of the Shoremen two years before. The reign of their arbitrary aristocracy was over, their monopoly of the mahogany trade soon to follow. With nothing left to lose, they sent a 'Petition by Settlers against Despard's Constitution' to the Home Office, which amplified their previous complaints to the most grandiose levels they could manage. Despard, they claimed, had made himself the 'sole and arbitrary disposer' of justice in the Bay, a 'sovereign-despot' who was 'above and at enmity with the laws and constitution'. There was now to be no law in the Bay but his 'sovereign will and pleasure'. 'Englishmen', they implored, 'can never brook the despotic government of an individual.' They had 'tasted the sweets of liberty' under British rule, and it was impossible for them to submit to a dictator who wished 'from the condition of free men to degrade them into that of slaves and bondsmen'.

The accusations the Baymen let fly were a mixed bag, many of them mutually contradictory, and many of them referring back to a language of the past that still had the ability to inflame. Despard was, in effect, a spectre from the bad old days of piracy, before the laws and constitutions of Britain were settled in its dominions, when might was right and planters and traders were at the mercy of the leaders of uncivilized criminal bands. Despard was such a man, 'destitute of the common feelings of humanity, of the most violent prejudices and passions, and of principles so arbitrary and despotic as to be totally incompatible with every idea of civil liberty'. He was an 'unlettered barbarian' who had torn up Burnaby's Code and plunged the Bay back into the era of buccaneers and desperadoes.

More than a pirate, the Baymen continued, Despard was also another spectre from the past: a Leveller, a fanatic from the revolutionary madness of the English Civil War who believed in destroying all private property, by force if necessary. His 'wild and levelling principle of universal equality' would spell the death of British interests in the Bay by destroying the distinction not merely between black and white, but between free man and slave. His 'career of despotism' had been boosted by inciting the motley crew to free Joshua Jones, and he had come increasingly to rely on the threat of his black militia. The Bay was now moving into the hands of a mob who were poised to sabotage the source of its wealth. 'The negroes in servitude,' the Baymen claimed, 'observing the now exalted status of their brethren of yesterday, would thence be induced to revolt, and the settlement must be ruined.' Already, they claimed, the Bay was unrecognizable, a 'land of famine, disease and death'.

This was an accusation well calculated to exploit the uncertainty within the Home Office about the rights of the black Shoremen, but one which was well wide of the mark. Despard's egalitarian tendencies, at this point in his life, were relatively modest. He himself had owned a slave for much of his tenure in the Bay; he had freed him by deed of manumission in 1788, citing 'good services done by him', including fighting alongside his master at Black River in 1782. It would be a mistake to read too much into either owning a slave or freeing him: both were standard practice, in the British, French and Spanish colonies and America alike. Nor, as the example of Joshua Jones demonstrates, was slave-owning confined to whites. The sentiments of universal equality Despard would express on the gallows would emerge later in life, though it may well be that the Baymen's unedifying example, by opening his eyes to the realities and abuses of power, played a role in their evolution.

Thus Despard was both pirate and Leveller, but the Baymen had a third accusation: he was a traitor to the Crown. He had seized power in the Bay, in their account, in collusion with the Spanish; far from seeking to protect their property, he had 'induced the Spanish officers to lay waste, pillage and plunder their provision grounds'. Despard's story that he had received an ultimatum from the Spanish, the Baymen alleged, covered the truth that he had been in cahoots with Spain against them all along. He had thus betrayed not only the Baymen but the Crown itself, by placing his local power at the disposal of the Spanish dominion and above his responsibilities to his own nation. Much of this was directly contradicted by Lord Sydney's own correspondence, which had time and again censured the Baymen for their infractions of the convention, but the Baymen had nothing to lose – and, perhaps, an inkling that a convenient fiction might somehow prove more useful to the government than an inconvenient truth.

As it happened, unrelated events halfway round the world conspired in their favour. By the time the Baymen's petition arrived at the Home Office, Lord Sydney had been replaced as Home Secretary by Lord Grenville. In this, Despard was doubly unfortunate. First, Grenville was not Sydney, and had no sense of the Baymen's history of hyperbole and ferocious self-defence. Second, he was William Pitt's cousin; the Prime Minister had appointed him because he was a far closer political ally than Sydney, who was subsequently marginalized in government. (His greatest contribution to posterity would turn out to be the convict settlement in Australia that was named after him in 1785.) Grenville, like Pitt, was aware of the Bay of Honduras Settlement first and foremost – perhaps exclusively – as a crucial and valuable source of mahogany. He was at least as diligent a Home Secretary as Sydney had been, and he read the divergent statements of Despard and the Baymen with puzzlement. But he was persuaded that action needed to be taken swiftly, not least by George Dyer, who was writing vigorously to the Home Office warning of the imminent 'destruction of the settlement' and even of 'a misunderstanding with the court of

LORD GRENVILLE.

Pub. Jan 22 1807. by James Cundee London.

William Wyndham Grenville

Madrid' if Despard were not stopped. Barely settled in his post and with eight colonies in the West Indies alone competing for attention with his home affairs brief, Grenville had enough to attend to without the threat that the Treaty of Paris might founder over a small mahogany enclave.

The Baymen's strategy was beginning to pay off. They were too remotely located for impartial intelligence to be easily gathered; they were too important to British trade to be ignored. Their persistent stream of allegations, however outrageous, had to be taken seriously. Grenville was faced with an awkward dilemma. There was much evidence from Sydney's time that Despard was acting commendably, but much recently arrived on his desk that seemed to presage catastrophe if he was not removed. Dyer was pressuring him; Grenville's secretary, Evan Nepean, was holding him off. 'Mr. Grenville does not feel himself sufficiently informed', he wrote, 'to dismiss Col. Despard from the office of Superintendent on the grounds of his alleged misconduct.'

A week later, on 2 October, Grenville reached his decision. He wrote to Despard, informing him that he would not 'deliver any decided opinion' until he heard from him, but that he did seem to have 'caused almost general dissatisfaction among the settlers'. Grenville, therefore, was sending Lieutenant-Colonel Peter Hunter of the 60th Regiment to the Bay to make an independent report. 'I am very far from meaning to intimate the smallest degree of approbation', he assured Despard, 'to those infractions of the Convention which you have represented to be so frequent and so glaring.' Despard, then, was to have a mediator, a disinterested third party, to referee the dispute.

But Grenville's suspension of judgement, for whatever reason, did not last. On 16 October he changed his mind, and wrote to both Hunter and the Governor of Jamaica informing them of his revised decision. Despard was to be suspended, and Hunter to be his temporary replacement.

Despard, meanwhile, was making slow and steady progress in regularizing conditions in the Bay. His Plan of Police was working smoothly, and he picked up his negotiations with the Spanish in a stronger position, haggling with them about how much land the Convention Town settlers should be allotted for cultivation and setting up plots of five hundred square yards each where they could begin subsistence farming. The news of his suspension, when it came, was a bolt from the blue, and a serious obstacle to his recent progress. This was something that could no longer be resolved locally; he realized that he could no longer avoid leaving for London to make his case and clear his name. 'It would be highly improper', he wrote to an officer friend in London, 'to push matters further than they have already been carried, which would be unavoidable were I to continue longer on the spot.' Without the authority of the Crown, he would be powerless to address the miscarriages of justice that were afoot.

But he could not leave until Hunter arrived, which would not be for another five months. Correspondence flew between Despard and the Home Office, bringing the differences of opinion between them into sharper relief. Grenville, as the pieces of the story fell into place, became more belligerent towards the Spanish, with whom diplomatic relations were currently strained by the distant Nootka Sound Crisis, where the Spanish had seized British fishing vessels in disputed Pacific waters. Keen to hit back at Spain, Grenville began to insist that Lieutenant Gual had had no right to destroy the Baymen's plantations; he should have referred the matter to his governor, who should have taken it up with Grenville. Despard, by the same token, should not have instituted his Plan of Police 'on the representation of the Spanish commissary'; he had allowed himself to be bounced into setting up a new system 'far more objectionable than that which has been abolished' by an aggressive foreign power. Despard had spent much of his tenure asking Sydney for a greater level of intervention from the British government; now, under Grenville, he was getting it, but not in the form he had anticipated. Under the letter of the treaty, the Spanish were within their rights, but Grenville's instincts seemed to be to pick a fight with them regardless.

Peter Hunter arrived on 11 April 1790. The next day, he formally announced Despard's suspension and his own appointment as acting superintendent, and declared Despard's Plan of Police null and void. 'The former system', he declared, 'is to be considered as standing upon the same ground as it did before the steps taken by Colonel Despard in May last.' The Baymen had finally succeeded in turning back the tide. Their old magistracy was to be restored, and disputes with the Spanish were no longer to be resolved by the Yucatán army but to be referred back to London. James Bartlett wrote to the Home Office praising Hunter for appreciating the 'Baymen spirit' in a way that Despard never had, and restoring their status as free-born Englishmen. Grenville also wrote secretly to Hunter asking him to ascertain the strength of the Spanish army in Yucatán, and to Jamaica alerting the governor to the possibility that he might have to send troops to the Bay at short notice. It was just like old times: the Bay was returning to Burnaby's Code, and the Shore was once more being put on a war footing.

Despard's response was unexpected. The restitution of the code meant that elections for magistrates needed to be held, and he surprised everyone by nominating himself as a candidate, despite having already announced that he was intending to leave by the next boat, and that his priority was to clear his name in Whitehall and be restored as superintendent. Hunter was extremely annoyed: such a step seemed calculated to 'keep up the old dissentions, and to create new ones'. But Despard had his reasons. The inquiry in London, he was already suspecting, would be no formality. The Baymen would appeal to the wealth of their trade and to the perfidy of the Spanish, aspects of the case that would speak more persuasively to Grenville than constitutional rectitude and the rights of blacks and mulattoes. He was beginning, perhaps, to appreciate that trade and war were for most politicians the only tangible evidence of far-flung colonies they would never visit. The greatest strength of his own position was that he had acted in the interests of the settlement as a whole, and the best way to back this up would be for the inhabitants to speak for him *en masse* as clearly as the Baymen had for their own minority interests.

Despard placed himself at the head of a slate of nine candidates, all of whom volunteered to stand on the simple platform he had drawn up for himself: of representing the interests of all the settlers, and pledging to abide by majority rule. His canvassers began to campaign enthusiastically in Convention Town, and among classes of inhabitants who had never voted before. Despard seemed to be enjoying his new challenge, and running it with military efficiency. Canvassers fanned out up the rivers and tributaries, down the coast to the turtlers and fishermen on the cays. The opposition quickly realized that they were being outflanked: a constituency was being mobilized that had never voted before, and that could not be counted on to return the usual candidates. Bartlett and the old

Baymen protested that this was illegal, but were unable to point to any provisions in the code to disqualify black or poor voters. It had simply, over the years, become the custom for the magistracy to nominate its own, usually on a turnout of a dozen or less.

A last-ditch move to stop the votes being counted was overturned by Hunter, and when the results were declared on 4 May they were more conclusive than Despard had hoped or the Baymen had feared. Two hundred and fifty votes had been cast, against a previous record turnout for magistracy elections of forty. Of these, Despard had received 203, and every candidate on his slate at least 150, including those of many of the old Baymen outside the magistrates' cabal. It was a massive landslide on a massive franchise, and an overwhelming mandate for his policies. Hunter received the verdict 'with astonishment'; the rump of dissenting Baymen responded to the news with horror. They petitioned London at once, charging that the vote had been maliciously skewed by the inclusion of 'ignorant turtlers' and 'men of colour', who knew nothing of the Bay's affairs and had been duped into supporting Despard on the basis of absurd promises to settle old grudges in their favour.

But it was a trump card for Despard, and everyone knew it. In the subsequent histories of the colony, which took – and continue to take – the Baymen's side, it has proved impossible to explain away. It has been called 'odd', 'inexplicable', 'extraordinary', the votes cast 'possibly in desperation'. After all, if Despard was an autocrat, a despot who rode roughshod over the established codes and best interests of the inhabitants, how could it be that the vast majority of them voted for him? Conversely, for Despard and his supporters, there could be no more definitive proof that the vocal Baymen represented a small and entrenched minority whose private interests were not shared beyond their immediate circle. It was a rhetorical triumph, but it would not prove to be an enduring one. Back in London, half a world away, it would shrink to a footnote in a campaign that would drag on, broaden out in unforeseen ways, and gradually come to consume the rest of Despard's life.

Despite fears expressed to Hunter by Bartlett and the other Baymen that he might be planning to stay and fight the Shoremen's corner, Despard had no intention of serving as a magistrate under the new superintendent. The vote, for him, was a referendum rather than a mandate for public service. He left the Bay on 3 June for Jamaica and London, intending to clear his name as quickly as possible and return as superintendent. He would, as it turned out, never be back.

Back in the Bay, it would become clear sooner rather than later that the problems with the post of super-intendent were endemic to the office rather than specific to Despard. After reinstating Burnaby's Code, Hunter became once more entangled with the Spanish authorities before being invalided out of service. The entanglement deepened, and contributed to the resumption of war between Britain and Spain in 1796. Thereafter the competing claims of authority between colonial governors, central administration and military command became ever more intractable. It was never established who the super-intendent of the enclave was ultimately answerable to: the inhabitants, the Spanish dominion that surrounded and partially included them, the Home Office, the government of Jamaica or the British army. George Arthur, who held the post thirty years later, was still complaining that 'the office is, and always has been, so very undefined as to deprive the Representative of the Crown of the authority necessary for the administration of public business'.

As the Baymen tightened their grip on the settlement, Burnaby's Code extended itself into a precise codification of race. By 1805, the voting qualifications for black residents had already become far more stringent than for whites; by the 1820s, there were seven legally distinct castes based on skin colour, from white to black, with a hierarchy of rights and privileges for which the inhabitants qualified depending on how much Anglo-Saxon blood they could demonstrate in their ancestry. The settlement stumbled on as an oligarchy, though an increasingly weakened one. By the 1830s, the Baymen were a spent force: the abolition of slavery, combined with their wasteful agricultural methods and the rise of industry, gradually made them less important to the British economy than Indian tea-growers, Birmingham railway builders or Welsh coal miners. The Bay itself remained a permanent bone of contention between Spanish and British military, until gunboat diplomacy finally converted it into the full colony of British Honduras.

Despard's period of superintendency in the Bay stands in sharp relief to the history that preceded and followed it. It was hardly the model for which he might have hoped: it never escaped its fate as a hybrid creature, consensual but not sovereign, self-determining within its own borders but non-existent outside them, and was ultimately torn apart by forces over which Despard had no control. But within its contradictions it came close to establishing principles that were unusual for the time, but which would become central to the conduct of government and empire in generations to come: racial equality, respect for international law, and democratic representation. For Despard, at this point, these were not products of a radical political ideology or acts of rebellion against the tenets of British rule. There is no indication that he doubted they were among the values that had derived from his own national culture and constitution, which he had spent his life thus far fighting to defend, and with which the government of Britain was in sympathy.

In London, he would discover otherwise.

PART TWO

The London Underworld

5

REVOLUTIONARY

When Despard arrived in London in the late summer of 1790, he was not planning on staying long. Like his visit in 1783, when he had attended the Colonial Office to discuss the terms of the Treaty of Paris and clarify its implications for the Bay settlement, this was a business trip with limited scope and objectives. He was intending to put his case against the Baymen, to demonstrate that their accusations against him were unfounded and based on the narrow self-interest of their arbitrary aristocracy, and thereby to win back the post of superintendent. He had brought with him a portfolio of glowing testimonials to his administration from all strata of Bay society, including several of the wealthy planters who had taken his side. He had also brought the results of his election as magistrate, to demonstrate the overwhelming mandate under which he was operating. In addition, he had some paperwork to process, including a backlog of expenses he had run up on official business and which he needed to have reimbursed. He took up lodgings south of the river, in Southwark, not far from the site where he would eventually meet his fate.

But London had some surprises for him, and he for it. Chief among the latter was that he now had a family, a wife and small child, and that both were black. His wife was named Catherine, and their son James. Despard and Catherine had probably met and married in 1784 or 1785 while he was patrolling the Shore, assessing how many British Shoremen were likely to arrive in the Bay enclave and hammering out the details of the new settlement with the Spanish garrison in Trujillo. It is also possible that she was responsible for nursing him through one of his many tropical illnesses, as Cuba Cornwallis had done for Nelson. Catherine's own background remains unclear: by one account she was the daughter of a Jamaican preacher, by another an educated Spanish creole. She seems to have been considerably younger than her husband. But what is clear is that she confounded the expectations and prejudices of those who met her. There was, as many were to discover, a great deal more to her than the colour of her skin.

The facts of Despard and Catherine's marriage, and their relationship up to this point, are confounded by a vagueness that appears almost to amount to a conspiracy of silence. The slender evidence that they lived together as man and wife in the Bay consists of a single letter from a Shoreman referring to Despard's 'family'. Yet this silence is in itself eloquent. The Baymen had been bombarding the Home Office with slurs about Despard, many of which had revolved around his partiality to 'people of colour' and his levelling tendency to make no distinction between races, yet they had never once referred to his wife and child. The silence was equally deafening from the other side. James Bannantine, Despard's secretary in the Bay, would later write a forthright and partisan defence of his super-intendent's career, yet he too would find no room to mention Catherine. She is also absent from contemporary histories of black people in Britain, which, around 1790, record servants, page boys, scholars, bare-knuckle boxers, abolitionists, freed slaves and prostitutes, but no black woman married to a British gentleman. The Despards, in ways of which they both seem to have been at least partly unaware, had formed a union that was not forbidden, indeed in some quarters theoretically encouraged, but which was unprecedented, and on which nobody wished to be the first to pronounce judgement.

Unlike the nineteenth century to come, the eighteenth had thus far been characterized by a general absence of ideological or scientific racism. The philosophy of the Age of Reason had tended to stress the unity of mankind rather than its differences, arguing that all people were created equal and were distinguished from animals by their intellect. The difference between humanity and the animal kingdom was only beginning to emerge with clarity from centuries of travellers' tales and myths of wild men, hairy tribes and speaking apes, and it was on the distinctness of humans as a species that new systems of scientific classification focused. The most authoritative text at the point when the Despards arrived in London was the German naturalist Johann Friedrich Blumenbach's *On the Natural Varieties of Man*, which had been published in Latin in 1776. Blumenbach developed ethnic categories and coined the term 'Caucasian' for the white race, but the thrust of his work was to separate humanity in general from the 'great chain of being', the pyramid of ever more advanced life-forms that rose from mollusc to ape, and to stress the singularity of the human condition. Blumenbach's overall conclusion was that, despite all its variations in geographical distribution and physical type, 'the human mind is one'.

The essentially shared characteristics of different races was not simply a matter of scholarly theory. When Captain James Cook sailed for the Pacific in 1769, his first rule of engagement was 'to endeavour by every fair means to cultivate a friendship with the natives and to treat them with all imaginable humanity'. Nor was Cook, enlightened as he was, an exception. His expedition's sponsor, the Earl of Morton, president of the Royal Society, had been specific in his instructions: 'They are human creatures, the work of the same omnipotent Author, equally under his care with the most polished European; perhaps less offensive, more entitled to His favour.' There had been black visitors to Britain, and black residents, since at least the sixteenth century, and many had been distinguished writers, poets and scientists. Some had been invited to the Royal Society, had delivered meteorological observations to the Academy of Sciences, and had become friends with the literati and the aristocracy. Particularly since 1783 and the end of the war with America, freed slaves and others who had fought for the British cause had boosted the black population to its greatest number ever, joining to form small communities with abandoned servants and black children who had been kept as pages by wealthy women and cut loose when they grew up. This population had its own small focus, around the docks of London.

But although black people were becoming familiar in some quarters, the aura of exoticism and strangeness lingered, and nowhere more acutely than in the idea of mixed-race marriages. These had rarely, if ever, been seen in Britain. It was perfectly well known that British officers and gentlemen in the colonies frequently had black mistresses, and that in many cases they had mixed-race children. Few spoke of this in polite society, yet it was permissible to do so, especially when framed in terms of an adventure on the far side of the world. The best-known example at the time was the Dutch adventurer John Gabriel Stedman, who had published the journals of his expedition to put down a mutiny in the Dutch colony of Surinam in the 1770s, during the course of which he had married a fifteen-year-old mulatto slave girl named Joanna. But she had not accompanied him back to Europe: he had lacked the money to buy her out of slavery, and had returned to Europe without her. His story was received at the time as a romantic tale of tropical beauty and sadness; a generation later it was adapted into *Joanna*, a potboiling anti-slavery novel.

Thus there was no explicit legal or moral reason why Despard and Catherine should not have married, nor why they should not have returned to London together. In fact the virtue of such arrangements was, in some quarters, being spoken of openly and to public acclaim. At the moment of the Despards' arrival, a black writer and preacher named Olaudah Equiano was touring England promoting his powerful and finely written autobiography *The Interesting Narrative*, which told of his childhood in Africa, his kidnapping by slavers and the horrendous 'middle passage' to the plantations of Virginia, where he eventually managed to earn the money to free himself. He travelled to the Caribbean, and even spent some time with the Miskitos on the Shore, before settling in London. Equiano's book was the *Pilgrim's Progress* of its day, a testament to the power of his Methodist faith, combined with a powerful plea for the abolition of slavery. Within it, he specifically raised the silent question of mixed marriage. 'Why not establish inter-marriage at home, and in our colonies?' he asked. 'And encourage open, free and generous love, upon Nature's own wide and extensive plan, subservient only to moral rectitude, without distinction of the colour of a skin?'

This was an appeal heard with generosity in the literary clubs, Wesleyan churches and abolitionist meetings where Equiano spoke, but many had their doubts, which they expressed largely among themselves. This is perhaps why the Baymen had made no reference to Catherine in their despatches to Grenville: they were aware that the ideals of racial equality and the abolition of slavery held a claim to the moral high ground back in Britain, and were wary of weakening their case with the suspicion that their complaints might be motivated by bigotry and a personal distaste for Despard's private life. Yet the informal racism of colonies such as the Bay was on the march; it was soon to be buttressed with the trappings of science and enshrined in codes of colonial practice across the globe. The now-familiar racial theory that humanity was a 'graded' hierarchy, with black at the bottom and white at the top, was already beginning to be formulated, and, perhaps not surprisingly, its earliest roots were among the planters in Jamaica.

Slavery, by itself, was not enough to generate racial science. The classical civilizations of Greece and Rome had depended on slaves, but these were usually of similar ethnic origins to their masters; the physical signs that distinguished them had been the result of practices such as shaving heads, tattooing or branding. The overwhelming divide in classical humanity had been between 'barbarians' – foreigners – and those employing the term. What was beginning to emerge in Jamaica while the Despards were living together as man and wife was a pseudoscientific rationalization of a society where two hundred thousand slaves, all black, were performing forced labour for a free population of little over ten thousand predominantly white masters.

Its first concrete expression was in the writings of

Edward Long, a Jamaican planter, who published a compendious work on the history and culture of Jamaica in 1772. Long was a Cornishman who had become a man of property through marriage, had set up in Jamaica and joined the Assembly; he was a fervent believer in the rights of the free-born Englishman, which in his view included the right to own and work slaves. Aware of the movement for the abolition of the slave trade, he produced a series of justifications for its otherwise undeniable cruelty. Black people were, he declared, 'void of genius', and 'incapable of making progress in civility or science'; to enslave a black man was analogous more to keeping a domestic animal than to enslaving a white man. In fact, slavery was a 'benign' occupation for Africans: productive work was the best moral therapy for them. Their life in Africa, revolving, as Long assumed it did, around human sacrifice and cannibalism, was far more benighted and depraved than life on the plantation, and furthermore the practice of slavery helped rid the African kingdoms of their criminal element (Long, of course, never visited Africa). His typology of the human race differed from Blumenbach's, linking man into the main chain of being with gradations from orang-utan to pigmy to negro to mulatto, creole and eventually to white. He asserted that mulattoes, like mules, were hybrids who were not fully fertile, and dismissed the evidence to the contrary as anecdotal. He was unimpressed with the work of learned black men such as Olaudah Equiano, whom he claimed were no more than animals who had learned to perform ingenious tricks.

When racial theory rose to scientific orthodoxy in the early nineteenth century, through the work of early anthropologists such as James Cowles Prichard for whom whiteness was an index of civilization, it would do so as part of the growing 'science of signs' and biological classification, and its prefiguring in the justification of slavery by Jamaican planters would be forgotten. Yet the theory that emerged would be far more enduring than slavery itself, and prove far harder to unpick. But in 1790 the question was far from settled, and by the same token the fact of the Despards' mixed-race marriage was one on which no judgement was overtly pronounced. It could hardly have passed unnoticed, yet, as Despard drifted ever further from the mainstream of London society, it would become impossible to tell how much of his exclusion was prompted or reinforced by the fact of Catherine's ethnicity. In the memoirs of the next generation of Despards, the story would be firmly rewritten: Catherine would be disowned in familiar Victorian terms as 'his black housekeeper' and 'the poor black woman who called herself his wife'; James would be ascribed to a previous lover and written out of the family tree. Yet the evidence shows that the Despards were deeply devoted to one another, the poster children for Equiano's appeal that intermarriage was entirely natural and skin colour irrelevant. Catherine would demonstrate abundantly that this was a marriage of equals: she was by various accounts intelligent, charming and beautiful – and, increasingly, Despard's greatest and most dependable asset in the last phase of his life.

It rapidly became clear that Despard's government business was going to take longer than he had anticipated. Unlike Lord Sydney, with whom Despard had developed a good shorthand understanding over the years, William Wyndham Grenville was new to the job; among the demands from the colonies, which formed only part of his portfolio, the internal affairs of the Bay settlement were of considerably less urgency to him than they were to Despard. Grenville's secretary, Evan Nepean, received

Despard's documents from him and submitted them to his minister for consideration. Days dragged into weeks; Despard waited in corridors and offices. It was an unfamiliar and puzzling situation for him. He had spent many years grinding through hard physical labour and military service, but very little time waiting idle at the discretion of others. He had no wish to make trouble or to cause a scene, but following the proper procedure seemed to involve sitting interminably in lobbies and waiting rooms to no effect. When his continued presence became embarrassing, Nepean's department handed him a series of odd jobs: consultancy on other colonial matters, reports to be considered and 'other affairs of government'. Whenever he returned from them, the deliberation on his own case seemed to have moved no further.

Grenville was not sitting idle, far from it. He and Prime Minister William Pitt, with others in their cabinet, were determined to preside over a machinery of government that was more unified, centralized and efficient than the unstable coalitions that had preceded them, and they were succeeding. Their programme of 'economic reform' was slowly but steadily replacing the government culture of bribes and sinecures with one of salaries and administrative transparency. The cabinet was taking a firmer grip on policy at home and abroad, and expanding their army of administrators to steer it with ever greater precision. They were driving up taxes at home, making large and risky borrowings, and pumping up the nation's military and economic muscle to pursue more aggressive foreign policies for greater financial gains. They were firmly focused on tax and war, the two most powerful instruments under the control of the House of Commons; it was these Robert Walpole had used two generations before to make the office of Prime Minister, previously little more than a jumping-off point for the House of Lords, the most powerful executive office in government. Pitt's predecessor, Lord North, had been uncomfortable with the role and office of Prime Minister, believing it to be unconstitutional; Pitt, by contrast, was determined to play it for all it was worth. He and his inner circle, by making tax and war the central drivers of public policy, were in the process of nudging the political system closer to that of today. As their administration forged on for its unprecedented length, through the Napoleonic Wars, it would amplify these tendencies into the distinctive character of British colonial policy for the next century: hard-nosed, practical, patriotic and imperious in tone, announcing itself with high-handed demands and threats but usually ready to strike a deal.

Within the grand scope of Grenville's plans, Despard's urgent petitions about the internal administration of the Bay were peripheral, even irrelevant. Grenville and his cabinet colleagues were already keenly aware that much of France and Spain's wealth, as well as Britain's own, was at stake in the Caribbean, and were assessing whether they might soon be in a position to enforce further claims to their advantage that would make the Treaty of Paris irrelevant. The fine points of how all this played out among subject populations in the distant colonies, especially the less wealthy, were becoming marginal details. Despard, from their standpoint, had ruffled the feathers of the only part of the community that really mattered: those who produced the mahogany. He might have been acting conscientiously and following the previous Home Secretary's orders, but priorities were changing, and he was not showing his authority and judgement in their best light by troubling his superiors with matters he should have been able to resolve *in situ*.

From where Grenville was sitting, there was little pressure, apart from the weatherbeaten colonel waiting alone in the corridor, for the Home Office to commit itself in any way. Better to wait, to observe how trade functioned without him, and see what other strategic interests might develop.

At ministerial level, Despard was pushing his case against the grain; at a lower bureaucratic level, Grenville's clerks had a long list of queries about his claims for expenses. There were thousands of pounds' worth of bills that had been drawn on the Treasury during his superintendency, including substantial costs such as food, shelter and relief for the starving Shoremen, and among these were many Despard had paid out of his own pocket. These added up to nearly £2,000, at least £120,000 today, more than half the salary he had received during his time as superintendent. Despard explained repeatedly that he had been administering the Bay with no more assistance than a secretary and a surveyor, and that Jamaica was far too distant to send for cash whenever it was needed. He had got into the habit of paying urgent costs, such as those incurred during the hurricane relief, out of his own pocket; the cash was there, and there was little else on which to spend it. He had also been dependent on others, usually the Baymen, for the basics: unable to get a proper residence built at public expense, for example, he had been forced to rent the Haulover personally at $25 Jamaican per quarter for the entire period. He had assumed that all these outgoings would be easily redeemed in due course, but the sums involved were, if not irregular, at least unusual, and he was kept busy over the weeks and months with demands for clarifications and further details.

Meanwhile, it was becoming clear to Grenville that the claim and counterclaim between Despard and the Baymen could not be settled without a full inquiry into the Bay settlement, and that this would be expensive, time-consuming and almost certainly divisive. At the beginning of 1791 he suggested a less expensive option: Despard should submit his own full account of events in writing. If he hoped that this would tie the colonel up for many months, he was disappointed. In March Despard returned promptly with a manuscript of over five hundred pages, which he headed *A Narrative of the Publick Transactions in the Bay of Honduras Settlement from 1784 to 1790*, and which is still preserved in the Home Office archives. It begins with a detailed list (numbered from one to seventeen) of the charges against him; it proceeds to tell the entire story of his superintendency in the Bay, the history of the settlement, the competing claims of ownership, his transactions with the Spanish, the critical flashpoints of Joshua Jones, the hurricane, and the disputes over the American smuggling vessels. It concludes with a specific complaint against the conduct of the Baymen's chief spokesman, Robert White, running to seventy-five pages.

Despard's record was exhaustive and loaded with verifiable facts, dates, transactions and letters; to attempt to contest it would have been a major bureaucratic undertaking. He explained that he had been acting throughout in the interests of the Crown and according to the specific instructions of the Anglo-Spanish convention and the Home Office, and was precise about the scope of the powers his office entailed. He was also explicit about the root cause of the Baymen's complaint: self-interest. They had been delighted to welcome Despard as their representative in 1784 and had given no indication at that point that he was, as they later claimed, a man 'of principles so arbitrary and despotic as to be totally incompatible with every idea of civil liberty'. If Grenville were to look at their objections to his superintendency, he would see that in each and every case they boiled down to the fact 'that they would not have it in their power to act in that arbitrary manner which they had heretofore done'. Furthermore, the course of action they had taken against him was illegal, libellous and, in several instances, designed to foment trouble with the Spanish authorities to the direct disadvantage of the Crown.

Despard concluded his report with a full account of the voting systems and elections during his tenure, to demonstrate objectively and numerically that the complaining Baymen represented only a faction within the established planters, and that the planters in turn represented only a small minority of the inhabitants under his protection. He explained that the elections of 1784 and 1786, which had given the Baymen control of the magistracy, were conducted either without polls or with a handful of votes; the more the polls were publicized, and the greater the number of people who voted, the more emphatically the Baymen were defeated, culminating in his overwhelming election as magistrate prior to his departure.

Despard might have felt that the elections were compelling evidence, but he was arguing at cross-purposes to Grenville's political assumptions. Before becoming Home Secretary, Grenville had worked as a junior minister on Irish affairs without ever being persuaded by the argument that Catholics should be allowed to vote. On his appointment to Secretary of State, he had had to stand for re-election to Parliament, and had done so without any electoral contest but simply at the cost of £316 4s. 4d., most of which had been bills for food, drink and hospitality for the freeholders of the borough he now represented. He was little interested in parliamentary reform at home, and even less in electoral representation abroad. He was an imperialist not in the later sense of believing that foreigners were best ruled by the British, but in his conviction that the prosperity of the colonies was beneficial to both sides. Once a colony prospered, in his view, it might progress not only economically but politically; eventually, it might aspire to the British system of government, at which point British armed force might be relaxed. Despard's argument, from Grenville's perspective, had the colonial enterprise back to front. The implication of Grenville's view was that the arbitrary aristocracy of the Baymen and those like them needed to be strengthened rather than weakened before the political system could become more inclusive.

Despard's report sat on Grenville's desk for most of the year; in October 1791, he finally communicated his decision. There was, Grenville informed Despard, 'no charge against him worthy of consideration', but he would not be reappointed. Colonel Hunter, who lacked Despard's constitutional resilience to the tropics, had been constantly ill and was returning home, but Grenville simply decided not to replace him. 'His Majesty', Grenville announced, 'has thought proper to abolish the office of Superintendent of Honduras'; from now on the local affairs of the Bay would simply fall under those of Jamaica. Despard would not be censured or disciplined in any way, but neither was there another commission for him at present. There were vague suggestions that he might, at some point, be given another posting, perhaps to the Barbary Coast of North Africa.

Despard protested the decision, but his case was slipping ever further from the Home Office's attention. Grenville's assessment of it was one of his last acts as Home Secretary before he was ennobled and, in November 1791, appointed Leader of the House of Lords and Foreign

Published by T. Chapman, 151, Fleet Street July 13, 1795.

Henry Dundas

Secretary. For years to come he would perform the crucial roles of swinging the consensus of the nobility behind Pitt and mobilizing the nation in support of the war with revolutionary France.

He was replaced as Home Secretary by Henry Dundas, who responded to Despard's pressure even less favourably than Grenville. Dundas had already made his reputation in his native Scotland as a tough enforcer of government policy, and was appointed to perform the same role in cabinet with Pitt and Grenville. Within two years, as Minister for War, he would be ruthless in exploiting the enemy's weaknesses in the Caribbean and consolidating the wealth and strength of the British planters; unlike Pitt and Grenville, he would even oppose the abolition of slavery on the grounds that it would have a detrimental effect on the planters' trade. When Despard persisted with his complaints, Dundas rebuffed him firmly. The accusations of the Baymen, Dundas warned, had not been 'done away with' by Despard's report; the Home Office might reopen their case if they saw fit. In the meantime, Dundas repeated, 'His Majesty does not conceive it will be for the advantage of His service to reinstate you.' Despard was to be maintained on half pay, with no promises of a new commission. His persistence had been rewarded with a slammed door.

Despard was by now in a very unfortunate position. He could not ply his trade other than in the British army; he could not be given a new post other than by the Home Office. He decided to take his case to Parliament, and to find an MP who might be prepared to represent him.

Thus far in his life, Despard had shown little interest in politics beyond that which had immediately concerned him; he might even have been accused of political naivety, a charge he would never entirely shake off. He had written in a letter to Evan Nepean three years earlier, 'I am no politician, *ni par goût, ni par métier*' – neither by inclination nor by profession. This was perhaps a disingenuous assessment – he had, after all, forged complex diplomatic relations, drawn up constitutions, administered an independent territory and organized, competed in and won elections – but it reflected his self-image as someone whose expertise lay on the battlefield rather than in the corridors of power. Entering the world of politics at this point, though, he made two discoveries that would dramatically alter the trajectory of his career. The first was that the issues he was attempting to raise were not confined to the Bay of Honduras: his conflict had been a microcosm of a struggle for electoral representation that had become a defining issue for Britain itself. The second, which followed from this, was that he was not alone: there were many, from his class and others, who were dedicating themselves to fighting for the same principles.

Since Despard had left Ireland for Jamaica, a great deal had changed in Britain's social and economic landscape, but very little in the fabric of its politics. The successful wars against France and Spain had increased trade and wealth, as had the profits from slavery abroad and a boom in manufacturing at home. A middle class of unprecedented size and sophistication had emerged, and it had turned previously insignificant villages into large urban centres; a previously static rural population had begun its irreversible drift into the new cities. Yet throughout all these demographic convulsions, the political system, set up by the Glorious Revolution of 1688, had remained static. For some this was a sign of its great strength; for others it was becoming a fatal weakness.

The British 'constitution', as it was universally known,

had emerged from the convulsive and bloody chaos of the seventeenth century to become, in the eyes of many both in Britain and around the world, the political wonder of the age. Its defining quality was that it was a 'mixed constitution', with power vested in three different strata of society: the King, the aristocracy (represented by the House of Lords) and the people (represented by the House of Commons). None of these, so the logic went, could be trusted to govern on their own. A monarch unchecked might become a tyrant; an aristocracy unchecked might become an oligarchy; a people unchecked might descend into anarchy. A mixed constitution, by contrast, allowed for each of the 'estates' to check and balance the others, and thus guarantee stability. While the rest of Europe suffered under the yoke of despotic absolute monarchies, Britain's constitution had tempered the powers of the King with those of his subjects, and had steered the ship of state to prosperity and victory.

But, constructed in the wake of civil war and violent insurrection, this was a system that explicitly favoured solidity over flexibility. Power had been concentrated in the centre, around the new Protestant monarch William of Orange; democratic participation was limited to the upper echelons of the propertied classes; a small metropolitan and aristocratic elite had taken on the authority and the responsibility of keeping the government of the country on an even keel. The role of the monarch had been made strong as a bulwark against the great political danger of its day, a seizure of power by the Jacobite dynasty backed by the Catholic French. Participation in the affairs of state had been limited to members of the Church of England, to guard against both Catholic influence and Puritan extremism. On the one hand there had been the threat of despotic monarchy being imposed from outside by war, on the other the threat of uncontrolled religious fervour running riot through the common people and toppling the structures of power. The new state had been conceived to steer a course between them.

But now that these dangers were past, it had become obvious to many that this was an arrangement that excluded the vast majority of the population from the affairs of state. The new middle classes were voteless; the wealthy and industrious communities of religious dissenters, Quakers and Nonconformists were excluded even from menial public office by the fact that they did not take the Anglican sacrament in church. 'Rotten boroughs', consisting of small landed estates, were at the command of their hereditary owners and could be won with a dozen votes, or simply on the nod. Such votes were routinely bought for cash, the seats available to the highest bidder. Where elections were contested, the qualifications for voting varied haphazardly between different classes of constituency: in a rural county a bar of property and income was set, while in London boroughs only members of the guilds and liveried companies were eligible. The anomalies of a county and borough system that had stood unchanged since medieval times were growing ever more apparent. Cornwall, as a result of a centuries-old electoral fix, returned forty-two of the total of 558 MPs on the basis of fewer than five hundred voters, while Birmingham, Leeds, Manchester and Sheffield returned not a single MP between them. All in all, a majority of MPs could be commanded by little over ten thousand voters in a population now pushing ten million.

There was little impetus for a radical overhaul of the system from the arbitrary aristocracy within Parliament itself. Many MPs were simply habituated to the idea of governing in their own self-interest, indeed dependent on it for wealth and influence, but some offered reasoned objections to any change. Many felt it was the job of government to remain constant while the world changed around it, that the current system enshrined hard-won rights for the people that might be jeopardized if it were even tinkered with. Stability, for them, was not a synonym for stagnation and inertia, but a great good that was the envy of the rest of the world. Parliament was also cushioned from the growing dissent by its belief that it and the people were on the same side. The central constitutional issue for those in office was the power of the King: they saw themselves as fighting on behalf of the people against the royal prerogative, the excesses of the civil list, the court sinecures and offices of authority, which remained in the gift not of the people but of the monarch. Parliament represented the people; the terms of that representation, such as qualifications for voting, were for them subsidiary to fighting what they already saw as the people's corner. As a result, outside Westminster, it was becoming clear to many that if they waited for Parliament to reform itself, they would, like Despard in the corridors of the Home Office, wait for ever.

Throughout the 1770s, while Despard was still digging trenches and repairing fortifications in Jamaica, the calls to reform the system had built towards a large popular movement. The change that was being called for would now be termed democracy, but it was more commonly discussed under the name of revolution. Originally a metaphor co-opted from physics and astronomy, this was a term with an overlapping set of political meanings. It could mean a recurrence or a cycle, a pendulum swing, a gradual correction in the nation's affairs; it could also mean a great change or sudden alteration, a tipping point whereby the old order might be replaced with an entirely new one. It by no means implied its modern sense of the forcible overthrow of the state. The Glorious Revolution, after all, had been a largely bloodless affair, effected by negotiation and treaty more than force of arms.

Revolution was, by and large, a genteel preoccupation. The most effective campaign for change at this point was being led by the Reverend Christopher Wyvill, a wealthy landowner from Yorkshire who believed, like many, that the government had become terminally corrupt and was wasting an unacceptable proportion of the people's taxes on keeping itself in the manner to which it had become accustomed. Wyvill saw Parliament rather as many Protestants saw Rome: a sinkhole of greed, depravity and entrenched privilege. He began a campaign called the Association Movement, 'from a detestation of corruption, from indignation at direct and open invasion of our rights', and organized large public assemblies across the northern manufacturing cities. He gathered thousands of petition signatures for sweeping changes to the electoral system, and for a reduction of Parliament's length from seven years to one to discourage politicians from feathering their nests. The association effectively focused the new, property-owning middle class, which had already begun to have an effect on state politics through its regional economic power, and the campaign was taken up within Parliament by the faction of Whigs whose hostility to the powers of the King extended to a commitment to wider reform in the interests of the people at large. It seemed as if such reform might finally be making its way into the mainstream of politics.

But in 1780, just as the Association Movement was gathering steam – and Despard was holding Fort Immaculada – a quite different type of public demonstration reawoke profound concerns about such extra-parliamentary activity. On 2 June, the Gordon Riots broke out across London. They were originally triggered by Lord George Gordon's opposition to the repeal of the law restricting Catholics from serving in the armed forces – a law that had, in fact, been routinely flouted for forty years – but it had quickly flared from anti-Catholic demonstration to full-scale anarchy. A mob stirred to action by rumours that there were twenty thousand Jesuits hidden in London's tunnels soon submerged its official leadership, the London Protestant Association, and spilled into a four-night orgy of looting and destruction during which prisons were emptied, all figures of authority were accused of being Catholics, and order was restored only when the army fired muskets into the crowds.

The Gordon Riots were in themselves nothing new – demagogue politicians such as John Wilkes had often called London mobs onto the streets in their proxy battles with authority – but their scale and the timing sent a salutary message to those champions of reform who were prepared to listen. Gordon's rioters shared no cause with the Association Movement; if anything, they demonstrated how powerful conservative and loyalist sentiment on the streets might become if the association's reforms were seen as a threat to stability. But they made the more general point that once any popular movement was begun, it was impossible to control the way it would develop. For the vast majority of the population, street demonstrations and riots were the sum total of politics, the only form in which they were allowed to participate in it at all. People rioted regularly against turnpike roads, prices, press gangs, Irish immigrants, workhouses, public punishments, taxes, foreigners, Catholics, calendar changes. The only factor they all had in common was that, once a riot had started, its original cause tended to be swept away in a tidal wave

The Burning & Plundering of NEWGATE & Setting the Felons at Liberty by the Mob.

Published 1st July 1780 by J Fielding & J Walker Pater Noster Row.

The Gordon Riots

of public disorder. It might be impossible to reform Parliament from within, but it might also be impossible to reform it from outside. While the fear of mob rule hung over it, the reform movement could never win the support of the politicians, or indeed the silent majority in the country; and yet no political reformer could or ever would be able to guarantee a popular movement immune to it.

The power of the association reached its high watermark without ever convincing the doubters in Parliament: even if 10 per cent of the entire British population had signed their petitions, as was claimed, that still left 90 per cent who were arguably opposed or indifferent. But the campaign for reform was nevertheless taken up from within Parliament by one of the youngest MPs in the House, the twenty-one-year-old William Pitt. Pitt's interest was not so surprising as it would later come to seem: his father had, after all, been the most distinguished commoner of the century, and had spent much of his life battling against an entrenched aristocracy. Pitt the Younger met with Wyvill in 1782 to hear the association's grievances, and asked the House of Commons for a committee to study the state of representation in the country. He introduced his proposal with an impassioned speech, asserting that 'it is the essence of the constitution, that people have a share in government by means of representation', and lamenting that this constitutional right had 'fallen so greatly from that direction and effect which it was intended' that it risked becoming an 'engine of tyranny and oppression'. He lost on the vote, but only narrowly, and was encouraged enough to meet Wyvill again and discuss whether their proposals might be modified to the point where they might satisfy a parliamentary majority.

But Pitt's leadership of the reform movement, and its last real chance of making headway in Parliament, came to an end the following year when George III astonished the House of Commons by asking the young man to become his Prime Minister. To the King's great alarm, Charles James Fox had finally succeeded in forming a government with the Whig faction under Lord North. Fox was George III's most hated and feared adversary, a man whose own father, having been denied an earldom the King had promised him, had habitually referred to the monarch as 'Satan'. Charles James Fox's 'inmost soul', in the words of Edward Gibbon, was 'deeply tinged with

William Pitt the Younger

democracy', and it was no secret that he wished to use his office to force a 'second Runnymede' to further curtail the powers of the monarchy. He had supported the American colonies in their struggle against the Crown, dressed provocatively in their brown and blue colours, and had ominously asserted in Parliament that 'countries should always be governed by the will of the governed'. George III, by mobilizing his bishops to vote down Fox's India Bill, had succeeded in engineering his downfall from office, but there was no obvious or even plausible replacement. Pitt accepted the offer of Prime Minister to the King to howls of ridicule and disbelief from the House of Commons, yet he would stay in the post for the next seventeen years.

But there was a compromise to be made for power. George took his vows to defend the British constitution as sacrosanct, and regarded calls to reform it as little short of treason. Pitt was publicly committed to the cause of parliamentary reform, and George was well aware that his protégé must not be seen as his puppet, yet a crucial part of the understanding between them was that Pitt would protect the King from the reforming tendency. The following year Pitt spoke once more for reform, his proposals this time watered down to the abolition of a few rotten boroughs. Fox and his Whig faction opposed the new motion on the grounds that it had become toothless, and Pitt lost by a greater majority than when he had lobbied for reform as a private member. The Association Movement, which had by now pinned all its hopes on the Parliament it loathed, began to wither away.

Thus, by the time Despard came to lobby Parliament, his claim that the will and the votes of the Bay settlers were being ignored was one that chimed strongly with the debate in Britain; but it was also one that had already run

Engraved by H. Robinson.

CHARLES JAMES FOX.

OB. 1806.

FROM THE ORIGINAL BY OPIE, IN THE COLLECTION OF

Charles James Fox

into the same brick wall Despard had met at the Home Office. Yet the campaign for reform was far from dead, and Despard found much common ground with those who were still pursuing it through other organizations that had sprung up to fill the vacuum left by Wyvill's association. Prominent among these at the time were men who approached the issue, as Despard instinctively had, not as a question of instituting a novel system of government but of reasserting the traditional rights and values that had always been at least implicit in the British constitution. It was among this milieu that Despard would find his most enduring political allies, although events would rapidly lead them all in directions they could not have anticipated.

It was, with hindsight, an odd time to join the struggle for political reform, on a cusp between the genteel agitation of the 1780s and the far more intense and bitter conflict to come. At this point, apart from the Foxite Whigs who were widely seen as having cynically played politics with the issue, the most forthright proponent of reform within the political system was John Horne Tooke, a former secretary to the Whig MP John Wilkes and veteran of the rabble-rousing 'Wilkes and Liberty' riots of twenty years before. Tooke was a lapsed parson who had recently been defeated in the contest for Fox's seat of Westminster; he would later become an independent MP, although he would subsequently be disqualified by a special act, still in force today, excluding priests from the House of Commons. He was a brilliant conversationalist, an antiquarian scholar and a waspish debater whose house at Wimbledon was the epicentre of reformist talk in London. It was also next door to Henry Dundas's, and the Home Secretary was regaled with anti-establishment wit through his open windows on summer evenings.

Outside the world of Westminster, the provincial debate

John Horne Tooke

that had been whipped up by the Association Movement was now being led by the Society of Constitutional Information, the brainchild of a Yorkshire landed gentleman named Major John Cartwright who had served in the navy but had declined to fight the American colonists on ideological grounds. Instead, he had become a major in his county militia, and had dedicated himself to writing pamphlets calling for government by consent and annual parliaments. Both Cartwright and Tooke were revolutionaries in the parlance of the day, but both were also traditionalists, even reactionaries, whose political views were rooted in the belief that the liberties for which they were campaigning had already existed in previous times, and needed only to be reasserted.

In doing so they were tapping into a vein of British political thought that had little currency in Westminster, but which pervaded the broader culture on many levels. It located the current struggle for political rights not as part of some progressive future, but in the nation's distant, even mythical past. As variously elaborated, it held that the original Anglo-Saxon inhabitants of Britain had lived in egalitarian harmony, self-governing through representative institutions and annual parliaments. According to this view, King Alfred and his successors, as England had been brought under the control of a single monarch, had preserved the autonomy of local jurisdictions and traditional practices such as trial by a jury of one's peers: the Anglo-Saxon kings had continued to submit themselves to an annual 'moot', or council of the people, which remained the ultimate source of their authority. But this civic equilibrium had been shattered by the foreign and aristocratic Norman conquest. Thereafter the 'Norman yoke', as it became known, had replaced the old system with land grabs and tyrannical rule, from which the British had occasionally managed to claw back fragments of their original inheritance through, for example, forcing King John to sign the Magna Carta. In some more mystical elaborations of the story, King Arthur, who had first united the Britons, was still sleeping in Avalon, and would one day awake to restore the nation's rights and lead its people back to their primeval happy state.

The notions of the 'Norman yoke' and 'lost rights' may have had little basis in fact – the evidence tends to suggest that Anglo-Saxon society was as highly stratified before 1066 as after it – but they were still remarkably pervasive during the eighteenth century. They had the dignity of antiquity, having been employed during the civil war by republicans such as John Milton, and they resonated with the common sense of even older folk-sayings: 'When Adam delved and Eve span, who was then the gentleman?' was a quizzical riddle that dated back at least to the time of the Peasants' Revolt of 1381. The idea of Britain as a land of traditional liberties also had distinguished champions abroad. It had been hailed as such by Voltaire, the greatest free-thinker of the eighteenth century, who had fled to England from the arbitrary persecutions of the French nobility and found 'a country where men think freely and nobly, unhampered by any servile fear'. Thomas Jefferson, too, firmly believed that by founding an independent America he was restoring his ancestral liberties, and he devoted much time to assembling evidence for his own Saxon forebears.

This idea of lost rights, though nebulous, derived rhetorical power from the way in which it radically short-circuited the claims of all authority, hereditary rule and land ownership, up to and including those of the King, by positing an illegitimate coup, centuries old, as a result of which all current power structures had been established.

But it also resonated with the more mainstream patriotic language of the Glorious Revolution. This was partly because the constitution that had emerged did indeed embody liberties – freedom of the press, an independent judiciary, trial by jury, habeas corpus – that had a genuine claim to natural justice; it was also because the revolution of 1688 had been presented at the time, in an age less enamoured with progress, as a triumph of tradition rather than innovation. Thus the language of 'lost rights' and the 'Norman yoke' combined its challenge to authority with an implicit conservatism that appealed to many who still feared the innovative and technocratic language of modernizing political reform. It was revolutionary in the sense of the wheel turning full circle, rather than an over-turning of tradition for its own sake. It was, like Despard, both conservative and revolutionary, a moral and patriotic response to injustice, to the spectacle of traditional codes of justice, honour and fair play being trampled by an arbitrary aristocracy. As he pursued his goal of justice for himself, Despard came to realize that it flowed into a wider stream of public debate about authority, legitimacy and liberty.

Despard, then, was finding some support for his cause within Parliament, but only from the handful of opposition MPs whose endorsement was more likely to confirm Dundas in his instinctive views than to prompt him to reconsider. But he also had another, and more pressing, problem to fight. On his arrival in London, he had begun to receive legal writs from the owners of the American vessels he had impounded in the Bay, demanding financial reparations for their losses. This was not uncommon practice; the common response, as in Nelson's case, was to avoid entanglement until returning to Britain, where it was a great deal harder to secure a conviction. Despard's defence was the one he had already offered to the Home Office: the ships had been trading 'equally against law and the interests of Great Britain' and he had had every right to confiscate their cargoes. He had already been cleared on this precise point by Lord Sydney in 1787. Since this accusation was part of the ongoing Home Office investigation, he was presumably counting on it being wrapped up in his favour in due course. But Grenville's delay, and Dundas's rejection of his complaints, had left him exposed. By the end of 1791, Despard was in dire financial straits. His expenses from the Bay had still not been paid, he had been obliged to hire lawyers to defend himself, and his salary had been halved.

Despard was not an extravagant man: he had, after all, spent the last five years living in a leaky shack in the jungle subsisting mostly on salt meat and whatever local food came to hand, and the only reason he was in London was to return to the same modest salary and spartan conditions. There was never any suggestion that he was financially dishonest or corrupt. Yet it is not entirely surprising that he should have ignored his financial affairs up to the point where he found himself in serious difficulties. His father had had a substantial landed income, and a reputation in the family for believing that 'his pocket had no bottom', spending money whenever he felt he needed to. Despard had moved straight from his care to that of the army, where as an officer he had simply requisitioned whatever was needed, used everything he found at his disposal and settled the paperwork later. He had clearly continued to do the same in the Bay, when the only money that was to hand was his own salary. Arriving in London for what he assumed would be a short stay, he had thought about his own personal finances as little as usual. But now legal bills had to be paid, and he had no money to pay them with. He owed, by his own estimate, a total upwards of £3,000, perhaps £200,000 today, and could not reclaim it without either action by the Home Secretary or a lengthy court case. Thus it was that in early 1792, unable to meet his bills, he was sent to the King's Bench debtors' prison in Southwark. Through little more than oversight and misunderstanding, he had somehow dropped through an invisible hole into the London underworld.

He was not alone, for this was the golden age of debtors' prisons. By law, the only people who could officially claim bankruptcy were insolvent traders; anyone else who, like Despard, had debts could be picked up and whisked into jail immediately, often without anyone else being informed of what had happened. After 1800, new laws would be passed to limit the number of debtors in prison, raising the level of debt required and offering rights of appeal. But in 1792 there were several debtors' jails in every borough. Had he been resident in London proper, he might have been sent to Newgate, or the Fleet, or Whitechapel; south of the river, the choices included the Marshalsea and the King's Bench. The latter was the usual destination for 'gentleman debtors', mostly gamblers and extravagant spenders – in the words of a judge at the time, 'men born to a property and a high station in life who by their folly and crime reduced themselves to wretchedness and loaded themselves with disgrace'.

This was a large category in an age when luxury and ostentation were an inescapable part of high society. Many gentlemen lived most of their lives in debt, juggling promissory notes and future inheritances against tailors' bills and IOUs scattered around their gambling circles. Richard Sheridan, who satirized the world of informal money-lending in his play *School for Scandal*, was

The King's Bench prison

constantly in debt, spending his wife's money and begging bailiffs to pretend to be waiters when his friends came round for dinner. He was also an MP, which meant that he had immunity from arrest for debt, but every time he appeared on the hustings the front row of the crowd was filled with traders waving unpaid bills at him. Many distinguished ladies also spent their lives lurching from one unstable financial arrangement to another. Emma, Lady Hamilton, while she was Nelson's mistress in 1803, had outstanding debts of £700 and a current account balance of twelve shillings and sixpence.

In the same way that debt was part of gentlemanly life, prisons such as the King's Bench were part of the gentlemanly world beyond their gates. Like the working-class debtors' prisons such as Newgate, they had criers, usually prisoners, who would show visitors where their friends were to be found for a small fee, and poor-boxes at the gates for those soliciting donations. But unlike Newgate, where many inmates had no better chance of paying off their debts than begging for coins to be dropped to them through the pavement gratings, King's Bench was set up to allow the financially embarrassed to generate the income to free themselves. The doors were locked only at nine at night; Catherine could visit Despard daily. During the day the inmates were also allowed to visit the local streets, within limits strictly defined by lamp-posts and parish boundary markers, and these districts hummed with money-lenders, lawyers and pawnbrokers. The local pubs were out of bounds, but some had special rooms built onto the side where debtors could adjourn.

Within the prison, rules were informal. The marshal, Mr Jones, had a reputation for making prisoners comfortable rather than punishing them; the few refractory ones were sent to Despard's final destination, the Surrey County Jail in Horsemonger Lane. Inmates were allowed to select any room that was free, and doubling up, if it was necessary, was arranged by a code that favoured the long-term residents. Inside the walls there were tap-rooms, wine cellars and bars, butchers, bakers, cobblers, tailors and a post office – as much a self-contained business district as a prison. Mr Jones closed down stalls that tried to pass off bad food on the prisoners, and 'a man in the King's Bench could lay out the little money he had to spend, to as much advantage as he could in any market in the kingdom'. The typical day of most inmates was taken up with arranging meetings with creditors, meeting friends, writing affidavits and bonds, gambling and drinking. Some prisoners claimed to have left King's Bench better dressed, better fed and far wealthier than when they went in.

It was not the place, though, to restore Despard's faith in the political system. Many of the debtors had some connection with government, and most had tales of corruption, dirty tricks, frauds, perjuries and briberies of which they had fallen foul or lacked the funds to exploit. Despard would have discovered quickly that he was not the only prisoner languishing in debt as a result of political revenge or bureaucratic incompetence. Another inmate from the same period reported prison gossip about Despard's persecutor, Henry Dundas, being in the habit of paying off his ex-mistresses with state pensions, and recalled leaving the King's Bench with the firm conviction that 'there is no tyranny so infamous as that which is carried on under the forms of law and justice'. For Despard, sitting out his time in a gentleman's prison must have been harder than fighting in the tropics. Time was against him in his struggle to clear his name and return to the Bay, and it had already become clear to him that there were broader miscarriages of justice afoot. He had never conceived himself as anything but a loyal servant of the Crown, yet he must now have felt uncomfortably as if he was being silenced.

He also found himself incarcerated at a point when the cause of political reform, for so long a background noise of pressure groups and factional interests, was being focused into the burning issue of the day through the lens of the French Revolution. By 1792, it was clear that France was exploding into an entirely new political configuration, one which was far surpassing the previous revolutions in Britain and America. The monarchy, and the entire ruling class, was rapidly becoming a thing of the past. The new force driving the nation forwards was one that had never before been part of any political settlement: the sheer weight of numbers of the common people. Any decision made by the newly constituted Assembly was communicated to them within minutes; if they disapproved, thousands of them would immediately take over the streets, threatening violence if their demands were not met. The only politicians left in power were those who could broker the people's will effectively.

This was an alarming state of affairs for Britain. As a constitutional monarchy with an elected Parliament, its situation was very different: most of the causes for which the revolution in France had been launched had already been enshrined in the British constitution for a century, and indeed the British system had been held up as a model by many of those who had led it. Yet the extent of the popular uprising in France had made it impossible to ignore the stubborn and persistent questions about how constitutional and representative the British system really was. The lower classes, the vast majority of the population who passed entirely beneath the radar not just of Parliament but of the reformers, were now leading the Paris Assembly. If the mass of the British people were to be consulted about the nation's political future, what might their answer be?

In January 1792, such an answer appeared, elegantly formed, passionately argued and expressed in the plain, simple language most political philosophy up to this point had deliberately avoided. Thomas Paine's *Rights of Man* was a fundamental attack on the British political system: the monarchy, the hereditary principle, the restriction of voting rights to the propertied classes, the right of any government to tax or wage war without the explicit consent of the majority of its population. It drove these arguments, too, far beyond the usual scope of politics, exposing the stifling effects of submission to unjust

Tom Paine, by George Romney

authority on society in general, and even family life in the home. Published in two parts, it was made available in cheap sixpenny editions that sold out immediately, and was republished in edition after edition as fast as the presses could turn it out. It was clear within weeks that there was no precedent for the number of people who were buying and reading it, which far exceeded what had been considered up to that point as the entire book-buying public. All across Britain, people reported that it was becoming impossible to find a shopkeeper, a craftsman, a manual labourer who had not heard of it; it was even on sale in the Outer Hebrides. Within two years it had sold an estimated two hundred thousand copies in a total population of ten million, and these two hundred thousand had been lent, passed on and read aloud to countless more. Despard read it in the King's Bench; it would become, by his own account, the closest thing he had to a bible, and would have a decisive effect on his trajectory from patriot to traitor.

Tom Paine was no youthful firebrand. He finished *Rights of Man* in his lodgings at the Angel Inn, Islington, on his fifty-fourth birthday – by the standards of the time, almost an old man. His defence of American independence, *Common Sense*, published back in 1776, had been a manifesto for how the rebel colonies might function as a republic, with the functions usually controlled by monarchy and hereditary government devolved to the 'virtue' of the people. But *Rights of Man* went much further, calling for a 'general revolution' and uniting the themes that had until this point tended to divide the British reform movement. Like Horne Tooke and Major Cartwright, whose Society of Constitutional Information endorsed and distributed the book, Paine found the roots of his system in the Anglo-Saxon heritage, an 'inheritance derived to us from our forefathers' which had been oppressed by the Norman yoke and 'ought to rescue itself from this reproach'. Yet he looked not just to the past, but to the future; not just to Britain, but to the wider world. He welcomed the example of the French Revolution as a sign of a new era in which the entrenched powers of despotism were on the wane, and all nations might be able to re-constitute their government by force of will and numbers.

Many of Paine's ideas were not new, though they were pulled together more skilfully and expressed more clearly than ever before. But the fifth section of the book, 'Ways and Means', laid out an original and practical template for how a new society might work. It would be driven economically by trade and private enterprise, not by state ownership, but instead of the population's taxes and man-power being channelled into wars that benefited only the wealthy, taxes might be redistributed for the good of the people at large. They might fund what we now recog-nize as a welfare state: old-age pensions, free education, maternity allowances, state-funded burials. Furthermore, the tax required might be raised not simply by head of population but by progressive increments levied on income. Here was not simply anger at the injustices of authority, but a careful critique of them, and a detailed blueprint for an alternative.

But, in the torrent of responses to *Rights of Man*, it was not the proposals for a welfare state that grabbed the headlines. Rather, it was Paine's insistence that there was no place for a monarchy in this brave new world. Monarchy was, in his view, 'the master fraud, which shelters all others'. The British monarchy was no more than 'a French bastard landing with an armed banditti and establishing himself King of England against the consent of the natives'; for all the fine talk of the Glorious

Revolution, 'the plain truth is that the antiquity of the English monarchy will not bear looking in to'. It had been an armed power-grab, and once established, like all monarchies, it had fixed its sights on acquiring absolute power, principally by waging war. 'All monarchical governments are military,' Paine observed; 'war is their trade, plunder and revenue their objects'. It is not the fault of the monarchs that they behave in this way; given the nature of hereditary power, how could they behave otherwise?

This was an uncompromising assertion, presented as inseparable from the broader argument, and it placed the entire book in territory that made many of the older generation of reformers profoundly uncomfortable. It pulled many of their disparate causes into a coherent manifesto, but it also co-opted them into precisely the assault on the King they had always been careful to avoid. Paine was arguing not that Britain's cherished mixed constitution was in need of running repairs, but that it was rotten to the core. He was announcing himself, in the terminology of the day, as a democrat – a far more extreme stance than revolutionary. A revolutionary might work for gradual change within the ruling system; a democrat was effectively calling for the murder of the monarch and the rule of the mob. A revolutionary could be a responsible member of society; a democrat was, in today's parlance, an anarchist.

It was not a position Paine adopted lightly. In private, he expressed doubts as to whether 'the proportion of men of sense, to the ignorant' was actually sufficient to make majority rule desirable; within *Rights of Man*, he cautioned that the overthrow of despotism was a sensitive business that risked backfiring in unforeseen ways. But the logic of his polemic, despite such cautions, was ineluctable. In following it to its conclusions Paine suspected that he would alienate many, and he was right. It confirmed the diagnosis of many of America's founding fathers that, in the words of John Adams, Paine was 'a better hand in pulling down than building'. Christopher Wyvill was quick to distance his waning movement from its 'pernicious counsels'. It was a book before its time, which pointed with unarguable clarity towards a future where democracy would no longer be the greatest threat to public life but its greatest virtue. Many of his ideas would become cherished cornerstones of this future, but he was launching them into a world that was not yet ready for the transition.

Thus the effect of *Rights of Man* was twofold, and contradictory; it was, in the phrase of the time, 'a sword sent to divide'. On the one hand, it gave the reform movement an impetus it had never had before, and spread the notions of electoral reform and participatory democracy to vast new swathes of the population; on the other, it guaranteed that whatever consensus emerged from it would be ignored by Parliament. For many, by the same token, it crystallized the sense that lobbying Parliament for reform had become a waste of time. Their old allies in the House of Commons had for a decade or more failed to deliver. Charles James Fox and Horne Tooke both talked a good revolution, none better. Fox was an astonishingly charismatic and articulate man, brilliant in dialogue and debate; his conversation, in the words of Georgina, Duchess of Devonshire, was 'like a brilliant player at billiards, the strokes follow one another piff puff'. Tooke, too, was, in the opinion of the essayist William Hazlitt, 'without a rival in conversation', his dinner parties legendary. Yet both were frustrating and ineffective conduits for the head of revolutionary steam that had been building up for so long in the world outside.

Tooke was a contrarian and pedant who would argue against any case that was put; it was terrifying to be cross-examined by him, but, in Hazlitt's assessment, he remained 'despised and feared by others, and admired by no-one but himself'. He would showily dismantle others' arguments and then 'talk treason with a saving clause', leaving the suspicion that he was 'unencumbered with a creed'. Fox, too, despite his brilliance, punched consistently below his weight in the House: over thirty-seven years as an MP he would spend fewer than two actually in power. He could work hard, but only in short bursts, interspersed with marathon bouts of gambling at cards, drinking and betting on horses; his grasp of racetrack odds was sharper than of many affairs of state. He had been a notoriously spoilt child, allowed to burn his father's state papers for pleasure and to paddle in bowls of cream; his parents thought 'the world would break his spirit soon enough', but, if anything, it had taught him how much he could get away with. On the sole occasion when political reform had come before the House, he had seemed more concerned to spike Pitt's guns than to work for an effective compromise. Subsequently he had referred to reform as a 'sleeping question' that might be woken only when it was politically expedient to do so.

Before the French Revolution and *Rights of Man*, the ebb and flow of the political process through such men as Tooke and Fox seemed to many, including Despard, the best that could be hoped for; after them, it seemed to many more, especially those undergoing their first real political awakening, not only absurd but insulting. Events in France had shown that real revolution could be achieved by popular will, and Paine had shown how, for the first time, the entire British population might participate in their own political future.

Promis'd Horrors of the French Invasion, *as envisaged by James Gillray*

But not everyone saw the French Revolution and its British apologists as a triumph of reason and brotherhood over despotism and fear. Many took from them precisely the opposite lesson: that any and all reform would inevitably lead to chaos and violent mob rule. The majority of the propertied classes had a vivid sense of what a revolution might mean in practice: gangs in makeshift uniforms requisitioning their houses, farms and other hard-earned assets for the public good; old scores and envies being settled under cover of the 'will of the people'. For them, a revolution represented not liberty but the most serious threat to it they could imagine. Much of the working class, too, especially in rural areas, was viscerally opposed to revolution. The traditional sense of British liberties could also be harnessed to a conviction that the dispensation of Parliament, Church and King was ordained by God, and worth dying to preserve. In the cities as well, crowds rioted as frequently for conservative causes as for progressive ones, often more so. The local magistrates, who were responsible for policing, often waived the usual constraints on law and order when violence broke out on patriotic occasions such as royal birthdays, Protestant festivals like Guy Fawkes Night, or in support of local causes they favoured. Priests and magistrates took the lead in organizing local defence militias, who paraded through the centres of towns under banners of 'Church and King'.

As the currents of revolution began to quicken, these forces of counter-revolution were at least as quick to organize themselves in defence of the status quo. They were also better equipped, better supported by local judiciaries, and a good deal more visible on the streets. When a former government lawyer named John Reeves began to advertise for volunteers to defend Britain's towns and cities from the revolutionary threat, William Pitt promptly summoned him for a meeting and encouraged him to set up his organization along lines that could be useful in forming a network of regional militias. Reeves' Association for Preserving Liberty and Property against Republicans and Levellers was franchised across the nation by 1792, an umbrella for the patriotic societies springing up to counter the enemy dupes and fifth columnists who they feared were, wittingly or not, plotting to open the floodgates to mob rule.

Increasingly, the loyalists took the fight to the revolutionaries in public. On 4 November 1788 the London Revolution Society, a network of moderate parliamentary reformers, had met at the London Tavern in Bishopsgate to celebrate the centenary of the Glorious Revolution under a banner reading 'A Tyrant Deposed and Liberty Restored'. Those present – MPs, Church ministers and other dignitaries – had signed a declaration stating that all political authority should be derived from the people, and committing themselves to the traditional liberties of trial by jury, a free press and free elections. In a final public flourish to the ceremony, the London Monument had been illuminated. Then, any controversy about the event was confined to the rarefied world of politics; by 1791, when the same causes were celebrated across the country by a similar network, the Friends of Liberty, the reaction to the French Revolution had made such meetings the targets of violence by Church-and-King mobs. MPs such as Fox and Sheridan were prevailed upon by the Prince Regent and others to stay away, and did so. At the Manchester meeting, handbills were scattered around the streets outside the venue, suggesting that 'the brains of every man who dined there would be much improved by being mingled with bricks and mortar'. In Birmingham, on Bastille Day 1791, widespread violence and destruction broke out; mobs stormed the reformer Joseph Priestley's laboratory and demolished it, calling all dissenters 'King-killers and levellers'. That November, the London Revolution Society's dinner guests included Tom Paine and French republicans such as Jérome Pétion; the company of 350 defiantly wore revolutionary tricolours and cockades. The old, patriotic language of liberty was being overwritten in a foreign tongue. The reform debate might have died inside Parliament, but outside it was flaring up into public conflict and violence.

It was in this new climate that an organization was founded of which Despard would become a prominent member. On 25 January 1792, the same month that *Rights of Man* was published, nine men met in the Bell Tavern just off the Strand in London to discuss the subject that had become a consuming interest to all of them: political reform. Their convenor, a man named Thomas Hardy, was forty years old, a jobbing artisan and cobbler who owned a shoe shop in Piccadilly. His colleagues were also working men, carpenters and engravers and tailors who were more interested in making contact with their fellows than in petitioning the great and good to intercede on their behalf in Parliament. 'The higher class', Hardy observed, 'have at all times made use of the middling and lower orders as a ladder to raise themselves into power, and then kick it away.' He asked each of his friends for a penny to fund a network of correspondence with other working groups around the country. His group considered naming themselves the Patriotic Society, to stress their benign intentions towards British liberties, but instead opted for the London Corresponding Society, and began to advertise for members. The number of members was to be unlimited; all that was required was the penny weekly sub and an affirmative answer to the question: 'Are you thoroughly persuaded that the welfare of these kingdoms requires that every adult person, in possession of his reason, and not incapacitated by his crimes, should have a vote for a Member of Parliament?'

News of the London Corresponding Society spread fast; within weeks, the numbers wishing to attend meetings had become unmanageable. Following the suggestion of a similar society in Sheffield, Hardy adopted a system whereby every time a local group reached sixty members, it divided into two smaller groups. Meetings took place on Sunday evenings; readings, in strict silence, were followed by discussions; eating, drinking and smoking were prohibited. Hardy and his colleagues struggled with the correct phrasing for a document that would announce the corresponding societies to the world at large. Eventually they agreed on an Address, which made it clear that they favoured 'reform, not anarchy', but that 'oppressive taxes, unjust laws, restrictions of liberty and wasting of public money' had made the current system of government unacceptable to the free-born Englishman. The remedy could only be 'a fair, equal and impartial representation of the people'. The Address was passed over to Horne Tooke, who arranged the publication of a thousand copies. Within six months, on the rising wave of sales of *Rights of Man*, the London Corresponding Society had two thousand members. Other similar societies in Sheffield, Norwich and Manchester were as large, perhaps larger.

It was 1794 before Despard was released from the King's Bench. The law suit against him petered out; he was found not guilty, just as Nelson had been, and as he had been convinced that he would. But he had not been as fortunate as Nelson. Both the charges against him – the Baymen's and the lawyers' – had been found without merit, and he was free, in theory without a stain on his character. In practice, though, his career had been seriously blemished: he had spent two years in jail, and had little or no chance of ever being asked to work again. As soon as he left jail, or perhaps even before, he decided to join the London Corresponding Society and become a full-time revolutionary.

Despard's conversion to politics was a dramatic change of career, but not an entirely puzzling one. He had always been a practical man; now, politics had become an urgent practical problem. His particular experience in diplomacy in a society patched together from disparate worlds of military rank, social class and ethnic origin made him well suited for bridging the alarming divides that were opening up in British politics. His interest in electoral representation had developed because it was the most effective tool for demonstrating that the system he had set up in the Bay was based on consent, and was thus practical. His extended stay in London had edged him across an invisible divide he had not even known existed; he had looked for support in the places where he expected to find it, and it had not been forthcoming. Now, his insistence that authority should be based on consent – which he had, like many Britons, held as an unquestioned assumption – was indeed being echoed, and powerfully, from every quarter of society. Another British revolution seemed to be stirring, and his experiences since his return had left him in little doubt as to which side he was on. There was a new force in politics, with a powerful manifesto and a massive weight of numbers behind it. This was no lost cause – at least, not yet.

6

TERRORIST

When Despard was released from the King's Bench in 1794 he was, once again, a man out of time. He had joined the ranks of the gentlemen parliamentary reformers late in the day, after the main parade had gone by; he had spent the 1780s fighting his own parallel battle in ignorance of the wider debate in Britain. Now, at the age of forty-three, he was entering the heady world of imminent revolution with firm commitment, but also with little more knowledge of the political world than an idealistic convert half his age.

He was, too, stepping out into a world where the debate had once more moved on. In 1792, following the French Revolution and *Rights of Man*, it had seemed to many as if the nation's political framework might be up for discussion. But by the time Despard stepped free from prison, the debate had been shut down; in its place, battle lines had been drawn. In France, declarations of liberty and fraternity had been followed by news of anarchy and mass murder; in Britain, the antagonists had dug into their positions, and the middle ground had swung decisively behind the status quo. In 1789 it had seemed as if France was converting to the British constitutional model; by 1792 it was clear that its leaders were, like Tom Paine, hoping to consign the British model to the dustbin of history. Thus the cause for which Despard had chosen to fight was already being forced underground, its supporters risking prosecution as enemies of the state.

The tipping point had been the declaration of war between Britain and France in 1793, which in turn had been precipitated by the execution of Louis XVI. With the British nation on a war footing, the cause of revolution, tied as it now was to France, had become a matter of public security, and the publication of anti-government sentiments had edged into sedition. The flashpoint, and the test case for the reach of the government's security powers, had been the fountainhead from which so many of these sentiments had flowed. Tom Paine's calls in *Rights of Man* for an end to the monarchy, combined with his praise of the French Revolution, now opened up him and those who published him to prosecution. A trial of the author on grounds of seditious libel had been mounted at the request of the Home Office; Paine had written the Home Secretary a letter of caustic insolence in which he referred to George III as 'his Mad-jesty' and which he signed off: 'I am, Mr. Dundas, not *your* obedient servant, but the contrary'. As the trial loomed, Paine skipped the country for France. He was found guilty *in absentia* by a special jury and pronounced a traitor; he would never set foot in Britain again. Despard's bible, and that of the London Corresponding Society, was burned in town squares up and down the country, Paine crucified in effigy under the banners of Church and King.

During Despard's incarceration, too, a concerted effort had been made to discourage gentlemen of the higher classes from revolutionary activity. It had begun in Henry Dundas's native fiefdom of Scotland, when dozens of corresponding societies met for a highly publicized British Convention in Edinburgh; the crowd had been broken up by the local magistrates and militia on grounds of public order, and those of social position and influence had been prosecuted with striking severity. A distinguished barrister, Thomas Muir, had been found guilty of seditious libel and sentenced to deportation for fourteen years; the Reverend Thomas Fysshe Palmer, formerly of Eton and Cambridge, had been banished for seven. Neither had expected more than a fine, or a few weeks in jail at the very most. As it turned out, Muir would eventually escape from Botany Bay via Havana and Spain to France, losing an eye in the process, while Palmer would die as a Spanish prisoner of war on the island of Guam in the South Pacific. The message was clearly received and understood, and the gentlemanly sector of the movement, many of them veterans of the lobbying and petitions of the 1780s, left the corresponding societies in droves. Despard, committing himself to the cause when he did, was conspicuous, and probably more so than he realized.

He was joining the movement at the point when its business was being observed by a rapidly growing number of government spies and informers. The beginning of the war had seen the passing of the Alien Act, designed to prevent French revolutionary Jacobins from infiltrating the London masses. The declaration of war had seen thousands of French pouring into Britain through Dover and the Channel ports, and there were indeed secret agents among them, though most of them were spying on their own aristocratic émigrés. The Alien Act set up a new bureau of the Home Office known as the Alien Office, with special agents detailed to observe public meetings and increased government powers to make visitors register their presence and to question and arrest suspicious characters. To these were added a new spy ring of Home Office recruits, including several placed within the London Corresponding Society – or LCS, as it was becoming commonly known – who reported to a Committee of Secrecy overseen by Dundas and Evan Nepean at the Home Office. Their names were protected from the committee by initials and aliases; they were paid very well indeed, and many of them survived for years without their cover being broken.

The arrival of war also extended Dundas's reach in other ways. He could call on the Post Office to open letters; he could cull suspicious information from customs and local officials. He also had the main London militia, the Bow Street Runners, at his disposal; their role was ill defined in law and could be extended in times of emergency, and he ran a separate secret service out of their offices. The combination of all these channels meant that he had intelligence in quantity, though its quality remained an ongoing problem. Some of his agents were plea-bargaining criminals, others had grudges and scores to settle, and most of their reports were impossible to corroborate. The LCS, for example, had probably been infiltrated to some extent almost from the beginning, but by 1794 there were several agents inside different divisions and committees, most of whom were unaware of one another and whose reports diverged wildly; their various accounts of one another's activities were the closest to a tool that could be used to separate the wheat from the chaff. Thus Despard was a marked man from the moment he left the King's Bench, and the reports filed on him over the next few years constitute much of the evidence, reliable or otherwise, for his movements.

Despard stepped into the fray, too, at precisely the time that the net was tightening around the movement's leaders. On 12 May 1794, the LCS's founder, Thomas Hardy, had been woken by a pounding at the door of his cobbler's shop at No. 9 Piccadilly. Six police and Home Office officials had stormed into the house, terrifying Hardy and his pregnant wife, and had begun ransacking his flat for books and papers, and turning his storeroom upside down; as Hardy commented later, 'they expected no doubt to find treason hatching among the boots and shoes'. He was hauled off to Newgate prison, along with several other high-ranking LCS members; the manifestos and documents in his oak bureau were confiscated to be pored over for evidence of sedition. Horne Tooke, who had arranged the publication of the LCS manifesto, was also arrested and imprisoned in the Tower of London. Charges had been expected, but none materialized. Instead, on 23 May, Pitt announced that the right of habeas corpus was suspended, and that Hardy and his confederates were to be held without trial at His Majesty's pleasure.

The right of habeas corpus, which specified that no British subject could be held arbitrarily without trial or the right of appeal, was one of the sacrosanct pillars of the Glorious Revolution of 1688. Throughout the eighteenth century it had been held up as one of the prime elements of the British constitution that distinguished it from the despotic monarchy of France, where a *lettre de cachet* was all that was required to keep an enemy of the King rotting in a dungeon indefinitely. Its suspension seemed to those in the reform movement to be a calculated assault: not only were new liberties not to be granted, but the most cherished ones were to be removed. It was not only a massive shock to the constitutional system but, as it turned out, the first of a series of measures that would soon come to be known as 'Pitt's Reign of Terror'. New offences would be introduced for those who maintained and promoted dissenting political opinions, and a new category would be created for those found guilty: terrorist.

As with Despard's own epithet of 'unfortunate', part of the reason why 'terror' made its way into the language so quickly and extensively was that it was rich with irony and ambiguity, capable of meaning different things to different people. Its overt model was the Jacobin Assembly's recent proclamation that 'terror is to be the order of the day' in the new French revolutionary politics, by which it was meant that loyalty to the nation would now be demonstrated by state requisitions, personal sacrifice and summary justice for enemies of the revolution. 'Pitt's Reign of Terror' was a term coined by Fox's opposition to imply that Pitt was using the same terror tactics as France to turn moderate reformers into criminals, riding roughshod over the rights of free speech, lawful assembly and freedom from arbitrary imprisonment. The term spread rapidly through the reform movement, which shared the sentiment: Major Cartwright and other moderate reformers dubbed their former ally Pitt 'the English Robespierre', a warmongering tyrant whose home front was the war on his own people. But loyalists and Church and King patriots also began to use the term with approval: a Reign of Terror was exactly what was needed to preserve English liberties from the fifth column of king-killers. If the government was not prepared to take the lead in suppressing them, there were plenty in the local justice system who would.

The suspension of habeas corpus was not the only emergency legal power Pitt had in store. There were many, and most of them were ready to be published, but he feared the public outcry if he were to unleash them all at once. He was also balancing the opposing pressures of hawks and doves within his own government. The moderate Whigs grouped under the Duke of Portland had split from Fox's faction over their support of the French Revolution and their opposition to the war; Portland was threatening to set up a third party, but Pitt badly needed his support. He was compelled to reshuffle his cabinet, and offer Portland the post of Home Secretary. Dundas was furious, so Pitt had to create a new post, Minister for War, to allow him to keep control of military strategy and maintain the coveted title of Secretary of State.

Dundas took Evan Nepean with him, and Portland settled into the nest of spies. Richard Ford, one of the Bow Street magistrates, quickly made himself indispensable to him with his files of 'all examinations in treason, sedition and conspiracy', particularly on members of the LCS. The reports of subversion increased – more secret meetings and, unreliably and often implausibly, tales of revolutionary militias assembling and drilling in the London slums. Portland had been a supporter of the French Revolution when the Bastille fell, but his ardour had cooled considerably since 1792, and he would quickly become as keen an advocate of terror as Dundas had been. Unlike the century's previous wars with France and Spain, this was also a war of ideas, which was being fought on more fronts than simply the military. On the ideological front, organizations such as the LCS were powerful and unpredictable players. Never before had the mass of the British population been so well informed, so politically engaged, and at such risk of conversion to views closer to those of the enemy than their own nation.

In the country at large, too, Pitt was not seeking to create divisions so much as to claim the middle ground. Ratcheting up the apparatus of state control was, he felt, necessary to keep the peace. Had he done nothing, many loyalist militias were clearly prepared to take the law into their own hands. It was precisely the sort of people who felt themselves in greatest danger from Tom Paine's ideals who were in charge of the county towns and the judiciary. Already magistrates in many parts of the country were handing out draconian sentences to suspected 'terrorists' on little evidence, or convicting them of rioting when they had been defending themselves from beatings by Church and King mobs. Just as the guillotine was the French Assembly's attempt to maintain a state monopoly on terror, so Pitt felt it necessary to hold terror out of reach of the magistrates and the mobs. It has often been argued that his Reign of Terror marks the point in his career when he moved from pragmatic, centrist power-broker to committed and ideological anti-Jacobin, but it may equally be argued that his most profound volte-face came before his career as Prime Minister had even begun, when he abandoned his first cause – political reform – in exchange for power.

Thus, in late 1794, Despard cannot have been entirely unaware of the direction in which he was travelling, or the dangers into which it might lead. Yet there is no reason for believing that he hesitated in his decision to commit himself to a cause that was already shading from dissent to treason. The reasons that would be offered after his death were few, and simplistic. He was mad; he was bent on vengeance against the government; he was a stubborn martyr to a lost cause. Yet he had other motives, and more plausible ones. The causes to which he was committing himself were far from deluded; they were, after all, causes that would come to be held universally in free nations, though by no means as quickly as he might have imagined. It was the first time in history – and, it was reasonable to assume in 1794, perhaps the last – that the British people might have the opportunity for root-and-branch reform of their public life. Such reforms had popular support, and had already taken place in Britain's great neighbours to the east and west. The issues that had sparked them had been the nub of his own question: whether nations should be run by an elite or by democratic consent. If ever there was a time for everyone, no matter what their background or abilities, to throw themselves behind a political cause, this was surely it.

It is worth considering, also, what else he might have done. It was clear to him by now that the only career he had ever had was over. He was certainly bitter about it, and with good reason. He had done nothing wrong, even by the account of his enemies. His conscience was clear, and his character, officially at least, unstained. Yet his years of digging ditches, building fortifications, risking his life in battle and sweating out dozens of tropical fevers had been rewarded with the coldest of shoulders. Even the money due to him had been withheld. His country was now at war, and he would not be invited to defend it.

He might, as many of his class did, have parlayed his rank and distinguished military record into an advantageous marriage, and become prosperously settled. But Despard was not about to become a character in a Jane Austen novel; apart from anything else, he was already happily married. His was an awkward and unusual position. Had he been living in feudal Japan at the time, he might have been recognized as a familiar archetype: the *ronin*, a samurai without a master, a loose cannon, dangerous to his former superiors and a valuable asset to any plotter. In Britain, he was an anomaly: a man out of time, a patriot without a nation.

He might have turned to his family. The estate he had

hardly visited since his youth still existed; he might have retired to it, been offered a management post or a small-holding, and eked out a life on a modest income. Yet this, too, was a distant option; he might not even have considered it for a moment. He had barely seen his family for twenty years. His father had died, and his brothers were scattered around the globe on military service. In the meantime, his life had become a constant upward trajectory towards more responsibility, more testing of his mettle, more danger, an ever broader vision of his role in the world. If self-preservation and living to a ripe old age had been high on his priorities, he would not have lived the life he had. From his first military engagement on the San Juan, he had disregarded his personal safety for a higher calling, and he had continued to do so without ever knowing defeat.

The personal danger into which he was now placing himself seems to have occupied his mind very little. It probably occupied Catherine's a good deal more: espionage reports reiterate that she was worried about the risks he was taking, and the trouble into which he might get himself. After a while he would begin to use a separate flat in Camden Town, of which she was unaware, for his revolutionary business. He might not have fully realized how serious this revolutionary business was becoming; he might not have understood exactly what it would finally cost him. He might well not have cared.

It was late October 1794 before Thomas Hardy, Horne Tooke and their collaborators were informed of their fate. By this time, their imprisonment had become the central and public focus of the Reign of Terror, and the barometer of how it was likely to unfold. Mrs Hardy, pregnant and suffering greatly under the shock and stress of her husband's arrest, had been terrified out of her wits by a loyalist demonstration that had taken over the streets of London in June; although she had patriotically illuminated their Piccadilly house, the crowd had still attacked it, and she had suffered serious injury while escaping. In August she had given birth to a stillborn baby and, in the middle of writing a letter to Hardy entreating him to keep up his 'faith and patience', had subsequently died herself. Fox's Whigs had maintained the parliamentary pressure on Pitt, demanding again and again that he reveal to the House his intentions towards the prisoners. Eventually, Pitt had pronounced. They were to face a charge of high treason.

High treason was a piece of English law a great deal older than habeas corpus, but one which had barely been wheeled out for fifty years. It had originally been codified in 1350, under Edward III, drawing on older traditions from at least a century before. It contained various clauses, including 'compassing or imagining the King's death', violating the wife of a king or an heir to the throne, levying war in the king's dominions and 'adhering to the King's enemies'. The government's case against Hardy was now becoming clear. It had, it now seemed, already been spelled out by Grenville when he had recommended the suspension of habeas corpus to the House of Lords. He had claimed at the time that the raid on Hardy's shop had revealed evidence of a conspiracy whereby 'all supremacy was to be destroyed', and 'all property was to be aggregately divided, and the present royal family was to be murdered'. This charge had now been turned over to the judiciary to be proved.

The treason trial opened at the Old Bailey on 29 October. The charges and prosecution evidence against Hardy continued for three days, adding detail after circumstantial detail to the case that the LCS was an organization that 'compassed and imagined the King's death'. The society, it was asserted, had condoned Tom Paine's writings, and thus his calls for an end to the monarchy; members of corresponding societies in the provinces had allegedly been found stockpiling pikestaffs; witnesses had heard threats against His Majesty being made; letters found in Hardy's shop had included plans for riots and insurrections, and plots with the enemy across the Channel. It was a case woven from threads of insinuation, some gossamer thin, but amounting to a grand tapestry of treason.

But the defence was equal to it. It was conducted by Thomas Erskine, a Scottish barrister and Foxite Whig MP, in a speech that would be long remembered as one of the most important ever made against the Crown. Erskine moved easily from engaging the judge on the detail of the law to persuading the jury that the evidence presented a selective, credulous and unrepresentative picture of a decent and legal public society. If the prosecution had hoped that the previous conviction *in absentia* of Tom Paine would deter Erskine, they were wrong: he raised the question of *Rights of Man* and addressed it explicitly. The book did, he freely admitted, include some strong statements against the monarchy, but they were subservient to Paine's main argument, 'which was to maintain the right of people to choose their own government'. This was a view that it was perfectly proper to hold, and it was on this basis that the LCS had promoted Paine's work; indeed, they had specifically distanced themselves from his extreme democratic views in print.

Erskine's speech was a marathon. He had been overworked and ill before it had begun; by the end, he was croaking it to an assistant who had to relay it at an audible volume to the judge. In his balanced summing up, the judge stressed that high treason was a serious and legitimate charge, but that 'clear and convincing' proof was needed to substantiate it. The jury deliberated for three hours before finding Hardy not guilty. The court was dismissed to find a huge and joyous crowd assembled outside the Old Bailey, who carried Erskine in triumph to the pub. Hardy, though, was in no mood to celebrate. He shook off the crowd, and took a carriage to St Martin's graveyard to visit his wife.

There were still eleven more traitors to try. The next was Horne Tooke, against whom the charges were the same, and whom Erskine was also defending. This time the prosecution took more care in selecting the jury, quizzing them about their political views; Erskine, rattled, turned to Tooke and whispered, 'By God, they are murdering you.' But the case against Tooke was even more insubstantial, at times bordering on the risible. It transpired that Tooke had been aware that one of his colleagues was a spy, and had amused himself with dramatic asides about far-fetched revolutionary plots. He stressed throughout that he had a long record as a supporter of moderate reform – and, in so doing, fuelled mutterings among the LCS rank and file that he was exonerating himself by implying the possible guilt of others. Tooke, too, was found not guilty; after him another high-ranking member of the LCS, John Thelwall, received the same verdict. The show had plainly come to an end. The remainder of the prisoners were released, and the jurors dismissed.

The treason trials of 1794 were a public humiliation for the Pitt administration. The first and most important salvo of the Reign of Terror had been a damp squib, and had highlighted a major and largely unsuspected obstacle that would plague all terror measures to come: the expression of the will of the people via the jury system. The use of the state apparatus in this way had made the accused seem honourable and upstanding members of society, the government a paranoid and maleficent body dependent on cruel legislative measures and dubious informers. The verdict was a propaganda coup for the reformers, and the LCS, over the coming weeks, received a considerable surge in membership, though one even more liberally sprinkled with spies than before.

Among the new intake was a tailor from Charing Cross named Francis Place whose memoirs, written fifty years later after a long and distinguished career in political reform, offer the closest to a personal portrait of Despard during this period. Place had first become involved with the LCS after organizing a strike of leather breech-makers in 1793, and had been galvanized into political activism by Thomas Hardy's arrest and the suspension of habeas corpus. 'The violent proceedings of the government frightened many people away,' he recalled, but many others, including himself, 'considered it was meritorious and a duty to become members now that it was threatened with violence'. The LCS that emerged was a little leaner than the first flush of 1792, but also fitter, as 'those who joined it were men of decided character, sober, thinking men, not likely to be put off from their purpose'.

Place and Despard met early on; both were members of the Central Committee, which was composed of the delegates elected by each local division. For Place, one of the attractions of the LCS was that he met 'many clever, inquisitive, upright men, in most if not in all respects superior to any with whom I had hitherto been acquainted', and he and Despard became close friends. Place had fallen on hard times: as a senior member of the LCS, and before long its treasurer, he found his shop boycotted and his gentlemen customers dwindling. He could hold on to his few accounts only by cutting his fees to the bare minimum, and was still plagued by late payments and defaulted bills. He considered going to France, but instead moved with his young family into the spare room of another LCS member, John Ashley. It was here that Despard would frequently come to visit, and, as Place recalled, 'those visits were very advantageous to me in intellectual and moral points of view'. Despard's reputation in the LCS as a whole seems to have been that of a gentleman of integrity, selfless commitment to the cause of the underdog, great intellectual ability and, from their point of view, invaluable experience as a man at ease in the many levels of society they were attempting to influence. Soon other qualities would become apparent, over which his colleagues would be more divided.

The failure thus far of the Reign of Terror was only one of the government's troubles, which mounted alarmingly through 1795. Pitt and Dundas had both been counting on a short war. France was weakened by the revolution, internally and externally chaotic; the British strategy had been to strike hard at her colonial wealth and wait for the new republic to collapse in the face of political wrangling, food shortages and encirclement by hostile monarchies. But the Jacobins had taken the offensive, announcing a new policy of *levée en masse*, the model for modern military conscription, whereby every citizen was obliged to take up arms and all the nation's resources were dedicated to the war effort. French revolutionary armies had swept through Europe, defeating far better-equipped Austrian forces with sheer force of will and ideological fervour. Against all this, Britain was ill prepared. Taxes were hiked up, new levels of conscription were rigorously enforced, and local food shortages began to produce riots. Public hostility to the government and even the King became impossible to ignore. A mob protesting against conscription and shouting 'No war, no Pitt, cheap bread!' surrounded Pitt's house in Downing Street and pelted it with stones, breaking his windows; Despard was among those hauled into custody and later released without charge. Several times, while en route to the House of Commons, Pitt was hissed, booed and pelted with missiles. In October, George III's cavalcade was surrounded by a hostile crowd while travelling to the state opening of Parliament; according to some reports, there was shooting, and an attempt to drag the King from his carriage. After this incident, the royal carriage was bullet-proofed.

Pitt's response was to ratchet up the Reign of Terror still further. Earlier in the year, the suspension of habeas corpus had been renewed; although its application had thus far been disastrous, not to have persevered with it would have been too obvious an admission of failure. In November 1795, Pitt read two new bills to the House. The first, the Treasonable Practices Bill, expanded and clarified the old medieval code of treason. This specifically prohibited the 'actual or contemplated use of force to make the king change his counsels', and 'intimidating either Houses of Parliament'. The second, the Seditious Meetings Bill, set stringent controls on the legality of public meetings, and limited their numbers to fewer than fifty. These 'Gagging Bills', as their opponents described them, were bitterly opposed in Parliament by Fox, Erskine and their Whig faction; they reminded Pitt about his own meetings with Christopher Wyvill in 1782, and asked whether these should now be considered retrospectively as treason. Outside Parliament, the opposition was even more voluble. Ninety-four petitions comprising 130,000 signatures were presented against the bills, and a protest meeting in

Regent's Park – as far as anyone knew, the last such public meeting that would ever be held in Britain – drew a crowd estimated at nearly four hundred thousand. But the passage of the bills through the chamber was a formality, and both received royal assent in December.

Even within the inner circle of government there was unease about whether the 'Two Acts', as they were now formally known, were constitutional, and whether they ran the risk of delivering the moral high ground to the reformers. Conciliatory voices such as William Wilberforce stressed that they were a 'temporary bulwark' whose only purpose was to 'preserve British liberties'. More hawkish ministers such as Dundas were unapologetic. 'I think it is absolutely necessary to define what sedition is', he insisted, 'and apply to it the proper punishment.' In a time of crisis, it was perfectly proper for the government to 'assume the illegality' of all popular meetings. In private, Pitt was explicit about why he had forced them through: he expected civil war. Without them, he feared, there would be serious unrest, insurrection and possible revolution. The country's only hope was for him to tighten the reins of power and attempt to hold on for dear life. His prediction to Wilberforce was that 'my head would be off in six months were I to resign'.

What was conspicuous to all was that the Two Acts were specifically targeted against the LCS and other Paineite societies, the maximum of fifty participants in a public meeting, for example, set so as to make the LCS divisions of sixty illegal. Though the acts were, as it turned out, rarely used, they did not need to be: their thrust was to make treason much easier to prove against those who disagreed with government policy, sedition against those who met to discuss it. Whether used or not, they were effective. By closing off the option of legitimate debate, they forced the corresponding societies around the country further underground, effectively declaring them illegal societies and a *de facto* terrorist network.

Although the word 'radical' was not commonly used in politics until the 1820s – the term favoured at the time was the more damning 'British Jacobin' – it would be used retrospectively to describe what these societies became after the Two Acts were passed. From this point on, the reform movement would begin to take on some of the sinister character with which its enemies had invested it. Its members would be increasingly persuaded by the view that, as Mahatma Gandhi would put it much later, 'an unjust law is itself a species of violence' to which a violent response might be morally justified. Despard's personal transition from patriot to traitor would remain contested, but the Two Acts marked a watershed where the burden of proof shifted, and he would be presumed guilty rather than innocent.

The Two Acts had the same effect, also, on the other radical society that was rivalling the British corresponding societies and would soon converge with them, overtake them and sweep them into conflict on a far grander scale: the United Irishmen.

Ireland was still a colony, and one where the struggle for self-government had run as long and almost as deep as America's. The political landscape that had emerged there after the Glorious Revolution made Britain's system of patronage and rotten boroughs look like a model of modern democracy. Ireland's five million inhabitants made it half as populous as Britain, yet a majority in its parliament could be commanded by little over a hundred voters. Its Catholic majority – over three million – had no votes and were barred not only from government but from the professions, and even from land ownership. Its million Presbyterians, many of them middle-class and concentrated in the northern province of Ulster, could vote if qualified by substantial property ownership, but were barred from high office. Its Anglicans, among whom were the Despards – under half a million in total – owned 80 per cent of the land and controlled its parliament and all its public institutions. Unlike America, which was taxed from Westminster, the Irish parliament could run its own revenue system as it chose.

When the war with America broke out, there were many in Ireland who supported their fellow colonists, and they came close to dragging their country into the conflict. In 1778 an American warship, the *Ranger*, sailed into Belfast harbour unopposed, to a joyous welcome. Presbyterian and Dissenting communities formed drill militias, the Irish Volunteers, called for liberty and began to arm themselves for their own war of independence. During one of Fox's brief spells in power in the 1780s, his Whigs had won some concessions for the Irish parliament along the lines the Jamaican Assembly had sought, making it theoretically more of a partner to Westminster than a subsidiary. The new parliament under Henry Grattan remained pre-dominantly Anglican but removed some longstanding prohibitions on Catholics, such as their right to buy land. Yet, despite a probable majority at this point in the British Parliament for more such changes – many of the opposition, including Pitt, were in favour – the rock against which Fox and Grattan's reforms had foundered was George III. The King was implacable: the core of his oath was that he would never again allow a Catholic ascendancy in his lands, and he regarded the calls for liberty in Ireland as a direct affront to his rule. The Grattan parliament had taken small steps towards such liberty, but not nearly enough to defuse the tensions. The armed volunteers failed to disband, and the middle-class reformers, Presbyterian and Catholic, remained united with the huge Catholic majority against aristocratic and British rule.

In late 1791, just as Thomas Hardy was preparing to set up the LCS, a Dublin lawyer named Wolfe Tone set up an organization with similar intent, and called it the United Irishmen. Tone and many of its leading lights were Protestants, but the organization was conceived to appeal across the religious divide to the new class of landowning Catholics. Tone presented his new society to the public with an explanation of its name and a declaration of its intent, that 'in that club, for the first time in Ireland, Dissenters and Catholics were seen together in union and harmony'. The United Irish members were drawn from the professional and landowning classes, a social profile closer to Wyvill's associations than to the artisans and tradesmen of Hardy's LCS. They began to publish a magazine, the *Northern Star*, which promoted Tom Paine's republican ideas and campaigned against the injustice of the Irish parliamentary system. It was distributed in Britain, often through the same channels as *Rights of Man*; it is likely that Despard encountered it, and possible that he was among the United Irishmen's early members. Like Paine, the society was open in its support of the revolutionary French Assembly, and even opened up informal diplomatic relations with it.

Thus the political configuration in Ireland was in many respects parallel to that in Britain; the most salient difference was that there was, and had long been, a much larger armed and militarized population underlying the struggle for reform. To this was now added the possibility that Ireland might become the first serious theatre of war

Wolfe Tone

between Britain and France. British intelligence reports strongly suggested that the French and the United Irish were jointly planning for an invasion of Ireland, and also that the British army would have little chance of defending the colony against the combined force of a foreign army and an insurrectionary populace. The United Irish, according to the same intelligence, were well on the way to transforming themselves from a political club into an armed militia. The gentlemanly sector of the movement had, as in Britain, declined as the progress of the French Revolution had become more alarming. Wolfe Tone had left for America; by some accounts, the United Irish were almost moribund by 1794. But the ranks had subsequently begun to swell once more, and their old division and committee system was converted into a military command structure of armed revolutionary cells. The old volunteer militias were secretly realigning themselves behind the United Irish front. Across the country, stashes of pikes and guns were now at the disposal of secret societies known as the Defenders.

The effect of the Two Acts on the United Irishmen was both to drive them underground and to accelerate their trajectory towards armed insurrection. Tone himself was no ideological zealot: he believed that 'if a nation wills a bad government, it ought to have that government', and that 'we have no power, and we have no right, to force men to be free'. But he was convinced that there was 'a spirit rising among the people which never appeared before', and that the time for polite discussion with an intransigent parliament was fast running out. Large areas of Ireland were falling under the shadow rule of the Defender movement, and the pace of communications between the various hotbeds quickened. Membership was now sealed with an oath of secrecy, which committed members to the overthrow of the Irish government.

The initial British response was one that would become successful, and subsequently notorious, following the Act of Union with Britain: to fund and arm the anti-Catholic Orange Order in an attempt to divide and rule by splitting apart the Protestant and Catholic interests the United Irishmen had brought together. But more was needed at this stage, and it soon came. In Defender heartlands such as Connaught, the British army began burning down houses, torturing suspects and press-ganging hundreds into the British navy. The Two Acts were complemented by an Indemnity Act and an Insurrection Act which were rushed through the Irish parliament, one protecting magistrates from legal redress in cases including torture and murder, and the other setting the death penalty for administering illegal oaths.

The combination of the Two Acts and the advanced revolutionary plans of the United Irish had a divisive effect on the LCS. The first caused its numbers to drop again from the recent peak after Hardy's trial; the second began to polarize its remaining members between political reform and armed struggle. Just as the government's prosecution of the war had blurred the line between political debate and military action, so the same line was becoming blurred for those who opposed them. By 1796, Francis Place was becoming disconsolate that 'the whole character of the society was changed'. The central committee's first response had been to cut the size of local divisions from sixty to forty-nine, so as not to fall foul of the Seditious Meetings Act. But members had still drifted away, thinking it too dangerous to meet in any number. Many of those who had stayed were expecting quick results, being 'of opinion that ministers would not be able to surmount the difficulties and would therefore be forced to concede a reform in the House of Commons'. Place, though, recalled that 'I had no such expectations'. In his view, 'good and cheap government' would only come with electoral representation; until that point, oligarchical rule would always find more ways of running itself expensively into the ground, and 'would carry on to a standstill if necessary'. Despite all these pressures on the organization, eager members also insisted on starting up a magazine, which Place, as treasurer, insisted they could not afford. He was right, and they began to run up debts.

It was at this point that Place and Despard began to epitomize not the unity of the LCS but its contradictions. Place was a politician by nature, a committee man, for whom the reform movement was essentially about forming consensus, presenting petitions, promoting political views and negotiating with those in power. Despard was not without skills in these areas, and had shown a real appetite for drafting constitutions and organizing elections in the Bay, but he was also a man of action; now, action was on the horizon, and almost certainly getting closer. He had quite likely been a member of the United Irishmen since its genteel days under Wolfe Tone; now, it seemed, they were to be at the vanguard of a conflict many had long predicted. If so, then there might well come a moment, like the moment when he had freed Joshua Jones, when there was no longer any alternative to physical confrontation.

It is unlikely that Despard, or anyone in the LCS, made a sudden decision to abandon the political process for insurrectionary violence. Francis Place later stressed that the vast majority of members were reasonable men, with only a small minority of hotheads prepared to countenance physical force, but such a clear dividing line can only be drawn with hindsight. For most in the movement, what changed as the 1790s progressed was not their beliefs or goals, but the channels that were open to them to press those goals forward. Had armed insurrection broken out in Britain on the scale it would in Ireland, the vast majority of them would have taken up arms. The differences between them were differences of degree, based not so much on ideological commitment either to physical force or to the political process as on their constantly evolving views on how far things had gone, or were likely to go.

There were, nevertheless, various factors that marked out Despard as more likely than others to become involved in physical force. The most obvious was that this was his own professional area of expertise. The LCS and the British reform movement in general were sorely lacking in military skills; apart from Despard, they had perhaps no other member of high officer rank, and certainly none with such a distinguished record of combat. Moreover, the particular area of expertise in which Despard was unexcelled was in pulling together motley crews, soldiers of various backgrounds and little or no conventional fighting experience. It is entirely possible that part of him, at least, was yearning for the chance to do so. Nelson, for example, since they had last fired their cannons together, had spent years perfecting the technology of battle – designing faster, lighter and more effective guns and ships, with an often obsessive attention to engineering detail – and had refined his command into the most technically brilliant the world had ever seen. Despard, by contrast, had transformed a bunch of irregulars typically seen as the dregs of the British army into an unbeaten fighting force that had secured a new territory for Britain, but he had subsequently been whisked away from military command. He had a great deal still to prove, and an increasingly worthy enemy to prove it against. He was still, in his view, fighting for exactly the same cause: the rights and liberties of the British people, which the government of the day seemed intent on dismantling.

Yet military expertise does not imply bloodthirsty motives – quite possibly, in Despard's case, the opposite. If the LCS and the United Irish were moving towards armed conflict, his military authority could be invaluable not only to incite them but also to hold them back. He and Francis Place might, in fact, have been united in not wishing to see the movement destroy itself in a foolish rush to arms that would see them easily crushed and the entire movement discredited; but in this event it would be Despard, and not Place, who would be in a position to stop it. Of the many explanations that would be offered for Despard's subsequent actions, most would be less plausible than this one.

But there was another factor that might have set Despard on a different course from Place. Events since the Two Acts had spotlighted not only the military dimension of the struggle, but also the Irish dimension. Despard's attitude towards his own Irishness seems to have evolved around this time. There is little indication prior to 1796 that his Irish roots were important to his sense of identity. His family were from the ruling Anglican class, virtually a foreign population among the ethnic Irish. He returned to Ireland rarely, if at all, after his childhood, which was spent on a landed estate and in a few cloistered institutions. It is possible that he sensed the injustice of Irish politics at an early age, but his essential trajectory was away from his home and family towards a new life in ever more distant colonies from which he returned rarely and reluctantly. Yet there is little doubt that, from this point on, he felt the suffering of the Irish people keenly and – whether by inheritance, or rediscovery, or conversion – identified with their struggle as if it were his own. Ireland was still a colony, and in this sense its struggle was one that was alien to most of the LCS, but entirely familiar to Despard. It may even be that he discovered a certain symmetry between his roots and his cause. The Irish were the Shoremen of Britain, and thus the people for whom he had sacrificed his career. Now, it turned out, he was one of them after all.

If his motives are unclear, so is the question of what Despard's sympathy with the Irish cause meant in practice. It would be claimed later by British intelligence that he was already complicit by this stage in plotting an invasion of Ireland in conjunction with the French government and the Irish terrorists, but these sources are partial, contradictory and in other details wildly inaccurate. It is equally possible that he was a good deal more ambivalent. The revolutionary movement might have seemed from some angles to be converging with that of the Irish, and the Irish with the French, but there were also those within it who felt little kinship with this larger struggle. Tom Paine had, after all, been forced to flee for his life from France just as he had from Britain. As the French Revolution progressed, its ideals seemed to be drifting ever further away from those which Thomas Hardy and Wolfe Tone had celebrated five years before. The Thermidorean revolt, which had ended the rule of Robespierre in 1794, was characterized by the heavy-handed restoration of order and martial law; its rising star was the prodigiously talented young general Napoleon Bonaparte. War was shaping revolutionary France, much as it was shaping Britain, into a centralized, repressive, militaristic state, increasingly in love with imperial pomp and ever more draconian in its suppression of dissent among its own people. Essentially pacifist Paineite radicals such as Francis Place were already wondering whether the cause of democratic political reform would be any more favoured under Napoleon than under Pitt.

Wherever Despard stood on all these questions, he certainly went to ground after 1795. According to intelligence reports, he and Catherine moved from lodging to lodging every few months: St George's Fields, Soho, Belgrave Street, Berkeley Square. He might also have frequented safe houses used by the United Irish in the outskirts of London. He had long disappeared off his family's radar. In May 1796 his brothers John and Andrew had a brief correspondence about him; John was unable to furnish Andrew with his address. 'I have had no account of Marcus', as they still called their youngest brother, 'since July, when the newspapers mentioned his being taken up and carried before a magistrate for being amongst the mob that was breaking Mr. Pitt's windows.' 'I should not be surprised', John commented, 'to hear of his having gone to France, as his political sentiments agree perfectly with those of that country.' If a sentimental attachment to the Irish cause was rooted in Despard's childhood, it seems not to have rubbed off on the rest of his family. For them, his politics were those of a hostile foreign power. 'In my opinion his whole conduct for several years has been very foolish,' John added. 'Had he possessed some prudence he might now be in comfortable circumstances, instead of which I fear he is in great distress, as with his extravagant ideas, the price of his commission could not last long.'

How Despard supported himself financially during this period is indeed a mystery, though by no means the greatest one. When he emerged into the spotlight two years later, there would be other, more pressing questions to ask.

On 21 December 1796, the shadow politics of France, Ireland and the British underground came abruptly into focus when a large French fleet became visible in the waters of Bantry Bay on the south-west coast of Ireland, in striking distance of the crucial military and naval garrison at Cork. There were forty ships, with a total of almost fifteen thousand men on board, including the senior French general Lazare Hoche and none other than Wolfe Tone. Tone, it was now revealed, had left America for France earlier that year, and had succeeded – as much by naive honesty as cunning diplomacy – in convincing the French Directory that, given military support, the Irish would side with France against Britain. Ireland, he had told them, was ripe for becoming an independent republic, and for playing its part in encircling Britain.

The fleet drifted towards shore on a favourable wind, and waited for the command to attack. It never came. Lazare Hoche's frigate had become separated from the main force, and by the next day the weather had turned to squally rain and snow, with a bitter gale blowing off the coast. The French held tight through Christmas; the squall turned to roaring gales and even hurricanes. By 27 December the fleet had cut their cables and returned to France, harried by British warships out of Portsmouth.

Bantry Bay made several things very clear. A sustained French invasion would, according to all sides, wrest Ireland from Britain's grasp. Most of her forces were in Ulster, tied up with the suppression of the Defenders and the United Irish; Cork would fall, and with it the rest of the south. Thereafter the rest of the country would, in the assessment of the Irish parliament, wait 'not an hour' before rising up to support the invading forces. Wolfe Tone bitterly regretted that the forces of nature had confounded an attack that could otherwise not have failed. 'England', he reckoned, 'has not had such an escape since the Spanish Armada.'

For the British government, relief at the outcome was less potent than the shock of what might have been. The war was beginning to look unwinnable. Britain was running out of allies, the rest of mainland Europe suing for peace. England itself was running out of allies within Britain: signs were that the Scots would no more fight to the death for Church and King than the Irish. The north of England, too, was no longer to be relied on: war had hit industry hard, and there was mass unemployment and rising discontent. The City of London was wavering: the national debt had skyrocketed to its highest level in history, and the directors of the Bank of England were warning Pitt of a run on their cash stocks, perhaps even a collapse of the currency. Pitt sensed the writing on the wall, and gathered his cabinet to discuss suing for peace. Grenville and Portland opposed him bitterly, arguing that the war machine had to be cranked up to full throttle. It was do or die: if Britain lost the war, British society as they had always known it would be over. It was the closest the administration came to a rift at the heart of power. Arguments were loud and furious; Grenville stormed out of cabinet on several occasions and threatened to resign. Pitt caved in, and Britain soldiered on in an atmosphere of deepening dread.

On 16 April 1797 came the most dreadful blow of all. On a clear, beautiful morning, Admiral Lord Bridport, commander of the British navy's Channel Fleet, arrived at Spithead, off Portsmouth, where his ships rode at anchor in an orderly phalanx, decks freshly painted and flags fluttering in the breeze. He sent orders out, through the hive of tugs and rowing-boats that dipped and darted among the warships, that the Channel Fleet was to weigh anchor and sail to engage the French. Every single ship refused. Instead, they ran the red flag of mutiny up their masts and declared that they would no longer obey orders until their demands for minimum pay and conditions were met. If they were not, they warned, they would sail across the Channel on their own and join the French.

Bridport and the Admiralty responded with furious threats: if the ringleaders were turned over for execution without delay, the rest of the men would be spared. But the messages came back calm and considered. There were no ringleaders; this was a collective decision. Conditions in the navy were no better than slavery. The majority of ordinary sailors were not there of their own free will: they had been press-ganged, shipped out of debtors' prisons, rounded up in London and Ireland and marched on board in chains, prohibited from shore leave because their masters knew how many of them would desert at the first opportunity. They were subject to beatings and whippings at their captain's whim, half-starved, and their meagre pay, the level of which had been frozen since the reign of Charles II, rarely arrived. Many of the officer class sympathized with their plight, yet they had exhausted all legitimate means of complaint and received nothing but broken promises. They were conducting their action peacefully, guaranteeing that the ships would be perfectly maintained and that no officers would be harmed. But they were not moving until their demands were addressed.

As news of the Spithead mutiny spread, it became clear that the majority of the British population supported the navy's demands; it even began to look as if this was a flashpoint around which sullen resistance to the ever harsher demands of war might coalesce into open revolt. Pitt, agonized by the paralysis of the fleet so soon after the crisis at Bantry Bay, capitulated to the mutineers' demands. Tentatively, the mutiny began to unlock, officers allowed on board the ships and seamen coming ashore to discuss terms. But the Admiralty's bad faith was soon exposed: crucial reforms were delayed, and it became clear that they planned to break both mutiny and promises without remorse. The stand-off at Spithead was resumed, and the mutiny spread to the fleet protecting London at the Nore, in the Thames estuary. Here, despite the moderating influence of its spokesman Richard Parker, a Scottish schoolteacher who only months before had been bundled out of a debtors' prison and conscripted at Leith, the mutiny turned violent. Ships that attempted to break the blockade were fired on, their crews killed. After several days of stalemate, the 'floating republic', as it was becoming known, began to sail up the Thames, threatening the population of London.

This turned out to be a terminal miscalculation. The population of London, now transformed from supporters of the cause to its potential casualties, swung behind the government; the army, meanwhile, was able to remove marking buoys and strand the fleet in the muddy estuary where they could be besieged and starved out. The mutiny collapsed in a tangle of recriminations and accusations of conspiracy. The government claimed that the sailors had been put up to it by subversive elements – the LCS and United Irish – but found little convincing evidence; the sailors claimed in turn that the violence had been sparked by government agents planted on the ships. To begin with, Richard Parker was to stand trial for high treason, but Erskine was limbering up for another public defence along the lines of Hardy's and Tooke's, and the government switched the trial to a closed court-martial. Parker was convicted and hanged, blaming the 'turpitude' of his masters and sadly concluding that 'I ought to have known mankind better'. Pitt intensified the Reign of Terror once more with a Seduction from Duty Act, making sedition

Richard Parker presents the sailors' demands at the Nore

among the armed forces a capital offence. Wolfe Tone, who had tried and failed to persuade the French to act quickly and the United Irish to offer the floating republic their flag and support, mourned for the brief remainder of his life 'that precious opportunity, which we can never expect to return' in which 'the destiny of Europe might have been changed forever'.

Just as the French and Irish had been slow to exploit the chance of war, so the parliamentary opposition found themselves unable to snatch the opportunity for peace. Fox attempted to lead a rebellion against the war party, but many of his former supporters deserted him, fearing that events had gone too far for him to hold back the tide of violent revolt the fall of Pitt's administration would unleash. The point had been passed where a change of faces in government could rescue the country from its crisis. The Foxites took the controversial step of boycotting Parliament, refusing to dignify Pitt with an opposition. The LCS attempted to fill the political vacuum by co-ordinating mass peace demonstrations around the country, and announced a London assembly at St Pancras. All police leave in the capital was cancelled, and the army put on standby; three thousand gathered, but the meeting was broken up by magistrates and the armed forces. Francis Place, who felt that by now the society was being run 'very absurdly', resigned as treasurer. Despard, if a subsequent informant's evidence is to be trusted, was busy recruiting and organizing for the United Irishmen in London's Irish pubs.

Pitt, now lashed to the wheel of war, launched a massive drive to win the patriotic support of the nation. Parishes were enlisted to round up local militia support; Dundas offered subsidies to volunteer societies that were already up and running. A propaganda campaign was launched through newspapers, such as the *True Briton*, promoting 'the real rights of man': social order, paternalism, religious charity and state protection. A new paper, *The Anti-Jacobin*, was founded by Pitt's colleague George Canning, to which Pitt, Grenville and others contributed. Its opening editorial announced that 'the existence of a Jacobin faction, in the bosom of our country, can no longer be denied', and asserted the urgency of countering its 'vigilant, persevering, indefatigable and desperate' plans. To do so it hired the services of caricaturist James Gillray, who had previously lampooned Pitt on many occasions with characteristic savagery. Gillray eventually tired of the creative compromises involved in taking the government shilling, but for a while turned his obscene and prodigious talents to blackening the French and their Jacobin allies.

The patriotic campaign's tone was one of brittle nationalism in the face of adversity; behind its bluster, bile and bigotry lay a sobering acknowledgement of the nation's desperate straits. It was a great success, increasing the national and volunteer armies by as many as three hundred thousand new recruits, and its mood of embattled defiance united many more against the republican enemy. If there was mass discontent with the government and the war, there was mass support for them too, even in their darkest hour.

During the winter of 1797, the Duke of Portland's Home Office began to receive ever more concrete and alarming information from Samuel Turner, one of their most prized undercover informants. Turner was a lawyer and long-standing mole within the United Irishmen; he had recently become a member of a new executive, the Ulster Revolutionary Committee, which was apparently charged with attempting to co-ordinate an Irish uprising with a

Voltaire instructing the infant Jacobinism: *James Gillray, for* The Anti-Jacobin

French invasion. But the society, Turner reported, was divided. One faction, led by Thomas Emmet, was building its strategy around the French plans, but a vocal minority, led by Arthur O'Connor, was convinced that the Irish had the manpower to begin an uprising alone. According to British intelligence submitted to the Committee of Secrecy, they had calculated that they had the remarkably precise figure of 279,896 men under arms, outnumbering the British army by five to one. The O'Connor faction had been on several missions to England, where they had been meeting with a new society named the United Britons – at various times and places also called United Englishmen – which seemed to be a faction from within the LCS who had committed themselves to paramilitary action. One of the linchpins of this new configuration, according to Turner, was Colonel Edward Marcus Despard.

O'Connor's companion and envoy on his trips to London was a priest named James O'Coigley, and Turner had been privy to some of the conversations between them. In their discussions, they had revealed that there was to be some kind of uprising in London, which would be the cue for the French to launch their fleets and support the revolutionaries, first in Ireland and then on the British mainland. Some 'hubbub', it appeared, was about to go off.

On 28 February 1798, O'Coigley, O'Connor and three companions were arrested at Margate, just as they were about to sail for France. Father O'Coigley was caught redhanded: in his pocket was an 'Address of the Secret Committee of England to the Executive Directory of France'. 'With the tyranny of England,' it declared, 'that of all Europe must fall.' If the French were to attack Britain, 'myriads will hail their arrival with shouts of joy'. This was the first concrete evidence of the type of conspiracy the government had insisted was real for so long, and they announced it to press and public with gravity and quiet satisfaction. It was a triumph for the intelligence services: they had not only foiled a plot against the security of the nation, but had netted O'Connor, the ringleader. The case was to be heard in May, and the charge was to be high treason.

The Home Office sprang into action, arresting the other conspirators Turner had fingered in the plot. On 12 March, Despard was picked up and held in solitary confinement. But doubt was cast on the merit of the intelligence when his brother John, now a general, was also arrested and, according to witnesses, 'dragged from his family in a most inhuman manner and kept prisoner for several days'. This was less than a triumph for the intelligence services, and, in the recriminations and inquiries that followed, Edward Marcus was also released. Subsequent intelligence claims about Despard's activities would, and will always, need to be weighed against the fact that after four years of surveillance they were still able to arrest his distinguished and well-known brother by mistake.

But Despard would not be free for long. On 18 April, following three weeks of intensive surveillance, a meeting of the United Britons was raided at the George pub in Clerkenwell, and all nineteen participants were arrested. Despard was not among them. According to Francis Place, he and Despard had been together that night, and had known that there were spies about. The two of them had disagreed over what course to take. Place was by now of the view that the entire business with France and Ireland was no more than a destructive diversion. The French Directory had betrayed the revolution, and were no more their friends than Pitt was. The LCS had originally considered naming itself the Patriotic Club; it ought, for its own good and that of the country, to support the government in its war against a tyrannical enemy. Despard's views on this point are not recorded, but he and Place needed to agree on what to do about the United Britons. Place suggested reporting them to the magistrates, but Despard objected, 'as it would appear dishonourable'. He proposed, instead, that they should go to the meeting themselves and, as Place recalled, 'expose its mischievous tendency' and talk the members out of any reckless actions they had planned. In the event, for whatever reason, they did neither; but it would make little difference to Despard.

The next evening, the LCS Central Committee met in a pub in Drury Lane. Place was absent but had at the previous meeting proposed his idea that they should support the war effort. Just as the committee was discussing which patriotic militia they might join, they too were raided by police. Sixteen were arrested; parallel raids on corresponding society meetings in Birmingham and Manchester netted several more. It was the last time the LCS would ever attempt to meet. The next day, 20 April, Pitt renewed the suspension of habeas corpus. Over the next few days, they rounded up those on their wanted list who had not been at either meeting; on 22 April Despard was arrested again and held with the others. Some were released, but more than thirty were held pending the O'Connor trial, where the grand sweep of the conspiracy was to be unveiled.

The trial, when it came, was the most public test of the Reign of Terror and the government's grasp of the secret war since Hardy and Tooke's acquittal, and once again the political opposition was ready to challenge them. Outnumbered and outmanoeuvred in Parliament, they had realized that the most potent weapons at their disposal were the remaining traditional British liberties: the independence of the judiciary and the right to trial by jury.

Charles James Fox, Richard Sheridan and Henry Grattan all spoke on O'Connor's behalf, insisting that his cause was that of political reform in Ireland, and that it was a just and constitutional one. The government was chasing shadows, attempting to make traitors out of honest men; there were now thirty more being held without trial and without any better evidence. By and large, the jury agreed. Of the five accused, only Father O'Coigley, who had been caught with the treasonable note on his person, was found guilty and hanged. The other four, including O'Connor, were acquitted.

The verdict was another propaganda disaster. Pitt was furious and, roused to insults by the Foxite Irish Whig George Tierney, ended up fighting an illegal pistol duel with him on Putney Heath. Both missed, and the crisis of honour was satisfied. The government had no doubt that they had foiled a genuine plot but were unable to demonstrate that the French, or indeed the United Irish, had any knowledge of it. They had produced exactly the type of smoking gun for which they had been searching for so long, only to discover that a jury was still more inclined to interpret it as the solitary initiative of a sadly deluded priest. They had apparently, and not for the last time, leaped too soon. Samuel Turner had to pretend to his United Irish comrades that he had fled to France, before settling in Hamburg to continue his reports on the international wing of the republican movement. His pay was increased to a comfortable £30 a month and he continued to operate for another eight years. His cover was never broken.

Government intelligence, meanwhile, was still reporting a flurry of United Irish activity; this time, they would not be kept guessing about its meaning for long. The British army had stepped up their policy of 'dragooning' the

The Great Rebellion in Ireland

revolutionary hotbeds in Ireland with arrests, torture and burning, a policy designed to 'strike terror' into the rebels. On 23 May 1798, the rebels struck back. In and around Dublin, the United Irish militias took to the streets armed with guns and pikes, halting the mail coaches to the provinces as a signal for the rest of the country to join the rising. The initial insurrections were mostly suppressed, but in provinces such as Wexford the rebels held off the British army and Protestant loyalists for days; more insurrections followed, and more reprisals. The violent struggle ebbed and flowed for weeks. On 22 June, Pitt, despite George III's fears that he was leaving Britain 'in a very naked state', sent a huge British army of a hundred thousand under Lord Cornwallis to put down the rebellion. Despite Cornwallis's attempts to hold his troops back, they used their overwhelming force brutally, making little distinction between soldiers, militias and the hostile civilian population. Over thirty thousand Irish died, a number that by anyone's reckoning exceeded the casualties of Robespierre's terror in Paris.

The size of the British army had been geared to the possibility of French intervention, but none had arrived. Two days after the rising, Napoleon sailed the bulk of the French fleet over to Egypt, the expedition that would end in his first disastrous showdown with Nelson. He had not heard about Ireland when he left, and afterwards bitterly regretted his lost opportunity; but the truth was, as Wolfe Tone had latterly come to realize, that he had little solidarity with the Irish revolutionary cause. For him, Ireland was a promising route into Britain, and nothing more. A small French force arrived too late, finding the republicans scattered into fragmentary pockets of resistance; after a few successful skirmishes they were surrounded by Cornwallis and withdrew. Wolfe Tone was discovered among the prisoners of war and arrested. This time there could be no miscarriage of justice: if standing on the prow of an enemy fleet and directing them into battle against his own nation was not treason, then the word had no meaning. The Irish cause of self-government, and the British response to it, had taken Tone in five short years from genteel reformer to unambiguous traitor. Certain of being found guilty of high treason, he cut his throat in his prison cell. The Irish government were outraged to be cheated of the ceremonial moment; the Lord Chancellor thought he should have been hanged 'severed throat and all'.

Despard and his confederates, meanwhile, had been shuttled between police stations and prisons and had ended up in Coldbath Fields, a new purpose-built jail to the east of the city in Clerkenwell. While the Great Rebellion in Ireland ran, there had been no thought of releasing them; once it had passed, there were many who were extremely curious to discover how much they had known, on what grounds they had been detained and whether they were going to be charged. The events of the summer had thrown the United Irish and United Britons into the spotlight. The 'hubbub' that had been whispered about in the spring had proved that the Dublin rising was planned, and that some of the planning had apparently been conducted in the underworld of London. Government intelligence alluded to an actual armed uprising in London, which was to be the cue for a French invasion; some of these whispers that suggested such a rising might be aimed at assassinating the King, and also mentioned Colonel Despard as its 'leading person'. But the absence of French support for the rebellion seemed to tell a different story: that if any of the terrorists had been expecting Napoleon to fight the Irish cause, they had been deluding themselves. Events had shown either that the revolutionary network in London was extremely serious, or that it was not serious at all.

The Home Office's Committee of Secrecy, when it reported to the House of Commons, took the former line. It had found, it claimed, 'the clearest proofs of a systematic design' to 'overturn the laws, constitution and government' of Britain and Ireland, a design that had been undertaken by a 'system of secret societies' in league with hostile foreign powers. The paramilitary cell structure of the United Irish, by the committee's account, was replicated in the Irish districts of London. There were forty divisions of United Britons, each of forty or fifty men, who were armed or in the process of arming, and had been ready to light the fuse of Irish rebellion with a rising in London, giving the United Irish their cue and also tying up British forces on their home turf. One informer claimed that Despard had estimated, in a pub, that it would be possible to gain temporary control of London with a force of 1,500 men, though many more – around fifty thousand – would be needed to make a serious attempt to hold it. The colonel was, by several informers' accounts, if not a fixture on the scene, at least regularly observed. He was distinctive in his gentlemanly dress and in his habits, which included constantly wearing a dark-blue greatcoat against the cold: he seemed not fully to have adjusted after his time in the tropics. He was easily recognizable in working men's pubs as the only customer carrying a green silk umbrella – a recent and genteel fashion – and drinking brandy and water.

Yet there were troublesome credibility gaps in this version of events. One of the unnamed informers on Despard, who had assembled an allegedly detailed picture of his movements and contacts, had reported that Despard's main connection with the United Irish was a senior member named Hamilton Rowan, to whom the colonel had introduced the informer and with whom he had continued to meet after the O'Coigley arrest. This was allegedly a contact about which Catherine had had deep misgivings; she had tried to discourage her husband from meeting him. Alexander Hamilton Rowan was a known republican and United Irishman, but all this was quite impossible: he had left Ireland for America several years earlier – before even Wolfe Tone – and had by nobody's account ever returned. Francis Place insisted that the Committee of Secrecy report had exaggerated proceedings 'in a most scandalous manner' – claiming, for example, that 'there were forty divisions of the United Britons in

London where there was not *one* such division'. The society, he maintained, had been 'only in an incipient state'; the meeting he and Despard had considered interrupting had been no more than an exploratory one to discuss whether such a society was worth establishing. Once again, the United Britons were either a serious paramilitary force or a figment of the Home Office's imagination.

While this debate rumbled on, it began to emerge that the conditions in which the suspects were being held in Coldbath Fields were spartan in the extreme. Despard was being held in a cell that was seven foot square, with no glass in the windows, no fire, no candle, no books or personal possessions, and set below ground level where it flooded when it rained. He was being sustained on nothing but bread and water. Catherine was not allowed to visit him in his cell, and could manage only snatched conversations with him through the bars. She had written immediately to the Duke of Portland, protesting that Despard was being held in conditions more typical for 'a vagabond than a gentleman or a state prisoner'. Portland had ignored her protest, so she began to petition his under-secretary. He promised to mention the complaint to his minister, but the summer came and went without response.

Catherine began to take her complaints to opposition MPs, just as Despard himself had done on his return to London. She had more success, rapidly locating the one man who was prepared to take up her case. The young independent MP Sir Francis Burdett, who had a reputation for speaking out against injustice and fighting the under-dog's corner, had also been looking into conditions in Coldbath Fields. At a dinner party he had been shown letters written by some of the thirty mutineers from the

Nore who were still incarcerated there; the letters had been written in tobacco juice (and, allegedly, blood), scrawled onto paper with skewers and smuggled out, and they reported the same conditions Catherine was attempting to bring to Parliament's attention. Burdett and Catherine joined forces to wring a response to these accusations out of Pitt's administration.

Sir Francis Burdett was one of a kind, and would remain so throughout the long and distinguished career in which he was in the late 1790s taking his first steps. He was, in William Hazlitt's words, 'a plain, unsophisticated, unaffected English gentleman' for whom 'there is no honest cause that he dare not avow, no oppressed individual that he is not forward to succour'. He was also, according to Hazlitt, 'a very honest, very good tempered and a very good looking man'. A baronet of noble family who could trace his ancestry back to William the Conqueror, he had entered politics in order to reform the injustices of the system and had been entirely comfortable with doing so by buying his seat in 1796 from one of the boroughs belonging to the Duke of Newcastle. His first cause had been vigorous opposition to Pitt's Reign of Terror, which he saw as unjust, counterproductive and fundamentally un-British. 'The war against the growth of French opinions', he argued, 'seems to me to be exactly the way to encourage them instead of destroying them.' In his view, 'a good and free government has nothing to apprehend, and everything to hope, from the liberty of the press'; by contrast, a regime which 'dreaded the scrutinising eye of liberty' was not government but 'despotism'. Britain, by allying itself with the unreconstructed monarchies of Europe against the French, was coming to resemble them.

Burdett was a great admirer of Charles James Fox – he had called him 'the wonder of the age' – but he did not sit with the Whigs. In June 1798 he had applied to do so, but they had blackballed him from membership. He shared some of their causes, but not all; his closest ally and political mentor was Horne Tooke. By instinct he was a conservative, though a radical one, who was more closely in sympathy with Tooke's idea that liberty was already enshrined in ancient and longstanding principles of British law. His adherence to Tooke's pedantic antiquarian views on this point was his only flaw, according to Hazlitt, who himself believed that liberty 'is but a modern invention', and in any case 'whether old or new is not the less desirable'. Excluded by the Whigs, Burdett had joined the LCS; by 1798, he and Despard were among the very few gentleman members who had stood their ground against the purges. He had known Despard before his imprisonment, and they would remain close friends right up to his execution. He was perhaps the closest of Despard's colleagues in his ideology, and certainly the one who would be boldest in taking risks on his behalf.

Burdett paid several fact-finding visits to Coldbath Fields during the autumn of 1798. He confirmed Catherine's stories about her husband's cruel treatment, and spread the word that more and more people, prisoners and public alike, had begun to refer to the prison as 'the Bastille'. Eventually he was barred from entering by a letter from the Duke of Portland, which also instructed the governors of Newgate and Tothill Fields to deny him access to their prisons. But Burdett was undaunted, and began to win over more politically respectable figures to his cause. In November he turned up again with John Reeves, the founder of the loyalist militia network, now the conservative magistrate for Middlesex. Reeves succeeded in persuading the governors to move Despard to an upstairs room with a fire, and to allow Catherine to visit

Sir Francis Burdett attempting to inspect Coldbath Fields
(James Gillray)

him. By this stage she was becoming distraught at his condition. His near-starvation diet had wizened him, putting years on his appearance. The early winter had been bitter, and he suffered the cold worse than most, his legs becoming ulcerated with frost.

When the suspension of habeas corpus came up for review in December, Burdett mounted a concerted attack against its current abuses. Catherine wrote a letter that was read in the House of Commons and subsequently reported in the press, detailing the conditions her husband had suffered, 'without either fire or candle, chair, table, knife, fork, a glazed window or even a book to read'. Another opposition MP, John Courtenay, endorsed her account, and added a flourish of his own. On the occasion of his visit, he had flagged down a carriage and asked the driver to take him to the Bastille. The carriage had set off, and Courtenay had checked his understanding of the destination. 'Oh yes, I know it,' the driver had assured him. 'Everybody knows the Bastille in Coldbath Fields.'

The government, far from conceding to pressure, went on the attack. The attorney-general, Sir John Scott, who had been responsible for pushing much of the terror legislation through Parliament, flatly denied that conditions in Coldbath Fields were anything like those that had been represented. He claimed to have spoken to a witness who had met Despard and found him satisfied with his treatment. As for Catherine's letter, according to Scott, Despard 'had not any knowledge' of it, and 'if he had, would have disapproved of it'. The implication was that there was mischief afoot, and that Catherine's letter was not what it seemed. 'It was a well-written letter,' Scott pointed out, 'and the fair sex would pardon him, if he said it was a little beyond their style in general.' Catherine's blackness remained, as ever, invisible; her gender was reason enough to suggest that she might be a pawn of subversive elements who were exploiting her plight for their own ends. George Canning seconded this opinion; Burdett assured the House that Catherine 'is not so illiterate as Mr. Canning would have us believe'. The attorney-general responded with an implied threat that 'there were some wives who had met with much indulgence, in not being taken up and confined as well as their husbands' – it would not be advisable for Catherine to press her case much harder. Burdett's report on conditions in Coldbath Fields was put to the House for recommendation, and failed by 147 votes to 6. Habeas corpus was suspended once more, and Despard still held with neither trial nor release in sight.

Throughout 1799, Despard, Catherine and Francis Burdett continued their lobbying to improve conditions in the prison, and made some small but slow progress. Despard was now allowed to read books, and he requested material on abstract mathematics and navigation. He wrote several times to the Duke of Portland, and once asked for his sentence to be commuted to transportation to Australia; Portland scrawled 'impossible' on the letter. During the summer, the government began to have second thoughts about keeping so many political undesirables confined in the same place, where they might 'continue the conspiracy'; the mutineers and revolutionaries were scattered around the provinces. In August, Despard was moved to Shrewsbury.

In the outside world, the Reign of Terror was yet again extended. New acts were passed that prohibited the LCS and the United societies by name; on the same day a new Combination Act was brought in, banning the assembly of workers for the purpose of negotiated demands or strike action. This was a strong measure, effectively extending the ban on political societies into the world of industry, and it would have the counterproductive effect of radicalizing sectors of the workforce that had previously shown little interest in politics. 'The republicans', one spy reported back, 'are drinking Mr. Pitt's health.'

It seemed finally, though, as if the crises that had combined to drive Britain towards collapse in 1797 and 1798 had begun to lift. Napoleon's departure for the Mediterranean calmed the immediate threat of Britain being invaded, and his famous defeat by Nelson on the Nile tipped the balance of war back towards Britain's favour. Trade with the West Indies was able to pick up as Britain capitalized on her naval supremacy, and the worst of the food shortages eased off. But it was not long before the pendulum swung back. All it took, initially, was a succession of two poor harvests in 1799 and 1800 to expose the brittleness of the new economy. Grain prices soared, doubling in six months; by the spring of 1800 there were serious food shortages once more, with large swathes of the population spending almost their entire income on flour and bread.

But it was the government's handling of the problem that turned it into another crisis. Portland, as Home Secretary, was reluctant to meddle with state distribution, taxation, quotas or maximum prices; his preferred solution was to allow the free market to send stocks to the parts of the country where they were most needed. But where they were most needed was not where they commanded the highest prices. Adam Smith's invisible hand diverted the food away from the poor, and large sections of the country began to boil out of government control. There were more naval mutinies as rations were cut to starvation levels. In the north, government spies reported mass assemblies listening intently to speakers explaining how the government was deliberately starving them, and why the only solution was for the country to make peace with France, and the people to seize power from the monarch. It was reported in the House of Commons that 'the walls of the manufacturing towns throughout the kingdom were too small to contain the quantity of sedition that was written' on them.

By September it was not only the provinces that were in outright revolt, but the centre of London itself. A mass meeting at the Haymarket swelled too large for the police to close it down, and erupted through the city for several days in scenes of looting and mass disturbance not seen since the Gordon Riots. George III was shot at in the Drury Lane Theatre by James Hadfield, a discharged soldier who later turned out to be a lunatic following his own messianic plan, but the crowds that assembled outside to witness the King's survival were not cheering but jeering. The government was convinced that the shadowy forces of destabilization, the LCS and the United Britons, were behind the explosion of demands for peace, democracy and revenge on the ruling class; they were convinced, too, that they were assisting the French in sending *agents provocateurs* to Britain to stir up the mobs. It was, once again, no time to free political dissidents who were safely under lock and key.

Yet among the starvation and the riots, it was Ireland, and political reform, that was finally to topple the Prime Minister. After the Great Rebellion of 1798, it had become clear that a new constitutional arrangement was needed for a hostile colony where the status quo could only be maintained by force of arms. There were essentially two options: either to relax the discrimination against the Catholic and Dissenting majority and allow the mass of the people more representation in their own affairs, or to extend the current military regime into a permanent state of martial law. The first had its passionate supporters in Parliament, among them Fox and Burdett, but the second had the weight of numbers to force it through. Pitt attempted to combine the carrot with the stick, offering limited emancipation for Catholics in exchange for extending direct rule from Westminster. But even this was too much for George III, for whom any concession to the Catholic population was a concession too far. It was, he claimed, 'the most Jacobinical thing I ever heard of!' He insisted that 'I shall reckon any man my personal enemy who proposes any such measure'. Pitt was left with no option but to resign.

It was not the end of the road for Pitt: he would be back for a final term in a few years' time, to steer the ship of state through its next crisis. But his great period of tenure was over. It had both risen and fallen on his original cause of political reform, a cause that had been otherwise conspicuous by its absence from Parliament during his office – and one on which, ironically, he privately shared more common ground with Despard than with most of his own party. He was replaced by his colleague Henry Addington, who steered a similar course but followed the prevailing wind by relaxing his predecessor's grip on terror. In February 1801, the suspension of habeas corpus came up for renewal once more; this time it was allowed to lapse.

Despard could now, constitutionally at least, no longer be held without trial. His imprisonment, like Pitt's fall from office, had been circumscribed by events in Ireland, even though his connection to them remained unproven. Yet he was not freed immediately. As soon as the suspension of habeas corpus lapsed, Portland issued an order for him to be transferred from Shrewsbury to Tothill Fields prison in London – modern King's Cross – where the formalities of arranging bail could be carried out. This was, as Despard and his supporters saw it, a ploy to throw some last-minute obstacles in the way of releasing the prisoners at a point when fears of United Britons activity were once more preoccupying the Home Office. Despard was asked to find £1,000 to guarantee his bail, and to drop any complaints about unlawful detention and prison conditions. He refused. He wanted a trial, a public showcase where his treatment could be weighed against the government's evidence, and he was quite prepared to wait in jail until he got it. But the government baulked at the prospect; instead, they rushed through a Habeas Corpus Suspension Indemnity Act to protect themselves against any such complaints. Sir Francis Burdett gave his personal guarantee for Despard's future conduct, and he was released in April 1801.

Despard was greeted, for the first time in nearly twenty years, with something approaching a hero's welcome. During his confinement his former secretary in the Bay colony, James Bannantine, had published his memoirs of their time together and the shabby treatment Despard had received from the government thereafter, and his version of the tale had become increasingly well known through Burdett's campaigning efforts. Despard, by Bannantine's account, had served his country with astonishing bravery and loyalty and had been laid low by malicious rumours and official penny-pinching, before being scapegoated by the government for his troublesome complaints against them. The memoirs of the future radical MP Henry Hunt, published some years later, suggest that this version of Despard's story was widely held, and Hunt even projected it forward into its final act with disturbing accuracy, helped, perhaps, by hindsight. 'He is too honest ever to gain redress,' Hunt claimed he was told at the time of Despard's confinement. 'If he would crouch and truckle to his persecutors, he might not only be set at liberty, but all that they have robbed him of would be returned. This, however, he will never do.' Despard, Hunt was convinced, would persevere with his claims for redress, but 'if he be troublesome, they will stick at nothing, and I should not be in the least surprised if they were ultimately to have some of their spies to swear away his life'.

The timing of Despard's release coincided exactly with an upswing in the public mood, and a lifting of the veil of war and terror that had oppressed the nation for so long. Within a few months of becoming Prime Minister, Addington negotiated a peace with France; the deal was eventually signed at Amiens in March 1802. It was greeted with a massive outpouring of public joy: crowds celebrated on the streets of London, and mail-coaches festooned with flags and with 'Peace with France' chalked on their sides spread the news up and down the land. Peace allowed Addington to scale back war taxes and army conscription, and to eliminate food shortages, and the spectre of food riots and insurrection faded, at least from public view.

But it was peace more or less on Napoleon's terms, and uncomfortably close to peace at any price. Fox, who had long led the opposition in condemning Pitt and Grenville's arrogant and intransigent diplomacy, declared it 'an excellent thing', and added mischievously that he 'did not like it any the worse for being so very triumphant a peace for France'. Grenville, Portland and Dundas were privately disgusted, stung by Fox's mockery; they considered it peace on dishonourable terms, with Britain forced to restore most of her conquests to France, Spain or Holland, keeping only Trinidad and Ceylon. Pitt complained that the public joy was 'undiscriminating': everyone was celebrating, but nobody was asking what the terms really meant. The hawks also thought it a weak peace that would be immediately infringed and disputed, and would last only until Napoleon had recovered enough strength to attack again. They would be proved right. In the meantime, a nation emerged blinking from the fog of war into the light of peace, and began to ask itself why it had acted as it did. Despard, emerging at the same time, was a beneficiary of the new mood.

An annual chronicle of character sketches, *Public Characters of 1801–2*, offered a crisp commentary on this cusp in time. It began with an essay on Henry Addington, and devoted a subsequent chapter to Colonel Despard, the *cause célèbre* of the Reign of Terror, which was already coming to be seen as an embarrassing, or perhaps unfortunate, bout of public hysteria. Despard, it maintained, 'has met with very harsh treatment', especially for someone who remained innocent of any charge and was released, not for the first time, without a stain on his character. It rehearsed his military and administrative career in similar terms to Bannantine's, and blamed Grenville for reducing him to penury despite his assurances that 'his services were not forgotten, and would receive their reward'. It reminded the reader that 'during the period of terror, when all men were taught to believe that some secret conspiracy was about to burst forth', Despard, 'a gentleman often employed in confidential situations', was arrested without charge and confined in freezing conditions where 'he was obliged, during the rigours of a hard winter, to jump from his table to his bed, and from his bed to the ground, in order to produce such an increased circulation of his blood as should diffuse warmth through his half-frozen veins'. 'In the course of this narrative,' it concluded, 'great care has been taken not to mention anything that might be deemed offensive'; but the thrust was clear. Despard began to be mentioned favourably in the press, the *Monthly Magazine* in 1802 becoming perhaps the first to dub him with the epithet 'unfortunate'. His detention, whatever else it might have achieved, had been no propaganda coup for the government.

It would become even more embarrassing the following year when Sir Francis Burdett stood for election in Middlesex, the sprawling, ever-expanding and slum-ridden constituency to the north and west of London proper. The incumbent, William Mainwaring, was a justice of the peace who had tried to block the investigation into conditions in Coldbath Fields, and Burdett used this to highlight his own platform of justice and reform. He refused to spend any money on his election campaign and began the polls trailing some distance behind his opponent, but as the fifteen days of voting progressed he received a massive groundswell of popular support for his brand of radicalism and his opposition to both of the main political groupings. Two days before polls closed, when he was still five hundred votes behind, a massive popular demonstration filled the Strand, Pall Mall and Piccadilly with his supporters chanting 'Burdett for ever! No Bastille!' When he pipped his rival at the post, the result was greeted by a mob singing the French revolutionary anthem 'Ça Ira' outside the King's palace at Kew. Political wits discovered to their delight that his name was a near anagram of 'Frantic Disturber', but outside the Westminster elite the epithet that clung to Burdett was 'the idol of the mob', the only man acknowledged to speak with their voice in Parliament. It was not forgotten that he had risen to this position through his support of Despard's cause. Robert Southey, who had followed the news of

Despard's incarceration with interest, observed that 'merely upon the ground of having raised his voice against this new species of punishment, Sir Francis Burdett has become the most popular man in England'.

Despard, meanwhile, was a good deal harder to locate. He and Catherine disappeared from the public eye. Some said that they had gone to Ireland, though the espionage report of such a visit is uncorroborated and, if it took place, his family were unaware of it. He had, once more, gone to ground, leaving little clear evidence of his state of mind. His request to the Home Secretary for a sentence of transportation had suggested that he might be through with the revolutionary struggle, yet his truculence in wishing to hold the government to account for his treatment seemed to suggest otherwise. In public, he was forgotten as Burdett took centre stage; behind the scenes, the government remained extremely interested in him. The secret service lost his trail until February 1802, at which point the Despards were rediscovered living in lodgings in Lambeth.

Thereafter, they were watched closely. The Home Office had begun to detect an increase in volume in the reports being brought to them about the United Irish and United Britons, which suggested that the societies had not disappeared in the wake of the Great Rebellion but had merely gone deeper underground, setting up hermetic cell structures unknown to all but the high command and thus harder to penetrate. Specific questions about Despard, though, continued to draw a blank. The consensus, according to the Home Office's informants, seemed to be that he 'does not feature very prominently'.

More worrying, or promising, was intelligence that was beginning to filter out from the battalions of army infantry that had recently been relocated to London to guard royal residences and public buildings. Here, it seemed, there was a conspiracy afoot. A trickle of soldiers came forward independently to inform the authorities that their colleagues were being infiltrated by a secret organization that was scouting out likely volunteers to participate in an armed uprising; some claimed its objective was the assassination of the King. The conspiracy was, by all accounts, already a large one: estimates suggested that several hundred infantry might already be involved. One soldier who had allowed himself to be led on, Arthur Graham, found himself in the Flying Horse pub in Newington being introduced to 'the Colonel that was confined so long in the Bastille'.

More flesh was put on the bones of this conspiracy by Thomas Windsor, a disaffected private in the Third Battalion of the 1st Foot Guards whose application for discharge from the service had been refused. He had joined the plot, hoping in part to find some evidence he could use to renegotiate his own position, and had stumbled upon a 'name of consequence' he recognized: Colonel Despard. He had signed up with the Home Office as an agent, and decided to undertake a little freelance entrapment, hoping to find a way of making Despard break his cover. He had sought him out in a pub in Tower Hill, engaged him in conversation, and offered to bring along some new volunteers to the cause. Despard had suggested a subsequent meeting in the Oakley Arms in Lambeth. He also, according to Windsor, outlined the object towards which all this infiltration was heading: the assassination of the King on his way to the House of Commons, which would be the signal for a broader conspiracy, spread across the length and breadth of the country, to make itself known, 'and that then the people would be at liberty'.

The Home Office swiftly collated all their related

intelligence but, to their disappointment or relief, Windsor's story failed to check out. Two other informants had been in the pub, and neither of them could confirm the story. One refused to comment, and the other told the government agents what he thought they wanted to hear but was unable to add any detail. But Windsor claimed that he had details of a time and place where all would become clear. There was to be a meeting at the Oakley Arms on 16 November, where Despard and the high command of the United Britons would be putting the finishing touches to their planned regicide. The Home Office weighed the evidence against the possible consequences, and decided that they would intervene.

Around nine o'clock on 16 November 1802, three Southwark policemen went to a prearranged location around the corner from the Oakley Arms, where they met a large body of Bow Street officers. The group burst through the door of the pub, declaring loudly that they had a search warrant, rushed *en masse* up the stairs to the club-room on the first floor, and threw open the door. There were thirty men inside, some in work clothes, some in regimental uniforms, and, conspicuous among them, Despard – the only person in the room dressed in the manner of a gentleman, and carrying a green silk umbrella.

Despard, at this point, allegedly shouted 'One and all, follow me!' and made his way towards the door, only to find it blocked by more officers coming up the stairs. At this point he stopped, and asked to see a search warrant. One of the Southwark constables waved one in front of his face, but refused to allow him time to read it; Despard, in turn, 'indignantly' refused to allow himself to be searched. Constables began searching the other men, and found 'unlawful oaths' in the pockets of three of them. The oaths were headed 'Constitution: The Independence of Great Britain and Ireland. An Equalisation of Civil, Political and Religious Rights; an ample Provision for the Heroes who shall fall in the Contest'. They affirmed that the bearers would 'endeavour to the utmost of my power to obtain the objects of this Union' and that they had sworn themselves to secrecy. The oaths constituted grounds for arrest under the new terror legislation. Despard was now searched despite his protests, but nothing was found on him. All were escorted from the premises to the cells of the county prison for examination.

Despard was once again in custody, and this time he would be charged. It would be high treason.

7

TRAITOR

The charge of high treason was slow to emerge. The day after the arrest, Despard was taken from the local prison to the magistrates' office, where he was interrogated by Sir Richard Ford, now knighted and promoted to chief magistrate. Ford had remained the chief spymaster and co-ordinator of intelligence reports on the LCS and its off-shoots throughout the 1790s; among his files were stacks of private correspondence from figures such as Horne Tooke and perhaps Despard himself, all confiscated, collated and even indexed. Ford was the man with the facts at his fingertips, but he was only the first link in the chain of inquiry that would now seek to hold Despard to account. The following day, accompanied by Catherine, Despard was transported in chains to Whitehall and examined for several hours by the Privy Council. No details emerged, but the interrogations were clearly making slow progress. The next day the Privy Council called him back for a further six hours of questioning. At the end of this he was committed to Newgate prison, still awaiting charges.

The government had many delicate calculations to make, and less damning evidence than they might have wished. On the one hand, they were convinced that they had foiled a serious plot, and an imminent one; on the other hand, as with O'Connor and O'Coigley, they had nagging doubts that they might have jumped too soon. Their evidence was partial in some crucial respects, and in others difficult to present in open court. Sir Richard Ford had many intelligence agents embedded in the plot, and he had to consider whether he could afford to blow their cover by summoning them as witnesses. Fine judgement was required in charging the conspirators: should some be released, in order to focus on those against whom the evidence of conspiracy was strongest? The most promising outcome of the raid was that they had caught Despard more or less red-handed, at a private meeting where illegal oaths had been recovered; yet some of their best evidence suggested that the plot predated Despard's involvement, and that he had become a player in it only recently, if at all. He was the most high-profile catch, and it was for this reason that Thomas Windsor had focused on him. Yet though he might have been caught red-handed, he might also turn out to be a red herring.

The newspapers had heard about the raid, and were sniffing eagerly for details, but the Home Office embargoed the story for several days. The first public reports alluded to a plot within the ranks of the armed forces, and suggested that Despard was likely to be charged under the Seduction from Duty Act, which had been passed after the naval mutinies. But by the end of November, a fuller story was confirmed. Despard was located at the centre of a conspiracy that rapidly became known as the Despard Plot. He, along with a dozen accomplices, was to face charges of high treason on the grounds that the plot had compassed and imagined the death of the King.

The details were sensational; as the *St. James's Chronicle* put it, of 'so shocking a description that we cannot mention it without pain and horror'. The plot was alleged to have reached an advanced stage; the purpose of the meeting at the Oakley Arms had been to fine-tune the arrangements before the King's journey to open Parliament the following week. Three Guards regiments had been secretly infiltrated, and were to act in conjunction with dozens of divisions of the United Irish and United Britons that had been covertly organized across London. The King's carriage was to be attacked, by some accounts using a ceremonial Turkish cannon that had recently been captured in Egypt and was being displayed in St James's Park, along the King's route. The King was to be assassinated, and this was to be the signal for the Guards who had been infiltrated to take control of the Houses of Parliament, the Tower of London and the Post Office. All communications out of London would be blocked, which, as in Ireland in 1798, would be the signal for the revolutionary cells and infiltrated regiments in the provinces to rise.

It was a high-risk strategy. The charge was shocking, and it immediately dominated the front-page news. Britain might be at peace, but if all this were true, she was still in mortal danger. If the Despard Plot were a reality, it was high treason by anyone's reckoning, more serious than any of the shadow battles of the Reign of Terror. But its grandiosity also aroused suspicion. It seemed implausible, calculated by its seriousness to stifle debate and to blacken the names of the accused. Despard had already been held for years and eventually released without charge; some had even predicted at the time that something like this might be on the cards. The trial would be at least as crucial to the government as Hardy's eight years earlier and, if the verdict went against them, at least as damaging. By the same token, if they could demonstrate the reality of the Despard Plot in court, they would have vindicated not only the pre-emptive action they had taken but the decade of terror that had preceded it. The dark days many had hoped were behind them had been brought back to life, and the verdict on Despard, one way or another, would rewrite their history.

It was Sir Francis Burdett, along with Catherine, who was the first to leap to Despard's defence. He enlisted his mentor Horne Tooke, who had subsequently become a fellow independent MP, to join him in starting a defence committee, which set up its headquarters at Tooke's house in Wimbledon. Tooke publicly proclaimed 'the innocence of the virtuous Despard'; Burdett began raising money for a defence fund and engaging a legal team. Thomas Hardy, the most famous treason trial veteran, also lent his support. The government was ready for this, and had informants well situated. John Moody, a shoe warehouse-man from Carnaby Street who had been a long-time double agent within the LCS and secretary to Tooke's election committee in 1796, managed to get himself engaged once more. Moody reported that funds were arriving from a small circle of wealthy sympathizers. Lord Cloncurry, an Irish peer close to the republican cause who had himself been imprisoned in the Tower of London, had given a donation of £700, which Burdett himself had at least matched. Burdett was allegedly rattled by what might come out during the trial, some of which, Moody reported, he feared might be 'damned awkward' for him personally.

The government was busy on several other fronts. By the new year of 1803 they were ready to call a pre-trial commission at the Sessions House of Surrey County Court in Horsemonger Lane, on 10 January. It would be presided over by the Lord Chief Justice, Lord Ellenborough, a staunch advocate of the Reign of Terror who was of the opinion that 'criminal laws could not be too severe', and prosecuted by the attorney-general, Sir Spencer Perceval, who would later become Prime Minister – famously, the only serving Prime Minister ever to be assassinated. The Sessions House adjoined the Surrey County Jail, and the surrounding streets were packed almost as tightly as they would be for the execution on the same site a few weeks later. A 'vast assemblage' of police and armed guards cordoned the building, and those with the coveted permission to attend the session had to fight their way through crowds that had assembled from before dawn in the hope of catching a glimpse of Despard.

When the colonel appeared under guard, he was 'dressed rather shabbily, with a plaid cotton handkerchief around his neck', but he impressed the crowd with the dignity of his bearing. Lord Ellenborough read the charge of high treason. He made it clear that he had 'no intention of directing' the court or biasing their judgement, yet he could not withhold his 'horror at the meditated consequence' of the plot. Despard, he announced, would be tried alone; the trials of eight of his confederates would follow. Of the men arrested at the Oakley Arms, around half had been freed, and four more, all soldiers, had agreed to turn King's Evidence in exchange for immunity from prosecution.

It was Despard who was the first to have his indictment announced, and to be asked who had chosen to represent him. He replied that Serjeant Best had been engaged on his behalf. William Draper Best was, like Thomas Erskine, a barrister and a Whig MP; he had been appointed serjeant-at-law in 1799 and was among the most highly rated advocates in the country. He had a reputation for quality rather than demagoguery, clever and pointed arguments rather than charisma or fluency, which made him more successful at the Bar than in the House. He came without Erskine's baggage of partisan conviction, which made him a subtle choice: seemingly conciliatory but signalling, perhaps ominously for the government, that the case was likely to be defended on the letter of the law rather than spirited appeals to the jury.

The government was also extremely busy with the selection of the jury, the crucial obstacle on which the previous treason trials had been wrecked. The gulf between the apparatus of justice and the jury of the people was, from the prosecution's point of view, by far the most problematic aspect of the case. Given the partial nature of their evidence, the verdict ran the risk of becoming a referendum on the Reign of Terror, for which their track record was very poor. The Lord Chief Justice's office circulated a list of the first hundred or so names in the jury pool to anyone who might be able to identify them and offer insights into their political sympathies. The recipients were instructed to identify any name with which they were familiar, and to grade it in the margin: 'G' for a good man and true, 'B' for a bad one, and 'D' for doubtful. The results might be regarded not merely as a striking example of the reach of the Home Office and magistrates' intelligence, but as a useful ballpark statistic in the ongoing dispute as to what proportion of the British population were loyalists or revolutionaries (bearing in mind that the qualifications for jury service still excluded the lower orders). Sixty-five of the list earned a 'G' rating, thirty-five 'B' (including one, a Southwark brewer named William Holcomb, 'very bad'), and ten 'D'. The list was adjusted accordingly, and after some tenacious haggling by the defence, the eventual jury comprised eight 'G's, three 'B's and a single 'D' whose views were unknown.

This was a crucial battle for the prosecution, and one which they secured effectively enough, although the eventual composition was only slightly loaded in their favour compared to a random sample. On 5 February the court reconvened for the preliminaries, and the jury members were sworn in. The clerk of the court concluded by asking Despard, 'How will you be tried?' Despard, unaware of the formulaic response required – 'By God and my country' – looked at him and replied, 'I suppose that has already been decided.' When made aware of his error, he apologized, saying that he meant no offence, he had simply found the question 'somewhat strange'. His response might simply have been truer than he knew; or he might have known perfectly well that it was the truth.

On Monday 7 February, when the trial began, the preliminaries had in theory paved the way for a straight-forward prosecution. Despard had been cleanly separated from the other defendants held after the Oakley Arms raid, and the case was to focus on him entirely. The charge of treason would be amply demonstrated if it could be shown that the Despard Plot had compassed the death of the King. The prosecution was in the hands of Sir Spencer Perceval who had a mountain of evidence, though much of it was complicated, some of it was self-contradictory, and most of it was unconnected to Despard. His task, as prosecuting counsel, was effectively twofold: to bind Despard into the plot that now bore his name, and then to bind the plot into an attempt on the King's life.

The indictment set out a series of 'overt acts' which, Perceval asserted, were all that was needed to weave

Despard, the plot and the crime of high treason insepar-
ably together. Despard had been present at the Oakley
Arms, at a meeting where soldiers had been seduced from
their duty, members of the society had been discovered
with illegal oaths, and the death of the King had not only
been compassed and imagined but planned in chilling
detail. This was treason on multiple grounds, old and new:
the newly treasonous offences of stirring up insurrection
in the ranks and membership of an illegal society, and
regicide, the heart of the time-honoured medieval code. All
of these, according to Perceval, followed directly from
Despard's undisputed presence in the club-room on the
evening of 16 November. This undisputed fact was,
Perceval argued, prima facie evidence of guilt. Everyone
else in the pub was 'from the lowest orders of society,
common soldiers, common labourers, and journeymen'.
'How', he asked, 'is this to be accounted for innocently?'
Despard was the only gentleman in company that was
'planning a most desperate act of treason to be executed
the very next week, by the lowest and basest of society'; he
could hardly claim that he was there by accident. More
plausible, surely, was the explanation that he was 'the
leader to whom the rest looked for advice'. The fact of his
presence, combined with his social class, was enough to
place him not only within the scope of the plot, but at the
very centre of it.

   Given that this was enough, in his view, to secure a conviction, Perceval was prepared to be generous towards
Despard's motives. There was evidence to come, he
admitted, that suggested Despard might have 'interfered in
restraint of the too great precipitation of his confederates'
– he might have been attempting to stop the execution of
the plot, or at least to delay it. But even if this was the case,
he was still guilty. He might have had 'influence and

authority to disperse' the assembled rabble, but his motive for doing so would have been that 'the time was not yet ripe'. Perceval was careful to soften the jury's expectations of the evidence that was to follow, to admit in advance that Despard's words and actions might not be spectacularly treasonous in themselves, but at the same time to insist that the charge of treason did not depend on anything beyond his presence in the room.

Focusing so narrowly on the conversation in the Oakley Arms had obvious benefits in clarifying the prosecution's case, but it also opened up, as Perceval acknowledged, a potentially serious credibility gap. The more Despard's role was highlighted, the smaller the plot became: by the prosecution's logic, it was necessary to believe that a handful of disaffected soldiers had seriously believed they could overthrow the state single-handedly. More problematically, it was necessary to believe that an experienced and battle-hardened colonel shared their delusion. Perceval attempted to help the jury with this problem by asking them to consider 'not how improbable its success appears to *you*, not how strange that a person should engage in so rash, so dangerous and so wicked a design, but how probable its success was likely to appear to *them*'. Once again, he was prepared to be generous to Despard's motives. This kind of endeavour might, to its perpetrators, appeal to 'the best exertions of virtue and patriotism'. He asked the jury to imagine that they themselves had 'been misled by all the nonsense and all the villainy which the French Revolution has set afloat in men's minds', that they had 'been almost solely with persons who had been enthusiasts likewise', and had been 'inflaming each other's passions, stirring each other's eagerness'; if this were the case, might it not be possible that, eventually, 'the same estimate of the probability of success would be formed'?

Perceval was doing his best to steer away from the possibility that there might be a genuine revolutionary underground in Britain by painting the most vivid picture he could of how a few deluded individuals might have convinced themselves that there was.

Once the charge had been carefully framed, the picture was ready to be filled in by the witnesses. The prosecution called several police officers to confirm Despard's presence at the raid, followed by various soldiers including those who had agreed to break their illegal oaths of secrecy in exchange for immunity from prosecution. These produced a good deal of circumstantial evidence: they had attended previous meetings where Despard was present, had witnessed the business of illegal oaths, and had heard other conspirators talking about how the assassination of the King was to be carried out, and the nationwide uprising that was being planned to follow it. There was enough of this to unmask the existence of some sort of plot, but little to connect it directly to Despard. The most substantial evidence against him came from William Francis, a private in the First Battalion of Foot Guards, who claimed that Despard had attempted to administer the oath to him, asking him 'what were my principles, and the desire of the cause that was going forth of taking the Tower'.

Francis, if he was to be believed, had enough to incriminate Despard single-handed. There had, he claimed, been a previous date for the plot, 6 September, but Despard had called it off at the last minute. 'There was nothing to be done,' Despard had allegedly said; 'he expected some money and news to come from France'. If true, this was treason in yet another ancient sense: 'adhering to the enemy in the King's dominions'. By the same token, if Despard was in collusion with the French

Directory, he was guilty of a good deal more than the deluded subversion the prosecution was attempting to prove. But the evidence was left to hang; Perceval was narrowing the beam on Despard, and leaving the wider panorama in darkness.

When it came to cross-examination, Serjeant Best did the same, focusing the spotlight on the character of the witness. Francis was forced to admit that he had previously been charged with desertion; Best also made him admit that his current confessions, if true, were likely to send his brother John, who had not co-operated with the prosecution, to the gallows. The jury could make of this what they liked, but Best asked them to consider whether Francis, who by his own admission had already sworn a solemn oath and broken it, was the kind of man they would be prepared to trust with their lives.

The most extensive testimony, and the phrase that was to grab the headlines, came from Thomas Windsor, the man whose evidence had triggered the raid and effectively brought the prosecution. Windsor testified that he had been an army and Home Office informer for some time, and was able to tie several of the accused directly into the plot, having attended meetings in a series of pubs scattered all over the city through which they had rotated randomly to avoid detection. He was aware to some extent of the division and cell structure of the movement, and of the presence of United Irishmen within it. He had first met Despard in the tap-room of the Flying Horse in Newington; the colonel had just ordered a shilling's worth of brandy and water. Being a well-known face, Windsor was able to listen to Despard talking freely. 'I believe this to be the moment,' the colonel had allegedly been saying. 'The people, particularly in Leeds, in Sheffield, in Birmingham, and in every capital town in England, are ripe. I have walked twenty miles today', he added, 'and the people are ripe everywhere I have been.'

Despard, according to Windsor, proceeded at this point to lay out the plot. 'His Majesty must be put to death,' he said, and then 'the mail-coaches were to be stopped, as a signal to the country, that they had revolted in town'. Later, addressing Windsor directly, he asked him to bring more men to a meeting in Tower Hill 'to consult on the best mode of taking the Tower, and securing the arms'. This was exactly what the prosecution wanted from Windsor: a first-hand link between the plot and the colonel. But it seemed they also had a particular flourish prepared. They cued him with the question 'Do you remember any other remarkable expression to have been used by Colonel Despard?' Windsor replied that he did. Despard had said, 'I have weighed the matter well, and my heart is callous.'

It was a phrase that stuck, although the defence would strongly deny that it had ever passed Despard's lips. It was a concrete admission, if true, that Despard had crossed the Rubicon that separated revolutionary sentiments from violent action, and that he knew he had. The jury was not, as Hardy and Tooke's juries had been, being asked to condemn a man as a traitor simply for holding political views and promulgating them among the public. Here was a man, and one of deliberate and serious character, who had made a rational and carefully considered decision to commit a desperate act. For whatever reason, whether cruel treatment or wounded pride or misplaced patriotism, Despard's heart was callous. It was on this ground that Perceval rested his case that the Despard Plot had been a clear and present danger to the nation.

The posthumous legend of Despard's madness, if its roots are to be found anywhere in his life, can be traced to the prosecution's case against him. There was no evidence of madness in his character up to this point, and none to come during the short remainder of his life, during which all accounts would stress his calm and dignity. His gallows speech, whatever else it might have been, was hardly a torrent of lunacy. Yet the picture the prosecution painted of the Despard Plot seemed to leave some form of delusion or mental imbalance as the only plausible explanation for his actions. How else could he have believed that, with a handful of turncoat privates and Irish labourers, he was in a position to decapitate the state and trigger a nationwide revolution of seemingly imaginary collaborators?

The truth was that the state had a great deal more evidence of the plot than they were prepared to reveal. They knew, for example, that the illegal oaths they had found were United Britons oaths: they were identical to ones they had found in Sheffield and Manchester in 1802, and virtually identical to the United Irish oaths that had been used to recruit the shock troops for the Great Rebellion in 1798. They knew, too, that there were divisions of the United Britons in the north of England that were indeed ready to rise had the London coup gone ahead. The previous summer there had been secret meetings in Yorkshire attended by up to a thousand conspirators, under the auspices of an insurrectionary committee sometimes referred to as the Black Lamp. They estimated the total membership of these groups in Yorkshire at around seventeen thousand; their hand had been detected in a wave of strikes and lockouts that had recently spread through the manufacturing towns. They had evidence that the northern underground had been manufacturing illegal weapons, and that there were at least a thousand pikes stashed in Sheffield alone. As many as fifteen years later, intelligence agents would meet

Yorkshiremen who had clear memories of the Despard Plot and their own readiness to join it. Their recollections were that they were well prepared, and that had the London insurrection been properly executed there would have been a serious regional rebellion.

They were aware, too, that these facts were not unknown to the circle around Despard in London. Several of the men arrested in the Oakley Arms were known United Britons who had been active while Despard was in Coldbath Fields. One, Charles Pendrell, was an old United Irish collaborator who they were certain was more deeply implicated in the plot than Despard, but they had released him to avoid exposing their agents. The organizational terms some of the soldiers had used – specific phrases such as 'executive power' – were immediately identifiable as United Irish. All this corroborated other pieces of evidence suggesting that Despard was probably on a secret, top-level committee that linked the United Irish to the United Britons. Despard's defence committee, according to the Home Office's informants, knew at least some of what was planned. In the mob activity that had accompanied Burdett's Middlesex election less than a year before, they had detected the co-ordinating hand of the United Britons and the United Irish. They reckoned that both Thomas Hardy and Francis Burdett had been approached and told of the plot, but that both had refused to get involved. Burdett, they had concluded on John Moody's evidence, had almost certainly known about the Oakley Arms meeting in advance: he had, after all, known many of the suspects ever since the days of his Coldbath Fields campaign.

But the sum of their intelligence still did not entirely add up. The pieces of the jigsaw they had assembled pointed to some kind of reprise of the plot they had thwarted in 1798 by imprisoning the most prominent members of the LCS and the United Britons, including Despard himself. Then, a London 'hubbub' was to have been a signal for a wider rising across Britain and Ireland, perhaps even a French invasion; in 1799, there had been rumours of a United Irish action planned for London; now, there was more evidence of the same. But it was partial at best. Apart from a few industrial towns in Yorkshire and Lancashire, there had been little evidence of insurrectionary activity in the regions at the time, and very little more had emerged subsequently. Most critically, the Irish rising of 1798 had had an indisputable international dimension. Wolfe Tone had travelled to France, lobbied the Directory, and turned up at Bantry Bay with a French fleet. If the Despard Plot was to make sense as the vanguard of a similarly serious rebellion, where was the evidence that France, or even Ireland, were to follow?

The evidence, such as it was, was almost entirely negative. France's dealings with republican cells in enemy kingdoms had, over the last ten years, slotted into a predictable pattern. In Holland and Belgium, as in Ireland, they had been glad to receive malcontents from hostile powers, and had learned as much as they could from them. But when they had been called upon to intervene, they had acted – or, more often, not acted – entirely in their own national interests. Many minor European countries had small governments-in-exile in Paris or, later, Hamburg; sooner or later, they had all become dispirited. Promises had been broken, enthusiasm had blown cold, diplomatic relations had eventually collapsed in pleading and recrimination. In 1798, the United Irish had undoubtedly been the supplicants most favoured by the Directory, yet Napoleon had still sailed for the Mediterranean just before they rose, leaving them to be slaughtered in their thousands. With hindsight, it had become clear that Ireland, however Catholic or republican, was for Napoleon a strategic route into Britain, and little or nothing more. Over the subsequent five years, the Irish in exile had joined the ranks of impotent coteries tugging petulantly at the mighty French sleeve. In 1798, a French invasion of Britain was all too real a possibility; in 1802, with the great enemies attempting to consolidate peace, it was not seriously plausible.

This empty frame was mirrored in the paucity of evidence linking Despard to any conspiracy with France. His name turned up in a few scattered intelligence reports, mostly on a United Irishman named William Duckett, who was based in the free city of Hamburg through which much of the traffic between the United Irish and Britons was diverted. But Duckett was plainly being ignored by the French Directory, and trying to impress them with Despard's rank to stress the calibre of some of the operatives who were prepared to commit themselves to rising. By the same token, many of the mentions of Despard in the United Irish correspondence were several stages removed from the colonel's actions; his name and rank were a talisman thrown around to impress, often by people who had never met him. Despard himself had, after all, asked the Home Secretary to commute his Coldbath Fields confinement to a sentence of transportation to Australia – hardly the act of a man who was hell-bent on staying involved in the revolutionary struggle. If there was a grand plot, it was obscure and doubtful, and Despard's role in it more doubtful still.

Finally, there was little evidence of any wider appetite for an invasion by Napoleon, even among the diehard political reformers. The Peace of Amiens had made it possible for British people to visit France for the first time in a decade, and many had done so; there was much to be admired, but also much to be learned about how brutally Napoleon was treating the populations of the countries he invaded. The First Consul was plainly no friend of liberty. Fox had made the trip, and had been welcomed with an effusiveness that had embarrassed him: he was unable to attend the theatre without receiving a standing ovation from the audience. He had been presented to Napoleon, who told him that 'I have long admired you', but Fox had not returned the compliment; he noted that Napoleon 'smiles with his mouth but his eyes never have a corresponding expression'. Napoleon, apparently, had expressed disapproval of trial by jury on the grounds that 'it might be so very inconvenient to a government'. Fox had replied that 'the inconvenience was the very thing for which he liked it'.

The same ambivalence had, by the time of the Despard Plot, turned most of the Paineite radicals and friends of the revolution against the 'Corsican Tyrant'. In William Wordsworth's lines, France 'had changed a war of self-defence for one of conquest', and 'become oppressors in their turn'. As Napoleon had increased his grip on power, Whig pressure for political reform had diminished. Burdett, who had also just visited Paris, might privately have kept some faith with him as the Spirit of the Revolution, but it was a view he never attempted to sell to the public. In 1798, when Napoleon had been a consul but not a figurehead, the causes of political reform and France were still sufficiently blurred, and united by opposition to Pitt's widely hated tyranny, to command some popular support. But by 1803, with Pitt gone and Britain at peace, a massive conspiracy to welcome in the dictator seemed like a fantasy. Even within the milieu of inveterate revolutionary plotters that Despard's prosecution had painted, it would have strained credulity to argue that Napoleon was still waiting in the wings, ready and willing to follow their lead.

There were, then, several overlapping reasons why the government had decided to make the case against Despard in the form they did. To throw open the floodgates to the evidence of a wider conspiracy would have had very awkward consequences. First, the evidence against Despard was, in the wider context, weak. Second, it would have created widespread alarm, even panic, to claim that there was a massive terrorist plot in progress. To arrest everyone they would have needed in order to stand their case up would not only have eliminated most of their spies, it would also have meant suspending habeas corpus yet again and locking up dozens, if not hundreds, on circumstantial evidence, just at a point when the last occasion this had happened was becoming generally accepted as a cautionary tale of paranoid over-reaction. More seriously still, official accusations that the French were plotting against the British Crown would have endangered the fragile peace. The alternative, given their belief that the plot was real but not deadly serious, was to push their discovery of Despard in compromising circumstances for all it was worth. A surgical excision of the most high-profile collaborator, they calculated, would be enough to scatter the threads of conspiracy to the winds; if they regrouped and wove together once more, the government would be at least as well prepared. Despard had been a thorn in their side for a long time; whether his grievances against them were legitimate or not was a story now too tangled to unravel cleanly. There *was* a plot, and he *was* involved, even if neither the plot itself nor Despard's role in it were quite as the prosecution had presented them.

To assemble the wider case against Despard was,

ultimately, to attempt to assemble a coherent image from a hall of broken mirrors. Some of the shards could be made to fit, but too many of them seemed to reflect entirely different worlds. Looked at from one vantage point, they revealed a vast international conspiracy whose extent was hidden in the shadows; looked at from another, some loose talk among a group of disaffected men in a south London pub. The disputed territory between these two perspectives was patrolled on one side by a group of government informers whose loyalty was uncertain and whose narratives were unreliable, and on the other by a network of collaborators bound by a solemn oath to take their secrets to the grave. The only way to offer a map through the territory was by proposing that Despard was himself deluded, as confused as the mapmakers themselves.

But Despard, if he had been reckless enough to get involved in a mad plot, had also been careful enough to commit nothing to writing, indeed to leave no physical trace whatsoever of any overt act of treason. The clear legal and moral line the prosecution was attempting to draw between politics and violence, if it was drawn at all, was drawn in darkness.

Serjeant Best, opening the defence, was happy to play the cards as the government had dealt them. The version of the story they had chosen had offered him some obvious targets, and it was on these that he focused. He began by making it clear that the sheer seriousness of the charge should in itself be no obstacle to proving Despard's innocence. It was an extraordinary accusation, one that 'freezes the blood', and which demanded extraordinary proof. Treason was a crime against the entire nation, and it was natural that it should arouse in the jury 'an interest of the most powerful kind, that which arises from fear of your own safety'. The charge itself must not be allowed to prejudice; they 'must guard against any presumption of guilt'. Nothing could be worse for the nation, or for liberty itself, than to allow any charge in itself to dictate a verdict.

From this point he led the jury to Baron de Montesquieu's 'inestimable' sentiment that 'nothing renders the crime of high treason more arbitrary than declaring people guilty of it for indiscreet speeches'. All manner of speaking can be interpreted as treason by those who are listening for treason, whether seriously meant or frivolously; loose talk might well have occurred, and in Despard's presence, but it did not constitute high treason. As the prosecution themselves insisted at the beginning, the charge would stand or fall on 'overt acts', and words do not constitute overt acts. The only overt acts in the frame were the illegal oaths found on three drinkers in the club-room, and the only connection between them and Despard was via William Francis, 'one of the most infamous men alive', who would do anything, including sending his brother to the gallows, to protect his own skin.

Having attempted to raise the standards of proof for Despard's involvement in the plot, Best turned his attention to the plot itself, perhaps the weakest link in the prosecution version of the story. It was, he argued, a preposterous scheme: 'fourteen or fifteen persons assemble together at a common tap-house, with no other fire-arms than tobacco pipes, form a conspiracy to overturn a government, resting upon the shoulders, and supported by the unshaken loyalty of almost as many millions'. This picture, as painted by the prosecution, was not to be believed. 'Not an atom of evidence' was presented to support the testimony of William Francis that the plot might have been larger in scope, encompassing foreign aid or enemy collusion. Whatever it was that the court was looking at, it was not a serious threat to the nation.

Best did not stake his case on denying that such a plot had existed. He did not need to: his only task was to extricate Despard from it. 'I have no doubt', he told the jury, 'that some men have conceived the detestable design of seducing the army from the allegiance of the King', but the very nature of the prosecution's testimony showed how far such a plan could hope to get. 'The moment they began their plan of seduction', as all the evidence thus far had shown, 'they found the integrity of the soldiers opposed an insurmountable barrier to their wickedness.'

The question, then, was why Despard was in the Oakley Arms if he was not party to the plot. It was a question Best was not obliged to answer, but he wished to offer an alternative to Perceval's slur that he was an 'enthusiast' for the cause, deluded by his 'wild and visionary' beliefs. 'It must be proved that he was an enthusiast,' Best insisted, and there were neither reliable testimonies nor written confessions that did so. Despard was, to be sure, 'a disappointed man, yet God forbid that disappointment should be supposed to engender treason'. More significant was that Despard was 'a soldier from his youth', and 'a man accustomed to form extensive schemes both of conquest and defence'. He had reached the rank of colonel not 'as rank sometimes is acquired, but by honourably serving in a dangerous campaign'. These were traits quite incompatible with the 'rash enthusiast', and ones that offered a far more likely explanation of why Despard found himself in the Oakley Arms that night. If there was a conspiracy – and 'it is not necessary that I should now say a word whether that traitorous conspiracy did exist, or did not' – Despard was exactly the kind of man the conspirators would look to to hang it on. His presence would bolster the credibility of their rickety plot, and allow those 'who were disposed to get rid of a treason which had attached upon themselves, and throw it upon the shoulders of another'.

As to why Despard should have allowed himself to be drawn in, Best again had a better explanation than deluded enthusiasm. He had been locked up without trial for three years, and released with no evidence against him; defence and jury alike 'have a right, therefore, to presume from this that he was wholly innocent'. Despard himself equally had every right to 'conceive himself an injured man'; he was also a fair-minded one, 'and was therefore induced by that sympathy which men feel to those who profess to endure the same evils as themselves, to give them his assistance'. This was explanation enough for why he should have had no qualms about attending an open meeting to listen to those with grievances, especially those from the army rank and file whose interests he had always defended. He was not to know that there were those in the company who were there under false pretences, men who had taken oaths and then broken them, and were now taking oaths once more to present yet another version of events to the court. If the jury considered the actions of these witnesses, sitting and listening coolly to wild plots of treason, then bartering the story for their lives – even, in Francis's case, at the expense of his own brother's – they would recognize the absurdity of privileging their testimony over Despard's.

Such was the case for the defence, and, Best concluded, it needed no testimony from Despard to support it. Apparently to the surprise of Burdett, Tooke and his defence committee, the accused would not take the stand. Despard spoke only briefly, to inform the judge that 'my counsel have acquitted themselves so very ably, and so much to my satisfaction, that I have nothing more to say'.

His defence had produced a neat match with the story offered by the prosecution, and one that was equally artificial. Both sides knew there was more to say, but the attorney-general had decided to narrow the focus solely on to Despard; the defence had responded simply by turning the narrowly drawn version on its head.

From the defence's point of view, evidence from Despard himself might have offered few benefits and many potential pitfalls. Although the Despard Plot as outlined by the prosecution was a contrived version, and in some repects probably a fabricated one, the true story of Despard's involvement was also probably more incriminating than the defence had let on. Despard was not a devious man; on the contrary, his personal standards of honour were exacting ones. Even the prosecution had flagged the idea that his role might have been to prevent a reckless and ill-timed attack, and there was evidence in their hands to support this theory. But Despard might already have been uncomfortable with the extent to which his own defence might be storing up trouble for his confederates. Five years previously, he had rejected Francis Place's suggestion of informing the authorities about the incipient United Britons on the grounds that it would be 'dishonourable', and he had spent most of the intervening years in prison as a result. Now, the stakes were even higher, and he might well have felt that Best had already said more than enough.

But those spectators disappointed by Despard's silence were to have an unexpected treat. Best proceeded to call a series of character witnesses on his behalf, of whom the first was to be Lord Nelson.

Apart from the King and the Prime Minister, both of whom were bringing the prosecution, it would be hard to imagine another living Briton whose endorsement could have carried more weight. Having defeated Napoleon on the Nile, Nelson had emerged as the undisputed military hero of the nation. He had recently been ennobled by Addington, who was keen to add some military gravitas to his administration as a bulwark against the accusations that his peace was a weak and impractical one. Napoleon was bullying Addington in a way Pitt would never have allowed, meeting accusations of rearmament and treaty infractions with bellicose threats: 'you mean to force me to fight for fifteen years more!' Nelson was already deeply involved in planning for the resumption of war, a campaign that would break cover when hostilities resumed in May, and would climax in his finest and final hour at Trafalgar. Yet, busy with secret affairs of state as he was, when Despard had written to him and asked him to testify on his behalf, he 'could not resist'. He had been as shocked as everyone else by the details of the plot revealed in the newspapers, and had been unable to believe that this was the same Despard he had last seen while being dragged down the San Juan River on the point of death over twenty years earlier. Like Despard, Nelson was a man whose sense of honour weighed heavily on him, sometimes at the expense of his political judgement. He had accepted without delay, and without fear for his reputation.

Although Nelson's career path had diverged spectacularly from Despard's, they had also run in parallel for some time. During Despard's endless wait for the Home Office to assess his case, Nelson had also spent fruitless weeks and months waiting in the anterooms of the Admiralty Office for a new commission. He, too, though largely apolitical, had been swept up in the reform debate of the early 1790s. His home county, Norfolk, was also Tom Paine's, and public disaffection and calls for revolution were too loud and prevalent for even a disinterested country gentleman to ignore. Nelson, like Despard, had ventured across the class divides, and had sought out labourers' opinions and listened to pub debates; he had been shocked to discover that workers' conditions were 'really in want of everything to make life comfortable'. But such political instincts as he had set him on the opposing side to Despard. The people might be downtrodden but, in his view, 'want of loyalty is not among their faults'; it seemed to him that what they needed was not a revolution but a more benevolent paternalism. He had supported Pitt in his sabre-rattling against revolutionary France, and had been delighted when war was declared. While Despard languished in the King's Bench, Nelson had begun to receive his now legendary string of naval commands, and the British people, from his vantage point at least, had fallen in squarely behind their leaders and against the enemies of monarchy and property across the Channel. It was the war with France that had finally split Nelson and Despard apart, turning one into a patriotic hero and the other into an enemy of the state.

Nelson's appearance for the defence was the biggest news of the trial; it would beat the 'callous heart' accusation to most of the headlines. It was also, by the same token, a serious problem for the prosecution, and they did what they could to keep his evidence short. When he began to launch into an extended testimony to Despard's military record, the Lord Chief Justice was 'sorry to be obliged to interrupt your Lordship', but asked him to limit his testimony to Despard's 'general character'. Nelson was brief, and poignant. 'We went on the Spanish Main together,' he told the court; 'we slept many nights together in our clothes upon the ground. In all that period of time no man could have shown more zealous attachment to his sovereign and his country than Colonel Despard did.' Nelson had 'formed the highest opinion of him at that time, as a man and as an officer' and, although they had lost touch, 'if I had been asked my opinion of him, I should certainly have said, if he is alive he is certainly one of the brightest ornaments of the British army'.

There was little that the prosecution could do in cross-examination but to force Nelson to restate a point he had already made, that he had not seen Despard for many years, and 'as to his loyalty for the last twenty-three years of his life, your Lordship knows nothing'. The same point was made with the other two character witnesses called by the defence, General Sir Alured Clarke, who had been acting Governor of Jamaica in 1789, and Sir Evan Nepean, now a baronet. Both were distinguished figures and unimpeachable character witnesses. Clarke called Despard 'a very loyal, good subject, and a good officer', and Nepean, whose great admiration for Nelson had perhaps persuaded him to testify, 'a respectable character' whose introduction to him at the Colonial Office was accompanied by 'such testimonials as made him hold a high opinion of him'. But both admitted that they knew nothing of his recent years; Nepean added that 'I know that he fell under the suspicions of government, and was imprisoned for a considerable time, and I supposed there was some ground for it, though I did not know what it was'. In the summing-up that followed, Lord Ellenborough was able to limit the damage to the government's case by stressing that none of the defence witnesses had been able to testify to Despard's character in recent years, or 'to exhibit to you his character in the same high and brilliant estimation' in which it had stood at the height of his career.

The summing-up also restated the evidence for the 'overt acts' of treason that had been testified to: the seduction from duty, the illegal oaths, the compassing of the death of the King. The jury were sent out, and returned in twenty-five minutes with a verdict of guilty. The fore-man added an unusual request: 'My Lord, we do most earnestly recommend the prisoner to mercy, on account of the high testimonials to his former good character and eminent services.' Nelson's intervention had made a difference, but not enough.

The verdict was no surprise; it had probably been secured by the jury selection as much as anything that had occurred in court. This and much else – the level of entrap-ment, the inadmissibility of much of the evidence – would in all probability ensure Despard's acquittal were the trial to take place today, but by the standards of the time it was no gross miscarriage of justice. To have caught Despard at a meeting in a Lambeth pub, in the company of working men and renegade soldiers carrying illegal oaths, turned out to have been enough. Treason was a charge with many clauses, and it is unlikely that Despard was in breach of none of them. The plot to assassinate the King might have been a headline-grabbing confection, and the extension of the treason code during the Reign of Terror might have verged on the unconstitutional, but in other ancient senses, such as 'adhering to the king's enemy in his dominions', the verdict might have reflected the truth. Just as Nelson was secretly engaged in plans for the resumption of war, Despard's presence in the Oakley Arms spoke of another secret war into whose covert and well-guarded ranks he was plainly initiated. It is hard to imagine that he had not at some point sworn an illegal oath of secrecy; it is harder still to imagine that he might have sworn one and not meant it. Others, such as Wolfe Tone, had already dis-covered how hard the times had made it to separate political dissent from force of arms, and in turn from conspiracy with foreign powers.

Had Despard testified, the outcome might well have

been different. His silence, combined with Best's rather technical insistence that he was not obliged to do anything more than pick holes in the prosecution's case, was judiciously conceived, but not best calculated to combat the emotive accusations that had been thrown at the jury. Where Erskine might have made a more assertive case for Despard as a man of honour unjustly persecuted by a government cynically attempting to cover up its mistreatment of him, Best's defence seemed evasive, one that attempted to hide behind the law rather than to use it aggressively and righteously. Had Despard also spoken in his own defence, his word as a gentleman in the company of villains would have changed the tenor of the case entirely, but this was a privilege he was ultimately not prepared to use at the expense of others who could not.

The following day, Despard's twelve confederates were tried by a new jury. Despite a procession of over a hundred character witnesses testifying that the accused were 'honest, sober and industrious' men with 'no improper political bias', the result was much the same. Charges were dropped against one, two were acquitted, and nine found guilty, of whom three were recommended to mercy and six handed the death penalty.

Despard was recalled to the court to stand alongside the men with whom he would soon be lining up at the gallows on the roof of the building next door. He was given leave to make a final statement. 'I have only to say that the charge brought against me is one which I could not have the most distant idea of,' he told the court. 'I have now nothing further to say than what I said at first: I am not guilty.' Lord Ellenborough then pronounced 'the dreadful sentence of the law', the solemn and gruesome ritual of hanging, drawing and quartering. In the silence that followed, Despard spoke once more. 'I beg your Lordship will allow me to say one or two words. Your Lordship has imputed to me the character of being the seducer of these men; I do not conceive that anything appeared in the trial or the evidence against me, to prove that I am the seducer of these men.' It was an interjection not of anger, fear or self-pity, but rather puzzlement that the trial could really be over, and high treason the settled verdict.

Despard and his fellow conspirators were returned to their cells in Surrey County Jail. The next morning, Thursday 10 February, the press embargo was lifted and the sensational news of trial and verdict burst into public view. The *Times* cleared all its news pages to run a detailed synopsis of the proceedings at 'extraordinary length' over sixteen full columns of tiny print, promising the reader that they were missing nothing 'of such moment as to give cause to the public to regret the omission'.

Opinions on the verdict were polarized, but most of them could still be contained within the spectrum of 'unfortunate'. For some this meant that Despard had, perhaps with the best of intentions, been in the wrong place at the wrong time; for others, that he had been maligned and conspired against from on high; for others still, that his actions had been regrettable and self-sabotaging. But if Despard was unfortunate, he also remained inscrutable. It was clear to almost everyone that there was more of the story to be told. For many, especially on the streets of Burdett's Middlesex, he was simply an innocent who had been framed by 'spies who had sworn away his life'; for others, he was going to the gallows with vital information that he was withholding from the authorities, or that the authorities were withholding from them. As the days progressed and the facts of the case were assimilated, Despard's silence came to loom larger than the commotion that had surrounded the trial. Detailed as the reports of it had been, they had raised more questions than they had answered. The version of the story that was of most interest was Despard's own, and the time left to him to reveal it was ticking away.

The authorities were less worried by Despard's silence than by the fear that he was about to break it to the public. He spent much of the time in his cell writing; Catherine visited him daily, and the jailers noticed that she was taking papers out with her. Sir Spencer Perceval was concerned enough to write to the Home Office. Despard's 'past habits', he pointed out, 'have been such as to fully justify any suspicion of mischievous intentions and plotting on his part'; he recommended that the prison officers should inspect what he was writing before allowing Catherine to leave with it. It turned out that Despard was writing a petition to the King, and that Catherine had arranged for it to be copied by a professional scribe. In it, Despard formally noted that he 'solemnly declares that he never directly or indirectly meditated or connived at any plan or attempt on the life of Your Majesty', and that he knew nothing of any words the prosecution witnesses had imputed to him. He concluded with a plea for clemency, 'to extend your royal mercy as in your wisdom you shall deem meet'. If Despard did not believe he was an innocent man, he was certainly doing a plausible imitation of someone who did.

Catherine was not counting on royal mercy alone to save her husband: she also paid a visit to Lord Nelson at the Hamiltons' house in Piccadilly. According to Lord Minto, the distinguished military attaché and future Governor-General of India, whom Nelson was entertaining, she arrived 'in great distress', and was clearly 'violently in love with her husband'. She presented Nelson with a letter from

Despard, and asked him for help; they discussed whether he might write a plea for leniency to the Prime Minister. After Catherine had left, Nelson read the letter to Minto; in it, Despard expressed his gratitude to Nelson, to whose testimony he attributed the jury's unusual plea for mercy. Minto, who was a vigorous advocate of direct rule in Ireland and shared the view of most of his peers that Despard was an unrepentant traitor, recalled that it was 'extremely well written and it would have been affecting from any other pen'. Nelson did indeed write to Addington; the Prime Minister told him later that 'he and his family had sat up after supper, weeping over the letter'.

It was probably this second plea from Nelson, combined with fears of mob violence, that persuaded the government to dispense with the disembowelling and burning of entrails, which had been pronounced as part of the sentence by Lord Ellenborough. Catherine's, and Nelson's, final service to Despard was to limit his punishment to mere drawing, hanging and beheading. Nelson also recommended that Catherine should be given a pension after her husband's death; it seems likely that this was considered, but that Despard's gallows speech was sufficient to rule it out. Instead, after his death, Catherine would be financially supported by a pension from Sir Francis Burdett. It was she who had first made contact with him, and won him over to Despard's cause; all her husband's subsequent support in his last years can be traced to her intervention. But this final settlement was for them both. Despard would have been more anxious about Catherine's financial security than about the manner of his own death.

In the meantime, it was not only the public who still hoped that Despard would reveal his secrets. The government was still in the dark, too; Despard's cross-examination by Sir Richard Ford and the Privy Council had clearly told them little. Now that sentence was passed, they were determined to make a final attempt. Ford approached the two clergymen, Protestant and Catholic, who were to give the prisoners their religious consolation before the execution, and asked them to do everything they could to extract final confessions from them. Their oaths of secrecy had thus far proved unbreakable, but, he hoped, fear of divine judgement might win out over them at the last. This had been tried previously with Father O'Coigley, who had asked for final confession from a Catholic priest before his hanging, although in the event he had revealed little of value. The chaplain of Surrey County Jail, the Reverend William Winckworth, was willing but not sanguine. The final warrants for execution had not yet arrived and Despard and the others were still hoping for a royal pardon; 'any attempt previous to the knowledge of their fate', Winckworth feared, 'would most probably defeat the whole design'. Only once they had 'entirely abandoned hope' might there be a final chance of persuading Despard to relinquish his secrets.

On the evening of 19 February the warrants finally arrived. The public pressure for a pardon had grown powerfully during the week, although it is unclear whether Despard and his confederates were seriously expecting it. The *Observer* reported that 'the unfortunate men received the awful intimation with the most perfect fortitude and resignation'. Not so Catherine, who had apparently believed – or hoped against hope – that pressure from Nelson and Addington might have brought a last-minute reprieve. Mrs Despard, the report stated, 'had almost sunk under the anticipated horror of his fate; she waited the whole of yesterday, in a state of expectation bordering on delirium; her feelings, when the dreadful order arrived, can scarcely be conceived – we cannot pretend to describe them'. She was allowed a final meeting with her husband during which, according to reports, 'the Colonel betrayed nothing like an unbecoming weakness'. Catherine went to Sir Richard Ford's office to plead once more for a stay of execution, but the wheels of state were already in motion. Despard would hang on the morning of 21 February.

The night before the execution, he had to make the best of the company he had: not Catherine, but the Reverend Winckworth. The chaplain asked him whether he had thought about the need for religious consolation; Despard 'mentioned that he had read a great deal of theology, and that he had made up his mind on religious matters'. Winckworth offered him the popular work *Evidences of Christianity* to read; Despard coolly returned the compliment by offering him a treatise on logic he had by his bedside. He gestured to his chains, and requested that the reverend 'would not attempt to put shackles on his mind as on his body'. When asked to expand on his beliefs, Despard explained 'that he believed in a deity, and that he supposed that outward forms of worship were useful for political purposes', but that 'otherwise, he thought the opinions of churchmen, dissenters, Quakers, Methodists, Catholics, savages or even atheists were equally indifferent'. His bible was Tom Paine's *Rights of Man*. Winckworth, in his report to the Home Office, concluded, 'I left the book on the table, but I fear he never read it.' Despard was 'very polite', 'never profane, nor did he at any point during his confinement speak disrespectfully or contemptuously of anybody', but he was not going to repent.

Winckworth was no silent witness, and the news of Despard's opinions spread fast. Though the beliefs he had communicated to the chaplain were, like Paine's, strictly deist – acceptance of a non-denominational supreme being, an immanent rather than an interventionist God – the niceties that separated this position from atheism were, as in the case of Paine and many others, ignored. The *Times*, in its leader the day after the execution, placed Despard's atheism centre stage in the entire plot. 'This bold, bad man', it wrote, 'would not have affected irreligion had that not been a distinctive, constituent character of the present unnatural conspiracies.' The evidence in court might not have furnished any connection with France, but Despard's view of religion had made the link plain. 'That atheism should be the foundation, and treason the superstructure, of Jacobin revolution, can excite no amazement; we have the example of France, that irreligion is the cause and prompter of every crime and disorder.' The roots of terrorism and treason were not to be sought in politics, law or justice, but in this cancerous disease of the soul.

The *Times* might have been justified, at least, in taking Despard's deism to be atheism in polite garb. There is no evidence that he ever showed any interest in religion, and some that he disliked it from an early age. As a young boy, he had been obliged to attend his elderly grandmother with coffee and bible-reading every afternoon; according to family tradition, he 'used to detest alike his grandmother, bible and coffee'. His pragmatic habits of mind were suited to making sense of the world without religion's explanatory frame. Mixing as he did with all creeds and colours throughout his life, commitment to a religious denomination would have seemed more often hindrance than help. He was not a man without morals, far from it, but religion was not among the forces that generated them.

During his final night, according to the warder outside his room, Despard paced around his cell. He then lay on his bed and, after some time, 'exclaimed with vehemence' to the empty room. 'Me? No, never!' he is supposed to have said. 'I'll divulge nothing! No, not for all the treasure the King is worth!' The warder rushed to his cell door, and asked him if he was aware that he had just spoken. Despard replied, 'Yes, and I said it that you might hear.' Relayed by Winckworth, the anecdote is perhaps apocryphal, but it chimes with the public sense of the melodrama that was playing out: Despard, his life winding down like a watchspring, forced to bow to authority but refusing to buckle, and unrepentant in taking his precious secrets to the grave. Amid the mystery, one fact had become entirely clear: not even torture could have wrung a single incriminating syllable from him.

The following morning Despard refused the offer of chapel. He was bound, and led from his cell. He shook hands with his solicitor, then stepped out into the prison yard. Awaiting him in the vacant cobbled arena was the procession of horses and carts, sheriffs and priests, keepers, constables and executioner, all ceremonially attired for their discreet ritual. And awaiting them, just as dawn was breaking, was Despard's hearty laugh.

Epilogue

THE UNFINISHED DESPARD BUSINESS

Despard's execution, and the unprecedented speech and crowd that had accompanied it, reverberated through press and public for some time. The editorial in *The Times* was matched by many others, drawing similar morals from the cautionary tale. Reverend Winckworth published an address 'to those who have imbibed the unhappy sentiments of the late Colonel Despard', warning against his theological errors and their treasonable consequences. Sermons were preached against him up and down the land; Hatchard's, the royal booksellers, published one delivered the following Sunday by the Reverend William Leigh at St George's Church in Hanover Square entitled *A Sermon on the Depravity of the Human Heart; Exemplified generally in the Conduct of the Jews, and particularly in that of Colonel Despard, previous to his Execution*. The biblical parallels of the event were plain to see: 'to the Jews were exhibited, at the crucifixion of the Messiah, a repentant and an unrepentant thief; to us Christians has also been displayed, and at the place of execution, one bold apostate traitor'. Despard was a 'traitor to his God, as well as to his King – to his religion, as well as to his country'.

The many who had taken a different moral from the spectacle also had their say, though their traces are more scattered and disparate. Despard's funeral speech was reproduced from *The Times* and sold in cheap pamphlets across the country. In Wolverhampton, a printer was arrested for producing 'inflammatory handbills' under the simple heading of *Colonel Despard's Address to the People*. In Leeds, a man named John Wilkinson was arrested for saying loudly in a pub, 'Damn the jury that found Colonel Despard guilty. I wish they were all at hell and that Colonel Despard's head was down the King's throat.' He was prosecuted for seditious libel but acquitted. The *Morning Post* gave voice to fears that such isolated explosions of dissent might be the tip of an iceberg, and that the state's use of extreme measures against Despard might backfire disastrously. 'Shall Despard's headless corpse', it wondered, 'walk into every tap-room, to make proselytes an hundred fold?'

There was still Despard's funeral to come, and with it more controversy. It turned out, presumably through Catherine's researches, that all Despards were entitled to be buried in the churchyard of St Faith's, in the City of London, an old parish church whose graveyard had been subsumed within the walls of St Paul's Cathedral. The Lord Mayor of London wrote to the government professing himself 'highly dissatisfied' that so conspicuous a disgrace to the nation should be interred within its most sacred resting place. Catherine co-ordinated a campaign on her husband's behalf for one final time. Sir Francis Burdett called for Despard's hereditary right to be honoured; Nelson, too, might have suggested to the Prime Minister that, now the deed was done, it would be impolitic to stir up further controversy.

The funeral was delayed until 1 March to allow James, the Despards' son, to return from Paris, where he was currently serving as an ensign in the French army – a detail that prompted some wild speculation about Despard's secrets involving traitorous dealings with Napoleon. In fact, James had originally signed up as an ensign in a British regiment, but had been expelled for fighting a duel with another cadet; his defection to the enemy might also have been prompted by the government's treatment of his father. As the appointed date drew near, tensions rose once more. The *Times* expressed concern that the event might be even more inflammatory than the execution had been. Noting the United Irish tradition of using funerals as occasions to display their force of numbers, they feared that 'a tumultuous assemblage of persons' might, 'under the specious pretence of attending a funeral', attempt a major disruption of the capital on a scale not seen since 'the example of Lord George Gordon's rioters'. Police and soldiers were once more called up in 'sufficient power to prevent any disturbance of the peace'.

The funeral, when it took place, was a modest one, a hearse and four carriages, and the crowd it attracted was substantial but largely quiet and reverent. They lined the streets from the Despards' last residence in Lambeth, across Blackfriars Bridge towards St Paul's, at which point they dispersed in silence. The only unexpected interruption came just as the coffin was to be closed for the last time: a French woman named Marie Tussaud, who had recently arrived in London, intervened to take a cast of Despard's face. Within the month the colonel would be on display, underlit by sinister blue light to suggest hugger-mugger conspiracy, in her new waxwork museum in the Lyceum Theatre, where the leading attraction was, and would remain for many years, her figure of Lord Nelson. Despard was the first of her studies 'modelled from the face after death'; its popularity would demonstrate to her that the British public shared the French taste for *grand guignol* horror. Despard would be a founding and long-running exhibit in her ghoulish 'Separate Room', which *Punch* magazine would later dub 'the Chamber of Horrors'.

Catherine and James were not entirely abandoned, thanks to Sir Francis Burdett; Catherine may also have been supported later by Lord Cloncurry, who contributed to Despard's defence and claims in his sometimes un-reliable memoirs that she came to live for some years at his home near Lyons in France. Later tradition in the Despard family is that she settled in Ireland, although she had no contact with the family, who never acknowledged her and James as relatives. But the Despard family recollections offer a final glimpse of James, in an anecdote told by General John, Despard's older brother, whose last contact with Edward Marcus had been when he was mistakenly arrested in his place. The general was leaving a London theatre in the company of another of his brothers when they heard a waiting carriage-driver calling the name 'Despard'. They made their way towards the carriage, which had been ordered in their name, 'and there appeared a flashy Creole and a flashy young lady on his arm, and they both stepped into it'. After this brief glimpse, James – and any future black Despards – melted into the night streets of London.

Despard's broader legacy also became, for a while, a thing of fleeting glimpses. In the short term, his public execution achieved exactly what the government had hoped it would.

By Permission of the Right Worshipful the Mayor.

LATELY ARRIVED FROM EDINBURGH,

THE GRAND EUROPEAN
Cabinet of Figures,

MODELLED FROM LIFE;—AND NOW

Exhibiting at No. 4, MARKET-PLACE, opposite the REIN-DEER INN:
Where the Citizens may be gratified with a View of all the SEVENTY Characters at once.

Madame Tussaud, Artist,

RESPECTFULLY informs the Gentry and Public of HULL, and its Vicinity, that
her unrivalled Collection has just arrived here.

The full-length PORTRAIT-MODELS of their Most Gracious MAJESTIES

Geo. III. & Queen Charlotte,

THEIR ROYAL HIGHNESSES
THE PRINCE AND PRINCESS CHARLOTTE OF WALES,
Duke of York—Prince Charles Stuart;
LIEUTENANT-GENERAL SIR JOHN MOORE,

Admiral Lord Nelson,
GENERAL WASHINGTON.

Right Hon. Ch. Js. Fox—Right Hon. Wm. PITT,

SIR FRANCIS BURDETT,

Right Hon. H. GRATTAN—Right Hon. J. P. CURRAN,
The Philanthropic Mr. ROSEBERRY, of Dublin,
Mons. TALLEYRAND—L'ABBE SIEYES,
COUNT DE LORGA,
The famous BARON TRENCK—The EMPRESS of FRANCE,
MADAME CATALANI, the celebrated Singer,
A SLEEPING CHILD—The ARTIST and her DAUGHTER.

AN EXACT LIKENESS OF THE BEAUTIFUL BUT UNFORTUNATE

Mary Queen of Scots.
JOHN KNOX, and JOHN WESLEY.

THE CELEBRATED
MRS. CLARKE.
A Coach and a Cannon,

Formed in Gold, Ivory, and Tortoise Shell,—to the Astonishment of the Spectators, is, with great Facility,
DRAWN by a FLEA!

The other Subjects composing this UNIQUE EXHIBITION, chiefly consisting of Portrait Characters,
in full Dress, as large as Life, correctly executed, may be classed as follows:

I. The late Royal Family of France, viz.
King, Queen, Princess Royal, and Dauphin, with M. de Cloise, Valet de shin.

Celebrated Characters of the past and present Times, viz.
Henry IV. of France—Duc de Sully—Frederick the Great—M. de Voltaire—Pope Pius—J. J. Rousseau—
Dr. Franklin—Bonaparte—Madame Bonaparte—Archduke Charles—General Moreau—General
Kleber—Ex-Consul Cambaceres—Eli Bey, and his Son, with a favourite Georgian Slave, and two
most beautiful Circassians.

II. Remarkable Characters:—Subjects, viz.
Mademoiselle Bruisee de Perigord, who formed the French Revolution.
Princess de Lamballe, who was murdered by the Revolutionary Mob in Paris.
Madame du Barri, the Mistress of Louis XV. who was guillotined in Paris.
Madame M. Antoinette, guillotined for relating to be the Mistress of Robespierre.
Charlotte Corde, who suffered by the guillotine for the Assassination of Marat.
Marat in the Agonies of Death, immediately after receiving the fatal Wound.
Heads of Robespierre, Foquelier, de Prince-the, Herbert, and Carriere, as they appeared after the guillotine.
A Soldier of the French National Guards, in full Uniform.
An old Coquette, who issued her Husband's Life away.
One of Bonaparte's Mameluke Guards.—Madame St. Clair, the celebrated French Actress.

III. Curious and Interesting Relics, viz.
The SHIRT of HENRY IV. of France, in which he was assassinated by RIVAILLAC; and an accurate
Portrait of Rivaillac himself, with various original Documents relating to that Transaction.
A small Model of the original French Guillotine, with all its Apparatus;
and two Picturesque Models of the Bastile in Paris;
(In which Count de Lorga was confined Twenty Years.)
One representing the Torture as at view from the time it showing, in the Revolution.
A real EGYPTIAN MUMMY, 3200 years old, in perfect Preservation.

Colonel Despard.

OPEN EVERY DAY, from ELEVEN in the MORNING till TEN at NIGHT.
Admittance, One Shilling.—Children under Ten Years of Age, Half Price.
N.B. A Free Ticket, (not Transferable) Four in. will admit a Person any Time during the Exhibition.

No. 4, Market-Place, Hull, }
February 24th, 1814. }

ROBERT PECK, PRINTER,
PACKET-OFFICE, HULL.

Nelson and Despard share the bill at Madame Tussaud's

Whatever confederacy of British Jacobinism had lurked behind the Despard Plot was scattered and, following a similarly small-scale and abortive uprising in Ireland the next year, seemingly abandoned. After the short peace of Amiens was ended and Napoleon emerged as emperor of France, the very notion of an international republican underground became a thing of the past. 'Jacobinism is killed and gone', observed the Whig MP Richard Sheridan, 'by him who can no longer be called the child and champion of Jacobinism; by Buonaparte.' Ten years earlier, France and Britain had represented alternative poles of the political future; as the war ground on, so France and Britain both gravitated towards a future few had foreseen and which neither people had chosen: the state as war machine, greedy for taxes and soldiers, the liberty of the people a threat rather than a promise and, at best, deferred to some unimaginable happier future. The tide of reform had seemed too powerful to hold back, but war had done the job. Many of the old radicals, such as Burdett, gradually came to believe that war was no more than 'an attempt to stifle liberty', engineered deliberately by corrupt elites on both sides to prolong their grip on power.

Yet Despard's causes did not entirely die with him. The torch of political reform, once the Whigs had abandoned it, was for a while carried almost single-handed by Sir Francis Burdett. He forced another Commons debate on extending the right to vote, but it gathered only fifteen supporters. Gradually he was joined by a few other radical MPs such as Henry Hunt, who had been a vocal critic of Despard's incarceration in Coldbath Fields. Hunt was, in Francis Place's opinion, 'the best mob orator of the day', though he also thought him a mischievous and dangerous loose cannon in turbulent times. Burdett and Hunt formed the core of a small independent lobby that presented itself as the defender of British liberties against the unconstitutional despotism of the government, and mentioned France and Ireland less and less. The rhetoric of reform was being overwritten once more, and was slowly shifting back towards the patriotic language of the previous generation.

Burdett also found a new and potent mouthpiece for his campaigns in William Cobbett. Cobbett, like Despard, had been a firm patriot who had fought for his country in the Americas; throughout his early years as a journalist he had been a staunch opponent of the French enemy and the Jacobin ideas that drove them. While covering Burdett's election to Middlesex, he had been appalled by 'a scene of confusion and sedition, such as never was beheld except in the environs of Paris during the most dreadful time of the revolution'. But a libel conviction against him for criticizing the government's Irish policy (also prosecuted by Sir Spencer Perceval) opened his eyes to the culture of self-interest and corruption that drove Westminster; his subsequent return to his rural roots brought with it a shocked sense of the injustices heaped on the working man by its economic policies. He became a champion of lost Anglo-Saxon rights and a critic of the Norman yoke, sentiments that transformed him, as they had many before him, from reactionary to radical. His newspaper, the *Register*, picked up the cause of political reform where it had been left hanging after the dissolution of the LCS. It sold, in its cheap twopenny edition, up to forty thousand copies a week, and the right of the people to a better system than 'Old Corruption', as Cobbett dubbed it, returned to the mainstream of political debate.

The clandestine world of secret societies and insurrectionary plots also resurrected itself, and within it

Despard's name had not been forgotten. Food shortages bit again and again, and food riots followed; mutiny in the armed forces recurred regularly; unrest in northern factory towns became endemic as new industrial processes squeezed the workforce. The Combination Act still made it illegal for workers to gather and form unions, so secret workers' organizations swelled the radical underground. Strands of the old Jacobinism, and of grand plans to rise and overthrow the ruling class, wove in and out of local protests over prices and disputes over working practices. Spies and *agents provocateurs* swarmed through this new underworld, often more numerous than the political subversives they were chasing, sometimes standing in for non-existent enemies of the state to see who might emerge to join them. Those who were genuinely involved became as careful as Despard had been to leave no traces of their overt acts.

In 1812, a new wave of insurrection swept through the provinces, with a new name for its perpetrators: Luddites. Mechanical shearing frames were putting thousands of traditional textile croppers out of work, and secret gangs of saboteurs began wrecking factories and mills under the cover of darkness and the cryptic signature of 'Lord Ned Ludd'. Luddism was urgently infiltrated, and its apparent ringleaders punished by death. During a raid near Wakefield secret oaths of affiliation were found, their wording identical to those that had been uncovered in the Oakley Arms. Anonymous threats began to arrive at the Home Office; one promised revenge for 'the blood of Despard'.

The end of war, after Waterloo, did not end the threat of revolution. Food prices remained high through controls that guaranteed profits to the producers while starving the regional poor, and popular discontent continued to flare into violence. The Home Secretary, Lord Sidmouth, felt that 'it will be fortunate if the military establishment which was pronounced too large for the constitution of the country shall be sufficient to preserve its internal tranquillity'. In 1817, government intelligence foiled a rural uprising at Pentridge in Nottinghamshire among labourers who believed that there were seventy thousand Londoners ready to rise at their signal. Its leader, Jeremiah Brandreth, had, it turned out, been present as a young man at Despard's execution; he too was hanged for treason, but without the ceremonial drawing or beheading. The scattered and excluded were beginning to find a shape and a voice, and it was a voice that had been heard before.

By this point it was becoming clear to many, even in Parliament, that the debates over political reform that had torn the country apart in the 1790s had not been resolved, only postponed. The next years brought two major and un-related events that entrenched the old oppositions still more deeply. In 1819, at St Peter's Field outside Manchester, a large crowd that had gathered to hear Henry Hunt speak were charged by a cavalry militia that killed eleven of them and wounded six hundred, many with swords and bayonets, while the brass band accompanying Hunt played 'Rule Britannia' and 'God Save the King'. Local magistrates were unable to stifle the public inquiry and national outrage that followed. The effect of the Peterloo Massacre was to test the laws against illegal meetings to destruction; it became clear that the British public would no longer support county militias dispersing unarmed crowds with lethal force. After Peterloo, the reform movement no longer needed to hide in the shadows, and mass public meet-ings began once more to pressure the rarefied world of Westminster to act or be overtaken by events.

But even if state repression was in retreat, violent

The Massacre of Peterloo! or a Specimen of English Liberty. August 16 1819

The Peterloo Massacre

insurrection was not. The following year, on 6 April, a plot to murder the entire cabinet while they were at dinner was thwarted after a violent struggle during which a guard was run through with a sword. The Cato Street Conspiracy, as it became known, had been infiltrated almost from the first, and the government had a better idea of how the plan was to work than most of those involved. It had the feel of pre-scripted action or self-fulfilling prophecy: it is often argued that the government, after the humiliation of Peterloo, deliberately allowed it to come to fruition to bolster their credibility. The story that emerged was oddly similar to the Despard Plot as the prosecution had portrayed it: an implausible and desperate action by a small group of men who believed that the country would rise in support of them once a

The Cato Street Conspiracy

symbolic blow at the heart of government had been struck.

What little is known of its leader, Arthur Thistlewood, also resembles the caricature of Despard as portrayed at the trial. Thistlewood seems to have been personally embittered, emotionally unstable and stubbornly acting out a perverse drama of personal honour that had already led to his being arrested for challenging the Home Secretary to a duel. He had also fought with the British army in the Caribbean before resigning his commission and imbibing revolutionary politics in France. Thistlewood was conscious of the comparison, and had warned his confederates that if they failed to act boldly 'this will be another Despard's business'. The Cato Street Conspirators were tried for high treason, and became the last men to be hanged and publicly beheaded. But the authorities had learned much since Despard's day. The drawing was omitted from the ceremony, and the crowd were barricaded so far back that they were unable to hear Thistlewood's final protestation that 'I die in the cause of liberty'.

The main effect of the Cato Street Conspiracy was to hold back the cause of political reform, alienating the middle-class supporters who were beginning to rally behind it in numbers not seen for a generation. In other ways, though, it added urgency to it: though it had had no chance of success, it raised the spectre of Despard's headless corpse once more, and of the unknown number of fanatics who might now be moved by government intransigence to desperate acts at the expense of their own lives. Public opinion was more restive and less pliable than it had been during the years of war. Hundreds of thousands of soldiers who had fought for their country were now demobbed and on the streets, and demanding a representative government in return for their sacrifices. As the industrial revolution snowballed, the absence of MPs for huge centres of population such as Manchester, Leeds and Birmingham became ever less defensible, and the expanding middle class were increasingly articulate and powerful in pressing the case for their own interests. By 1825, too, an increasingly well-organized and economically important labour market, assisted by the tireless Francis Place, had succeeded in forcing the repeal of the Combination Act.

By 1830, another revolution in France, overthrowing the absolute rule of Napoleon's dynasty, added to a powerful sense of *déjà vu*, and a growing dread that the turmoil of the 1790s would be revisited, perhaps this time with an outcome more unfortunate for the political establishment. At the same time, an economic upturn was gradually leading to a less polarized society, and a more inter-

Campaigning for political reform, 1831

nationalist British foreign policy – supporting the Greeks, for example, in their struggle against Turkish oppression – had made the nation a plausible champion of liberty on the world stage for the first time since Despard's early soldiering days. Constitutional reform no longer seemed like capitulation to an 'odious faction' in thrall to the politics of envy, but a broadly acceptable reflection of a new political maturity. Change, finally, was in tune with the times, and talk of an act to reform the parliamentary voting system for the first time since the seventeenth century came to occupy the centre stage of politics.

It was still to be a hard fight. The Reform Bill, drawn up under the new Whig government of Lord Grey in 1831, was watered down in a deliberate attempt to split the Tory vote, but it was still picked over and contested in every detail. The first attempt to force it through the Commons failed, blocked by those whose rotten boroughs were set to be dismantled; further concessions saw it through at the second attempt, only for it to be rejected by the House of Lords. The violence of the 'days of May' that followed far outstripped Peterloo: Nottingham, Derby and Bristol saw the worst mob violence in Britain since the Gordon Riots half a century before. It brought the threat of revolution as close as it had ever been; even ageing moderates such as Francis Place declared themselves ready to take up arms if the government persisted with the forcible suppression of its people. In Nottingham, the castle was burned down; in Bristol, where Queen Square was burned and looted, Despard's wax effigy, still touring in Madame Tussaud's travelling show, was nearly melted in the carnage. Marie Tussaud, trapped in a burning house nearby, suffered traumatic flashbacks to the terror that had followed the French Revolution. Fear of further unrest finally forced the Tories to support the bill, and Lord Grey presented it once more, this time explicitly commending it 'to prevent the necessity for revolution'.

Many of Despard's old colleagues were still alive to see it. Thomas Hardy had seen his cobbler's business shrink away after his trial for high treason and had struggled through hard times; he had survived for many years on a pension paid by Sir Francis Burdett. For him, at least in the euphoria of the moment, it seemed to be a vindication of his lifelong struggle. 'Revolution it is,' he wrote; 'the King and his ministers are now turned parliamentary reformers.' As such they 'were guilty of the very same crime' with which he himself had been charged under the Reign of Terror. For Burdett, too, the Reform Act was vindication enough of the causes for which he had struggled for so long. His youthful commitment to radicalism had already begun to soften with age: in 1821 he confessed that 'I begin to grow very aristocratic', and he had largely withdrawn from demagoguery and street politics. After 1832 he settled comfortably into old age as a high Tory, loyal to the Duke of Wellington. Burdett has perhaps been so little remembered because his career presents, from a modern political perspective, such a puzzling transit from the left of the spectrum to the right; but his politics were forged in an age that knew no such categories. In his own view, the traditional values of liberty and justice were his fixed star; all that changed were the commitment to liberty and justice in the world around him, and his personal appetite for fighting on the front line.

Others were not so content. The Reform Act had laid some valuable groundwork by redrawing the political map of Britain, which had stood unchanged for centuries. It had dismantled the most conspicuous of the rotten boroughs; it had replaced the inequality of a patchwork of voting qualifications with a single means test, the ownership of property with a rental value of £300 per annum; it had given MPs to the great new centres of urban population in the regions. Now the British electorate numbered 656,000, a larger proportion of the people than in almost any country in Europe. But these voters still represented only 10 per cent of the male population, a propertied middle class that had been permitted to join the traditional elite and whose interests would now be considered alongside theirs.

For Francis Place, still active in the reform movement, the ruling class had made the minimum concessions necessary to split the new bourgeoisie from the mass of working men. He rolled up his sleeves once more and began to draft a 'People's Charter', a 'new Magna Carta' calling for universal male suffrage without property qualifications. At the first meeting of the Chartists, who formed in the wake of the Reform Act, the sentiments of the old LCS would be repeated almost verbatim. The founding member, Thomas Cooper, warned them that they had too often been used as a ladder to power, only to be kicked away: 'don't be deceived by the middle classes again'. Among the Chartist founders was the great radical demagogue of the new generation, Feargus O'Connor, whose father and uncle had both been named repeatedly in Home Office intelligence reports as Despard's accomplices among the United Irish.

Finally, and far later than Despard could possibly have imagined, a new world was dawning where democracy dared to speak its name. But there were still long and hard battles ahead. It took another generation before continued pressure from the Chartists and others forced a second reform act, the Representation of the People Act of 1867, which enfranchised urban householders, adding a million new voters to the register and approaching the level of representation over which Despard had presided in the Bay of Honduras. It took another generation before the glaring anomalies resulting from these partial reforms were ironed out; and it took a century, and many more martyrs, before the process begun by the Reform Act in 1832 extended the same franchise to women as to men.

In the end, Britain had no revolution in the modern sense of the term, but one in the old sense of a slow turning. The ship of state inched through the shoals and reefs of popular unrest, adjusting its course as little and as late as possible and always bristling with force of arms. We are all now Pitt's and Napoleon's creatures, not Paine's or Despard's, in ways that could not have been confidently predicted before France and Britain went to war in 1793. In many ways, this was an outcome preferable to the convulsive change that engulfed many of Britain's neighbours. It was certainly advantageous to Britain's national standing: her dominance in the nineteenth century, and the growth of her empire, were in large part predicated on it. Nor is it a straightforward matter to wish it had been otherwise: the overthrow of the British state by violent means in the middle of the Napoleonic Wars was something few – perhaps not even Despard – would have celebrated. It is worth remembering, too, that Despard was perhaps the most egregious victim of the Reign of Terror, and to follow in his footsteps is to view it in its least flattering light.

Yet the revolutionary struggle that was defeated and subsumed has also emerged triumphant: democracy has made its way from treasonable creed to the most sacrosanct virtue in the political firmament. The movement for political reform in the 1790s may have been defeated, but it can hardly be said to have failed. Its causes, from freedom of the press to the abolition of slavery, the rights to trade associations and public meetings, the emancipation of women and religious tolerance, tax based on means and state provision for the poor, not to mention the right of common people to vote, have all joined the ranks of cherished democratic values. Some of these may have emerged subsequently from different contexts and different struggles, but, as far as those who were fighting for them in the 1790s knew, they were attempting to seize a chance that would never come again.

By this token, Despard, unfortunate as he surely was, cannot with the same confidence be judged irrelevant. In such a slow revolution as that which transformed British politics, it is never possible to be sure precisely what made the difference. He may have been a man out of time, fighting for a cause for which the world was not yet ready; but his disputed fate lived on, sustaining the memory that previous attempts to suppress reform had been fought fiercely and not always fairly. History has remembered him in connection with a violent attempt to overthrow the state, and one that failed dismally, but at the time it was by no means so simple to separate the allegations against him from the broader struggle for justice that tore Britain apart, and by no means so obvious which of two quite distinct Britains would emerge from it. Despard's precise connection to the plot that bears his name will never be entirely clear, except in the improbable event that he committed his final secrets to writing and they are yet to be discovered. Without them the rush to judgement, which must be suspended to understand his story in the first place, will need to be suspended indefinitely.

And even if Despard's treason is assumed, as it has been for so long, the judgement on him must still be a fine one. It must grapple with the paradox, rare in the history of treason, of an honourable traitor: a man who acted honestly and selflessly, believed himself innocent, refused to tailor his story for different sides and went to his grave betraying not a soul. We may, like Despard's prosecution, wish to draw a clear line between political opinion and violent acts of terror; but Despard's were times when people took up arms more readily, and the lines between politics and violence, democrat and terrorist, were often invisibly crossed. He was a traitor at a time when the British government had extended the definition of treason precisely because its meaning was contested, and had persisted with the new definition despite clear signals from juries that it lacked popular support. If Despard came to believe that no elite would willingly share power with the people without at least the threat of violence, he would be proved right. Even when they finally came, such liberties were not freely given: they still needed to be taken.

At the time, it was irresistible to read Despard's life and death as a cautionary morality tale. Today, if it has a moral, it is a good deal less clear. It may be that honour, bravery and a clear conscience are not enough to guarantee a good reputation; it may be that those in the right are sometimes better off keeping quiet; it may be the short, sharp and cynical 'trust no-one'. It may even be that the moral is not for Despard but for others: for example, that no government acting in its own best interests turns men like him into enemies. Yet it is hard to escape the suspicion that his life was no morality tale at all but a spectacle more like a car crash: a collision of the random and the inevitable, bad luck, driver error and the laws of nature, leaving behind useless fragments of criticism and blame, and a scattered debris of might-have-beens. It was not a burning ideological conviction, so much as a combination of happenstance and bad timing, and the injustices he chanced to witness, that set him on a collision course with authority, and ultimately with the tides of history. Yet even if what finally counted were forces beyond Despard's control, the direction he took was of his own choosing, and one from which, behind his apparent rise and fall, he never deviated. More accurate than any moral is perhaps his own laconic assessment of his fate, as he stood on the gallows facing the silent crowd: 'There are many better, and some worse.'

A NOTE ON SOURCES

The seriousness of the revolutionary threat in 1790s
Britain continues to be contested, and much of the
extensive secondary literature tends towards advocacy of
one of two opposing viewpoints. E. P. Thompson, and subsequent historians such as Marianne Elliott and Roger
Wells, have argued that the revolutionary movement was
well organized, ideologically sophisticated and founded on
a level of popular dissent that is under-represented in the
printed sources of the time and has continued to be underestimated by historians. Their archival work has been
groundbreaking, and has certainly undermined the
standard claim of nineteenth- and early twentieth-century
historians that the revolutionary threat was insignificant,
although the evidence they have unearthed is stronger for
some times and places than for others. There remains,
however, an opposing view, developed by historians such
as Ian Christie and Clive Emsley, who have maintained
that the revolutionary threat has now been exaggerated:
Britain remained overall profoundly conservative, most
public dissent was driven by local protests against food

shortages rather than by revolutionary ideology, and the legal measures of the Reign of Terror were rarely used and less significant than some have found them in retrospect. While the first view has persuasively demonstrated the previously unsuspected extent of some revolutionary structures, and the extent to which the government was prepared to go to suppress them, the second view has been strengthened by the likes of Robert Dozier and, more recently, Linda Colley, who have argued that the less visible forces of conservatism and loyalism in Britain have also been underestimated.

This book does not presume to referee between these two tendencies, far less to resolve the ongoing controversy. Some of the Despard archive makes interesting contributions to the debate (see, for example, pp. 307–8), but as each side has strengthened its case it becomes ever less likely that a definitive conclusion will be reached. The primary sources suggest that it was possible for people in different social worlds and at different points in the decade to come to wildly divergent conclusions about the seriousness of the revolutionary threat, and that aspects of both sides might, for different reasons, have been systematically under-represented in the historical record. It should also be noted that both tendencies, in their more extreme forms, edge towards self-contradiction. If the revolutionary threat was indeed serious, it becomes harder to argue that the Reign of Terror was gratuitously severe; if it was not, the unprecedented use of the state apparatus to suppress it was surely disproportionate.

The primary sources for Despard's story are in many cases as partisan as the history that has followed them. His military and administrative career in part one of the book is less contentious: much of it can be assembled from Colonial and Home Office correspondence, published as

Archives of British Honduras (1931), with which Despard's own manuscript account, *A Narrative of Publick Transactions in the Bay of Honduras Settlement* (1791), essentially concurs, and from which the Baymen's allegations against him, such as Robert White's *The Case of the Agent to the Settlers on the Coast of Yucatán and the Late Settlers on the Mosquito Shore* (1793), frequently diverge. In part two, Despard's own testimony becomes more sporadic, and the evidence for his actions is represented by two opposing types of primary source. Memoirs in defence of his conduct are typically based on his former secretary James Bannantine's *Memoirs of Edward Marcus Despard* (1799), a work of advocacy on behalf of his former employer, essentially factual but with enough omissions to suggest that it may not represent the whole truth. The picture of his clandestine activities is largely assembled from espionage reports submitted to the Home Office and its Committee of Secrecy, and retained as *Home Office Domestic Correspondence, George III: Letters and Papers* at the Public Record Office. These are demonstrably unreliable – in E. P. Thompson's pungent assessment, 'each word must be critically fumigated' – but they are nevertheless valuable, despite their inaccuracy on many details. The Despard family's private collection offers some useful insights not available elsewhere. Throughout part two, sources for the account of Despard's actions are indicated where relevant; they are assessed as far as possible in the context of his trial, the account of which is based on Joseph and William Brodie Gurney's *The Trial of Edward Marcus Despard for High Treason, Taken in Short-Hand* (1803), the fullest of the contemporary transcripts.

BIBLIOGRAPHY

Adams, Ephraim Douglass, *The Influence of Grenville on Pitt's Foreign Policy 1787–1798* (Carnegie Institute of Washington, Publication No. 13, 1904)

Anon., *A Description of the King's Bench Prison* (John McShee, London, 1823)

Anon., *Memoirs of the Life of Col. E. M. Despard, with his Trial at Large, and his Twelve Associates, for High Treason* . . . (A. Swindells, 1803)

Anon., *The Whole Proceedings of the Trials of Col. Despard* (4th edn, W. Flint, London, 1803)

Bailyn, Bernard, *The Ideological Origins of the American Revolution* (Harvard University Press, 1992)

Bannantine, James, *Memoirs of Edward Marcus Despard* (J. Ridgway, London, 1799)

Barty-King, Hugh, *The Worst Poverty: A History of Debt and Debtors* (Alan Sutton, 1991)

Bewley, Christina and David, *Gentleman Radical: A Life of John Horne Tooke* (Tauris Academic Studies, 1998)

Black, Clinton V., *History of Jamaica* (1st edn, Collins, 1958)

Black, Jeremy (ed.), *Knights Errant and True Englishmen: British Foreign Policy 1660–1800* (John Donald Publishers, 1989)

Bolland, O. Nigel, *The Formation of a Colonial Society: Belize, from Conquest to Crown Colony* (John Hopkins University Press, 1977)

——*Colonialism and Resistance in Belize* (Cubola Productions, Belize, 1988)

Brewer, John, *The Sinews of Power: War, Money and the English State 1688–1783* (Unwin Hyman, 1989)

Burdett, Sir Francis, *An Impartial Statement of the Inhuman Cruelties Discovered in Coldbath-Fields Prison* (London, 1800)

Burdon, Major Sir John Alder (ed.), *Archives of British Honduras* (Sifton Praed, 1931)

Calder, Angus, *Revolutionary Empire* (Pimlico, 1998)

Campbell, Major General Archibald, *A Memoir Relative to the Island of Jamaica* (1782, British Library King's Ms. 214)

Chapman, Pauline, *Madame Tussaud in England: Career Woman Extraordinary* (Quiller Press, 1992)

Christie, Ian R., *Myth and Reality in Late Eighteenth Century British Politics* (Macmillan, 1970)

——*Wilkes, Wyvill and Reform: The Parliamentary Reform Movement in British Politics 1760–1785* (Macmillan, 1962)

Cloncurry, Valentine Lord, *Lord Cloncurry's Recollections of his Life and Times* (James McGlashan, Dublin, 1849)

Colley, Linda, *Britons: Forging the Nation 1707–1837* (Yale University Press, 1992)

——*Captives: Britain, Empire and the World 1600–1850* (Jonathan Cape, 2002)

Cone, Carl B., *The English Jacobins: Reformers in Late Eighteenth Century England* (Scribner, 1968)

Conner, Clifford D., *Colonel Despard: The Life and Times of an Anglo-Irish Rebel* (Combined Publishing, 2000)

Cordingly, David, *Life Among the Pirates: The Romance and the Reality* (Little, Brown, 1995)

Cross, David A., *A Striking Likeness: The Life of George Romney* (Ashgate Publishing, 2000)

Dancer, Dr Thomas, *A Brief History of the Late Expedition against Fort San Juan . . .* (Kingston, Jamaica, 1781)

Davis, H. W. Carless, *The Age of Grey and Peel* (Clarendon Press, 1929)

Despard, Colonel Edward Marcus, *A Narrative of Publick Transactions in the Bay of Honduras Settlement from 1784 to 1790* (Public Record Office C.O. 123/10, appendices 123/11)

Despard family archive, *Recollections on the Despard Family* (Elizabeth Despard, c.1850); *Memoranda Connected with the Despard Family* (Jane Despard, 1838); letters, news clippings, genealogies etc.

Dickinson, H. T., *British Radicalism and the French Revolution 1789–1815* (B. Blackwell, 1985)

——*The Politics of the People in Eighteenth-Century Britain* (St Martin's Press, 1995)

Dobson, Narda, *A History of Belize* (Longman Caribbean, 1973)

Dozier, Robert R., *For King, Constitution and Country: The English Loyalists and the French Revolution* (University Press of Kentucky, 1983)

Duffy, Michael, *The Younger Pitt* (Pearson Education, 2000)

Dunn, R. S., *Sugar and Slaves: The Rise of the Planter Class in the English West Indies 1624–1713* (Jonathan Cape, 1973)

Elliott, Marianne, 'The "Despard Conspiracy" Reconsidered' (in *Past & Present*, No. 75, May 1977)

——*Partners in Revolution: The United Irishmen and France* (Yale University Press, 1982)

——*Wolfe Tone: Prophet of Irish Independence* (Yale University Press, 1989)

Emsley, Clive, 'Repression, "Terror" and the Rule of Law in England during the Decade of the French Revolution' (in *English Historical Review*, Vol. C, No. 397, October 1985)

——'An Aspect of Pitt's Terror: Prosecutions for Sedition during the 1790s' (in *Social History*, Vol. 6, No. 2, May 1981)

——*British Society and the French Wars* (Macmillan, 1979)

Equiano, Olaudah, *The Interesting Narrative* (1789; reprinted Penguin, 1995)

Finch, W., *Reflections on the Case of Despard and his Unfortunate Associates* (London, 1803)

Fitzpatrick, W. J., *Secret Service Under Pitt* (Longmans, Green & Co., 1892)

Floyd, Troy S., *The Anglo-Spanish Struggle for Mosquitia* (University of New Mexico Press, 1967)

Fry, M., *The Dundas Despotism* (Edinburgh University Press, 1992)

Fryer, Peter, *Staying Power: The History of Black People in Britain* (Pluto Press, 1984)

Gattrell, V. C., *The Hanging Tree: Execution and the English People 1770–1868* (Oxford University Press, 1994)

Gilmour, Ian, *Riots, Risings and Revolutions: Governance in Eighteenth-Century England* (Pimlico, 1993)

Godfrey, Richard (ed.), *James Gillray: The Art of Caricature* (Tate Publishing, 2001)

Goodwin, Albert, *The Friends of Liberty: The English Democratic Movement in the Age of the French*

Revolution (Harvard University Press, 1979)

Gurney, Joseph and Gurney, William Brodie, *The Trial of Edward Marcus Despard for High Treason, Taken in Short-Hand* (London, 1803)

Hazlitt, William, *The Spirit of the Age* (1825; reprinted Scolar Press, 1971)

Helms, Mary W., *Asang: Adaptations to Culture Contact in a Miskito Community* (University of Florida Press, 1971)

Hemmings, Ray, *Liberty or Death: Early Struggles for Parliamentary Democracy* (Lawrence and Wishart, 2000)

Hibbert, Christopher, *George III: A Personal History* (Penguin, 1999)

——*Redcoats and Rebels: The War for America 1770–1781* (Penguin, 2001)

Hill, Christopher, *Puritanism and Revolution* (Secker & Warburg, 1958)

Hobhouse, Christopher, *Charles James Fox* (John Murray, 1947)

Hodgson, Col. Robert, *Some Account of the Mosquito Territory, Contained in a Memoir Written in 1757 . . .* (Edinburgh, 1822)

Home Office Domestic Correspondence, George III: Letters & Papers/Supplementary, 1798/1802 (Public Record Office, H.O. 42/42–3, 65–6)

Honduras Bay – British Government Transactions January 1787–December 1790 (Public Record Office, C.O. 123/5 –123/9)

Hone, J. Ann, *For the Cause of Truth: Radicalism in London 1796–1813* (Clarendon Press, 1982)

Hope, James, *United Irishman: The Autobiography of James Hope* (ed. John Newsinger, Merlin Press, 2001)

Hostettler, John, *Thomas Erskine and Trial by Jury* (Barry

Rose Law Publications, 1996)

Hunt, Henry, *Memoirs of Henry Hunt Esq.* (T. Dolby, London, 1820)

James, C. L. R., *The Black Jacobins* (1938; reprinted Penguin Books, 2001)

Jones, Colin (ed.), *Britain and Revolutionary France: Conflict, Subversion and Propaganda* (Wheaton, 1983)

Jupp, Peter, *Lord Grenville 1759–1854* (Clarendon Press, 1985)

Keane, John, *Tom Paine: A Political Life* (Bloomsbury, 1995)

Lean, E. Tangye, *The Napoleonists: A Study in Political Disaffection 1760–1960* (Oxford University Press, 1970)

Leigh, Revd William, *A Sermon on the Depravity of the Human Heart; Exemplified generally in the Conduct of the Jews, and particularly in that of Colonel Despard, previous to his Execution* (Hatchard's, 1803)

Linebaugh, Peter, *The London Hanged: Crime and Civil Society in the Eighteenth Century* (Allen Lane/Penguin, 1991)

——and Rediker, Marcus, *The Many-Headed Hydra: The Hidden History of the Revolutionary Atlantic* (Verso, 2000)

Long, Edward, *The History of Jamaica* (1772; reprinted Frank Cass & Co., 1970)

Manwaring, G. E. and Dobrée, Bonamy, *The Floating Republic* (Geoffrey Bles, 1935)

Mintz, Sidney W., *Sweetness and Power: The Place of Sugar in Modern History* (Elizabeth Sifton Books/Viking, 1985)

Moseley, Benjamin MD, *A Treatise on Sugar* (John Nichols, London, 1800)

——*A Treatise on Tropical Diseases and the Climate of the*

West Indies (T. Cadell, London, 1787)

Observer, The (London, 3 February, 6 February, 10 February, 1803)

Oman, Sir Charles, *The Unfortunate Colonel Despard and Other Studies* (Edward Arnold & Co., 1922)

Paine, Thomas, *Rights of Man* (1791/2; reprinted Penguin Classics 1985)

Pakenham, Thomas, *The Year of Liberty: The Great Irish Rebellion of 1798* (Granada, 1982)

Palmer, R. R., *The Age of the Democratic Revolution: A Political History of Europe and America 1760–1800* (Princeton University Press, 1959)

Papers Relating to Jamaica, Presented by C. E. Long (British Library Add. Ms. 12,431)

Patterson, M. W., *Sir Francis Burdett and his Times 1770–1884* (Macmillan, 1931)

Philp, Mark (ed.), *The French Revolution and British Popular Politics* (Cambridge University Press, 1991)

Place, Francis, *The Autobiography of Francis Place* (ed. Mary Thale, Cambridge University Press, 1972)

Pocock, Tom, *The Young Nelson in the Americas* (Collins, 1980)

——*Nelson* (Bodley Head, 1987)

——*The Terror Before Trafalgar: Nelson, Napoleon and the Secret War* (John Murray, 2002)

Public Characters of 1801–2 (Richard Phillips, London, 1801)

Ragatz, Joseph Lowell, *The Fall of the Planter Class in the British Caribbean 1763–1833* (Century, 1928)

Robbins, Caroline, *The Eighteenth Century Commonwealthman* (Harvard University Press, 1959)

Royle, Edward, *Revolutionary Britannia?: Reflections on the Threat of Revolution in Britain 1789–1848* (Manchester University Press, 2000)

Shyllon, Folarin, *Black People in Britain 1555–1833* (Oxford University Press, 1977)

Southey, Robert, *Letters from England* (ed. Jack Simmonds, Cresset Press, 1951)

Stanhope, John, *The Cato Street Conspiracy* (Jonathan Cape, 1962)

Stedman, John Gabriel, *A Narrative of Five Years Expedition Against the Revoluted Negroes in Surinam 1772–1777* (ed. Stanbury Thompson, Mitre Press, 1962)

Stepan, Nancy, *The Idea of Race in Science: Great Britain 1800–1960* (Macmillan, 1982)

Tegg, Thomas, *Memoirs of the Life of Sir F. Burdett, Baronet* (London, 1804)

Thompson, E. P., *The Making of the English Working Classes* (1963; reprinted Penguin, 1991)

Times, The (London, 10 February, 22 February, 1803)

Veitch, G. S., *The Genesis of Parliamentary Reform* (Constable & Co., 1913)

Vickers, Tom, *Colonel Edward Despard: First Superintendent of the Bay Settlement (now Belize)* (privately published, 2001)

Wallas, Graham, *The Life of Francis Place 1771–1854* (Allen & Unwin, 1918)

Whelan, Kevin, *The Tree of Liberty: Radicalism, Catholicism and the Construction of Irish Identity 1796–1830* (University of Cork Press, 1996)

White, Robert, *The Case of the Agent to the Settlers on the Coast of Yucatán and the Late Settlers on the Mosquito Shore* (T. Cadell, London, 1793)

Worrall, David, *Radical Culture: Discourse, Resistance and Surveillance 1790–1820* (Wayne State University Press, 1992)

INDEX

THE AIR LOOM GANG
**The Strange and True Story of James Tilly Matthews, His
Visionary Madness and His Incarceration in Bedlam
By Mike Jay**

The Air Loom Gang tells the true story of James Tilly
Matthews, one of the most complex and bizarre ever recorded
in the history of madness. Confined in Bedlam, the world's most
notorious madhouse. Matthews believed his mind was being
manipulated by an 'influencing machine' called the Air Loom,
operated by a sinister undercover gang of French
Revolutionaries who were controlling the minds of politicians
and generals and plunging France and England into war. But
his case was even stranger than his doctors realized, for many
of the seemingly incredible conspiracies in which he claimed to
have been involved were, it transpired, all too real . . .

'A magnificent study of the "first case of modern
schizophrenia" . . . beautifully balanced and fiercely energetic
. . . *The Air Loom Gang* is an important contribution to the
historical debate, a paean to the logic of lunacy and a promise
that, at least for now, remote mind-control is probably no more
than a fiction. Probably'
Spectator

'Marvellous . . . free of academic jargon, delicately nuanced but
taut with drama, *The Air Loom Gang* is one of the most rewarding
works on madness and its history that I have ever read'
Literary Review

'Gripping as well as profound . . . Jay's narrative is structured
for maximum effect, and themes woven in strand by strand
until they run into a multi-coloured fabric'
Independent

'In this intriguing book, Mike Jay has taken a magnifying glass
to the archives and detected what amounts to a disgraceful
miscarriage of justice'
Daily Mail

0 553 81485 0

BANTAM BOOKS

THE MAPMAKER'S WIFE
A True Tale of Love, Murder and Survival in the Amazon
By Robert Whitaker

'Full of mystery and danger, bravery and tragedy, with a rapturous love story at its core . . . a marvellous read'
Dennis Lehane, author of *Mystic River*

In 1735 a team of French scientists venture into the South American wilderness to resolve one of the great scientific challenges of the time: the precise size and shape of the Earth. Scaling the Andes and journeying along the Amazon, the mapmakers faced all manner of danger. Madness, disease and violent death each took their toll, but one of them, Jean Godin, fell in love with a local girl called Isabel Grameson.

When the time came to return to France, Godin travelled ahead to ensure the way was safe for his new family. However, on reaching French Guiana, disaster struck and he found himself stranded, unable to return to Isabel. What followed lies at the core of this extraordinary tale – a heartbreaking twenty-year separation that ended when Isabel, believing she might never see her husband again, decided to make her own way across the continent. But what began in hope became hell on earth . . .

Drawing on his own experience retracing Isabel's epic trek as well as contemporary records, Robert Whitaker recounts a captivating true story of love and survival set against the backdrop of what many still regard as 'the greatest expedition the world had ever known'.

'An unlikely page-turner . . . as a testament to frustration, endurance and mutual devotion, this takes some beating'
Sunday Times

'In the brilliant tradition of Dava Sobel's *Longitude* . . . combines powerful story telling with excellent historical research, in a book that reads like a novel'
Alan Lightman, author of *Einstein's Dreams*

0 553 81539 3

BANTAM BOOKS

NELSON'S PURSE
By Martyn Downer

For nearly two centuries, a red morocco dispatch box lay forgotten in a castle attic. When Martyn Downer opened the box and broke its spell, he uncovered a cache of fascinating and intimate letters relating to the life of Britain's greatest naval hero, Horatio Nelson. As Downer explored the castle, he went on to find a treasure trove of never-before-seen objects, including Nelson' swords, medals, porcelain, guns and even the purse he was carrying on the day he was shot at Trafalgar in 1805, still containing its gold coins.

When Nelson died, these objects were passed on to his closest business associate, Alexander Davison, whose descendants had kept them without knowing their enormous historical significance. As Downer identifies each item and its provenance, fresh insights are revealed into the personal and domestic lives of Nelson, his jilted wife Fanny and his mistress Emma, Lady Hamilton.

Rarely, if ever, have Nelson and his circle been brought so vividly and palpably to life. *Nelson's Purse* is an extraordinary historical detective story that will change our view of Lord Nelson forever.

'Fascinating. The heartbreaking and dense web of relationships Downer unravels offers extraordinary insights into Nelson's private life. Downer's rich, highly personal account stands out among Nelson related books'
Daily Mail

'Downer has a good story to tell and does so in high style that will satisfy readers of historical novels with enough strange reality to intrigue those preferring non-fiction'
Literary Review

'Strewn with vivid images . . . Well-researched and well-written'
Sunday Times

0 552 15085 1

CORGI BOOKS

ARBELLA
England's Lost Queen
By Sarah Gristwood

'I must shape my own coat according to my cloth, but it shall not be after the fashion of this world, but fit for me'

Niece to Mary, Queen of Scots, granddaughter to the great Tudor dynast Bess of Hardwick, Lady Arbella Stuart was brought to the court as a young girl and acknowledged as her heir by her cousin Elizabeth I – her right to the throne equalled only by James VI of Scotland, Arbella could have been Queen, But her fate was to make her own forbidden marriage, to die a lonely, squalid death in the Tower and to be written out of history . . .

Drawing on a wide range of contemporary sources, including Arbella's own extraordinary, passionate letters, Sarah Gristwood's acclaimed biography paints a vivid and powerful portrait of a woman forced to tread a precarious path though one of the most turbulent, treacherous periods in British history, and in so doing rescues this 'lost queen' from obscurity.

'Utterly compelling and thumping good read . . . an exquisite jewel of a book' Alison Weir

'Fresh, vivid and beautifully detailed . . . conveyed with exactly the right mixture of suspense and sympathy. All her details tell'
Independent

'She teases out some vivid threads...and deftly weaves them into a startling, "pattern of misfortune" . . . The delights are in the detail, and Gristwood makes the most the them'
Daily Telegraph

'Carrying her learning lightly, Sarah Gristwood presents a powerful story of the Dynastic insecurity of the Tudors and Stuarts . . . This life of Arbella gives us perhaps what she was: a Stuart at the centre of the historical canvas, but a woman who lived on the fringes' *Sunday Times*

'Sarah Gristwood succeeds triumphantly...an enthralling account of an extraordinary life' *Spectator*

0 553 81521 0

BANTAM BOOKS

A SELECTION OF NON-FICTION TITLES
AVAILABLE FROM TRANSWORLD PUBLISHERS

15108 4	WITNESS TO WAR	Richard Aldrich	£9.99
81442 7	A POUND OF PAPER	John Baxter	£7.99
99065 5	THE PAST IS MYSELF	Christabel Bielenberg	£8.99
50590 4	THE DRAGON SYNDICATES	Martin Booth	£7.99
81418 4	CANNABIS: A HISTORY	Martin Booth	£7.99
99914 8	GALLOWAY STREET	John Boyle	£6.99
81506 7	GALLIPOLI	L. A. Carlyon	£9.99
99923 7	THE MYSTERY OF CAPITAL	Hernando de Soto	£8.99
99981 4	A PROFOUND SECRET	Josceline Dimbleby	£7.99
15085 1	NELSON'S PURSE	Martyn Downer	£8.99
81447 8	INTO AFRICA	Martin Dugard	£8.99
81194 0	GENESIS OF THE GRAIL KINGS	Laurence Gardner	£7.99
99850 8	THE RIGHTEOUS	Martin Gilbert	£8.99
50692 7	THE ARCANUM	Janet Gleeson	£6.99
81521 0	ARBELLA: ENGLAND'S LOST QUEEN	Sarah Gristwood	£9.99
81445 1	HIMMLER'S CRUSADE	Christopher Hale	£7.99
14975 6	CONFIDENT HOPE OF A MIRACLE: THE TRUE STORY OF THE SPANISH ARMADA	Neil Hanson	£8.99
81485 0	THE AIR LOOM GANG	Mike Jay	£7.99
81353 6	THE DEVIL IN THE WHITE CITY	Erik Larson	£7.99
15087 8	THE KING OF SUNLIGHT	Adam Macqueen	£7.99
81642 X	ANCIENT MARINER	Ken McGoogan	£7.99
81498 2	GENGHIS KHAN	John Man	£7.99
81522 9	1421: THE YEAR CHINA DISCOVERED THE WORLD	Gavin Menzies	£9.99
81657 8	ONE FOURTEENTH OF AN ELEPHANT	Ian Denys Peek	£9.99
14330 8	THE TEMPLAR REVELATION	Lynn Picknett & Clive Prince	£7.99
99886 9	WILFUL MURDER	Diana Preston	£7.99
77100 7	TO THE HEART OF THE NILE	Pat Shipman	£8.99
99982 2	THE ISLAND AT THE CENTRE OF THE WORLD	Russell Shorto	£7.99
81539 3	THE MAPMAKER'S WIFE	Robert Whitaker	£7.99